'An illuminating book that reaches beyond unrepresentative examples and management fads to take a nitty-gritty perspective on value-driven strategy.'
—Pankaj Ghemawat, Global Professor of Management and Strategy at the NYU Stern School of Business, and Professor of Strategic Management at IESE Business School

'By applying the evidence-based principles proposed by *Fad-Free Strategy*, Deneffe and Vantrappen enable managers to get a much better grip on customers' true preferences, including those for sustainable offerings, and on their attitudes towards the businesses supplying those. That understanding is critical for making strategic choices from which both business and society benefit. A must-read book for leaders of the future!'
—Paul Polman, former Chief Executive Officer, Unilever

'Building from one of the best summaries and critiques of classic strategy, *Fad-Free Strategy* goes beneath the covers and into the pragmatic detail of developing customer-driven approaches that will be valuable to all intelligent managers.'
—David J. Collis, Thomas Henry Carroll Ford Foundation Adjunct Professor of Business Administration, Strategy unit, Harvard Business School

'*Fad-Free Strategy* is a refreshing real-world approach to strategy that every smart manager must be craving for. It explains by means of real case examples how to translate an overall vision and ambition into specific customer-driven decisions. If you want to be more confident with the tough choices you make, this book is a must-read.'
—Hubertus M. Mühlhäuser, Chief Executive Officer, CNH Industrial

'This book shows — in line with its authors' no-nonsense attitude — how to take strategy from big ideas to very practical questions and evidence-based assessments, which is critical to ensure a strategy's successful implementation.'
—Eric J. Van den Steen, Royal Little Professor of Business Administration, Strategy unit, Harvard Business School

Fad-Free Strategy

Fad-Free Strategy provides a ground-breaking approach to making better business strategy decisions: more efficient, open to out-of-the-box opportunities and evidence-based. Most strategy books focus on Grand Strategy, the process that leads to high-level recommendations or, more accurately, hypotheses about where and how to compete. While this book briefly covers critical Grand Strategy practices, it deep-dives into Operational Strategy, the process of validation, adaptation and possible rejection of those hypotheses.

Operational Strategy is based on an in-depth understanding of customer preferences and anticipating the choices they make. Those choices rather than managers' ambitions determine whether a strategy will generate the aspired financial results. The book explains, by means of detailed real-world cases across industries, how to generate validated solutions to any strategic problem such as: how to enter successfully into new markets, either as an innovator or as a latecomer? How to defend one's position against aggressive new entrants? Or how to sustain margins when price is the only thing customers seem to care about?

This remarkable book contains expert advice from accomplished strategic advisors and thought leaders Daniel Deneffe and Herman Vantrappen. *Fad-Free Strategy* will be a useful tool for smart business executives at mainstream companies who are disappointed with strategy fads and simplistic solutions based on cherry-picked, anecdotal evidence from today's hero companies. It will also appeal to economics faculty members teaching graduate courses in business strategy who are looking for an economics-based strategy textbook that is both rigorous and comprehensive. The book's core ideas have been taught successfully in continuing and executive education programs at Harvard University and Hult International Business School.

Daniel Deneffe is the Managing Director of Deneffe Consulting and a former partner at Arthur D. Little. He is also a Professor of Strategy and Managerial Economics at Hult International Business School and teaches *Business Strategy in the Real World* at Harvard University's Division of Continuing Education.

Herman Vantrappen is the Managing Director of Akordeon, a strategic advisory firm. A former partner at Arthur D. Little, he has published numerous articles in a variety of journals, including *Long Range Planning, MIT Sloan Management Review, Strategy & Leadership* and *Harvard Business Review*.

Fad-Free Strategy

Rigorous Methods to
Help Executives Make Strategic
Choices Confidently

Daniel Deneffe and Herman Vantrappen

LONDON AND NEW YORK

First published 2020
by Routledge
2 Park Square, Milton Park, Abingdon, Oxon OX14 4RN

and by Routledge
52 Vanderbilt Avenue, New York, NY 10017

Routledge is an imprint of the Taylor & Francis Group, an informa business

British Library Cataloguing-in-Publication Data
A catalogue record for this book is available from the British Library

Library of Congress Cataloging-in-Publication Data
A catalog record has been requested for this book

ISBN: 978-0-367-24356-2 (hbk)
ISBN: 978-0-429-28198-3 (ebk)

Typeset in Warnock Pro
by Apex CoVantage, LLC

To my father (Daniel Deneffe)

To Kristien and Astrid (Herman Vantrappen)

Contents

Part 1
From Grand Strategy to Operational Strategy   1

1 The promises of a categorically different book on real-world business strategy   3

2 Grand Strategy as a lead-in to Operational Strategy   29

Figures

Tables

Boxes

Acknowledgments

The nature of the consulting profession makes that career consultants experience life as a succession of intensive bursts of intellectual activity: they get to know a client, understand his issues and then collaborate with him, only to take off toward the next assignment. Whether such flow is a curse or a blessing is for others to judge. What is certain, though, is that we are personally immensely grateful for the privilege of having worked with a vastly diverse range of firms across the world. Our first thanks, therefore, go to the hundreds of companies for the trust they bestowed on us and for their invitations to help them tackle their most pressing business issues. The intelligent conversations and energizing debates we had with their managers have been truly instrumental in formulating the applied concepts and concrete examples in this book.

Above all, these experiences taught us that there are some commanding principles that should underpin any real-world strategic business decision, that is, a decision that impacts the long-term health of the company AND makes management immediately accountable for results. We can testify that these principles apply across industries and products, for instance from the cheerfully cheap (lager beer) to the formidably pricey (3G telecom licenses); from the rather morbid (funeral services) to the most aesthetically pleasing (snow-white marble); from the downright mundane (garbage containers) to the forbiddingly sophisticated (advanced battery materials); or from the life-saving (pacemakers) to something else (life insurance). To all these clients, and to many others, we extend our most sincere thanks.

This book would not have been possible without the great opportunities we were offered through our past work with Arthur D. Little, the world's first management consulting firm. Ever since its foundation in 1886, Arthur D. Little has offered innovative solutions that help clients deal with major disruptions. We are most appreciative of the formative times we were able to spend with so many high-caliber people.

We would like to thank the many colleagues and associates, at Arthur D. Little and elsewhere, with whom we have worked on client assignments over the past 20+ years, especially René Groot Bruinderink, Bart Janssen and Marijn Vervoorn. Their constructive inputs, feedback and, at times, pushback enabled us to sharpen our own thinking and deliver greater value to clients. We are also indebted in particular to Hubertus Mühlhäuser, Petter Kilefors and Rick Eagar, whose vision, drive and leadership were instrumental in advancing the practice of strategy and innovation.

By the same token, we would like to thank the faculty and students with whom we conversed at the schools where we have taught, including Duke University's Fuqua School of Business, Harvard University's Division of Continuing Education and Hult International Business School. We could not have persevered without their friendly advice and probing questions. In particular, we thank Margaret Andrews (Harvard), Jim Anton (Duke University), Panos Kouvelis (Washington University in St. Louis), Rob Masson (Cornell University) and Mike Moore (Northwestern).

We are also particularly indebted to Peter Wakker, Professor of Decisions under Uncertainty at the Department of Econometrics of the Erasmus School of Economics (Rotterdam, The Netherlands), and elected four times best economist in The Netherlands. We would like to thank him for the countless discussions we have had on the methods we propose in this book. These methods are the practical embodiment of sound and empirically validated academic research. While taking sole responsibility for any potential remaining errors, we are grateful that we could check with him over and over again that the proposed methods have indeed the solid behavioral foundation that we claim they have.

We would also like to make a special mention of Pankaj Ghemawat, Global Professor of Management and Strategy at the Stern School of Business at New York University, and the Anselmo Rubiralta Professor of Global Strategy at IESE Business School. Long before we knew him personally, we were inspired as students and strategists by his writings about economic man, for instance through his seminal 1991 book *Commitment: The Dynamic of Strategy*. More recently we had the privilege and pleasure to collaborate with him on some aspects of globalization, and more broadly to benefit from his encouragement in bringing this book to its very conclusion.

Finally, we would like to thank Amy Laurens and Alex Atkinson at Routledge and to Kate Fornadel at Apex CoVantage for their confidence and the invaluable editorial support they have provided. Our gratitude goes also to Tony Barker for providing comments on the manuscript.

Daniel Deneffe and Herman Vantrappen

***

Acknowledgments are usually written after the completion of a book, but the following part was written halfway down the road so that my father, to whom this book is dedicated, would be able to read it. He was suffering from terminal cancer, and I knew that he wouldn't be around at the time of the publication of this book. Five weeks later he passed away.

I owe him everything for too many reasons, most of all for him being a genuinely good person. He gave me so much warmth as a child, despite his hectic schedule as a top lung surgeon and professor of medicine. He supported me all along and unconditionally, whichever way I performed. He expressed his total admiration for many achievements of mine, even the most basic ones. It was always so much fun to be around him too, with his very peculiar sense of humor and his passion for history and classical music. Finally, I just admired him all along. And in fact, every time I was asked the question whether I was "the son of" (I loved it when they asked), I heard this same admiration for his good-heartedness, and not just for his excellence as surgeon or professor.

Admittedly, he had a weak point in that he would make a terrible economist. But perhaps his weakness in economics was the flipside of his basic human caring. He was just too good for economics: he practiced surgery just for pure humane reasons.

For all these and many more reasons I am endlessly indebted to him.

Daniel Deneffe

About the authors

Daniel Deneffe

Dr. Daniel Deneffe is the Managing Director of Deneffe Consulting, a strategic advisory firm, and a Professor of Strategy and Managerial Economics. As a consultant, he advises companies worldwide in the areas of corporate and business unit strategy, marketing strategy and pricing excellence. Until 2013, he worked with the management consulting firm Arthur D. Little for 17 years, 12 of which as a partner.

He is on the Teaching Faculty at Harvard University's Division of Continuing Education, where he teaches Business Strategy in the Real World. At Harvard, he received the Dean's Commendation for Teaching Excellence twice. He is also a Professor of Strategy and Managerial Economics at Hult International Business School where he teaches in the MBA and EMBA programs in Boston, London and Dubai and holds the School's record of Professor of the Year awards. He has published widely in journals such as *Management Science, Harvard Business Review, International Journal of Industrial Organization, Managerial and Decision Economics*, and *Health Policy*.

Deneffe obtained his PhD and MA in Economics (Industrial Organization) from Cornell University (Ithaca, NY, USA) and holds a BA in Economics and Sociology from the University of Toronto (Canada). He started his professional career as a full-time faculty member at Duke University's Fuqua School of Business, where he taught in the MBA and EMBA programs.

Herman Vantrappen

Herman Vantrappen is the Managing Director of Akordeon, a strategic advisory firm. He serves large and medium-sized clients in a broad range of business sectors worldwide. Until 2012, he worked with the management consulting firm Arthur D. Little for 26 years, 19 of which as a partner. He was a member of the board of the firm's global Strategy & Organization practice. He was also the Editor-in-Chief of the firm's flagship journal *Prism* for 7 years.

He has published numerous articles in a variety of journals, including *Long Range Planning, MIT Sloan Management Review, Strategy & Leadership, Harvard Business Review, Nikkei Asian Review* and *Fortune*. He is also the author of the book *The Executive Action Writer* (CreateSpace, 2009).

Vantrappen holds an MBA from Tepper School of Business at Carnegie-Mellon University (Pittsburgh, PA, USA) and an MS in Engineering from KU Leuven (Belgium).

Part 1

From Grand Strategy to Operational Strategy

1

The promises of a categorically different book on real-world business strategy

One may wonder why people would write a book on business strategy when, at the time of this writing, a search for "business strategy" on Amazon generates over 40,000 book results.

One could argue that there is a perpetual need to update business publications, hence yet another book could just do that. That updating gap in the market is, however, already filled by the authors of the better-known strategy (text)books, of which 12th, 13th and 14th editions are not uncommon. The authors of established textbooks do go out of their way to revise their latest editions, using more recent business examples from the popular business press such as *The Wall Street Journal*, *Businessweek*, the *Financial Times* and the like. While some of these updates are likely to be driven by textbook economics and, specifically, by the desire to minimize head-on competition with one's own textbooks on the secondary market, the net effect of all this is that business strategy books and textbooks are continuously updated.

As a consequence, there was no point for us, as latecomers in this market, to come up with yet another business strategy book that would only marginally differ from the huge range of existing and well-established offerings by using just slightly different examples from the popular business press. Doing so would be too much of a head-on and insufficiently differentiated strategy to attract new readers. As a matter of fact, this book contains very few examples from that popular business press.

Trying to create a new strategic management theory is not our goal either, and definitely not a fad that disproportionately emphasizes one aspect of strategy at the expense of others. Such fads try to painfully identify anecdotal examples to "prove" the validity of the new approach and ignore the fact that an equal number of examples may exist that disprove their validity.

As an example, in the mid-1970s, the Boston Consulting Group (BCG) launched the idea that the experience curve was *the* key driver of profits: the more experience, as measured by cumulative volume over a certain period of time, the lower the marginal cost relative to competitors. Hence, a volume-based strategy was necessary to acquire experience and stay ahead of the game.[1]

In 1982, Tom Peters' *In Search of Excellence* popularized the concept of best practices. To be successful, companies had to imitate the practices and strategies of those companies that are currently successful. This assumes that there is such a thing as a magic formula (the one applied by the successful company) that always works. The reality points out, however, that these formulas apparently are not the sole reason for the success of the companies quoted in the book, as many of these same companies performed poorly after its publication.[2]

During most of the 1980s and 1990s, a number of advances in management theory were made. Michael Porter-style strategists emphasized the critical importance of analyzing the broader external environment (of which the existence of an industry experience curve was only one dimension) through industry analysis.[3] The core of strategy was to identify attractive industries and to properly position oneself in these favorable environments. Industry attractiveness became the overly emphasized dimension while, for instance, internal company capabilities were of secondary importance. Later on, particularly since the publication of Prahalad and Hamel's "The Core Competence of the Corporation" article (1990) and Collis and Montgomery's "Competing on Resources: Strategy in the 1990s" article (1995), the pendulum swung the other way.[4,5] Strategy was more about analyzing the internal capabilities of an organization than about positioning in attractive markets.

Coming next were strategies driven by vision, strategic intent or ambition, which relegated the other two dimensions (industry realities and internal capabilities) to the faraway background. An emblematic example is the

BHAG – Big Hairy Audacious Goal – idea (1994), stating that companies should formulate a 10–30 year transformative and emotionally compelling goal to progress toward an envisioned future.[6]

Other views include *Blue Ocean Strategy* (2004), where pretty much every strategy that was not based on discovering new market spaces and on a number of other very stringent conditions (e.g., increasing value and decreasing cost at the same time) was considered a solid no-go.[7] With such stringent conditions (the "five imperatives" of a Blue Ocean Strategy®, as the articles call them), it is not surprising that relatively few examples that satisfy all these conditions can be found.

More recently, Alan Lewis and Dan McKone have argued pretty much the opposite in *Edge Strategy* (2016), saying that it makes a lot more sense to investigate options at the edge of one's core business and grab incremental profits from overlooked opportunities that are right in front of us rather than to explore new terrains that mostly come at huge risks.[8]

Our goal is not to create a new grand theory or another management fad that takes yet another dimension of strategy out of proportion, and then tries to support that theory by finding anecdotal examples from the business press that apparently fit the mold. Consequently, our approach does not consist of selecting and studying companies that appear to be top performers, and then to generate an ex post explanation as to why the companies thus observed from a distance are actually doing better than others.

That approach constitutes the foundation of quite a few strategy books, including those written by some full-time academic experts. That they take such an approach is not surprising, since it is not their primary focus or interest to engage either in in-depth consulting projects or in actual business decision-making. That approach has a number of disadvantages.

First, recommendations stemming from observations about the most successful companies are not generalizable. That is, it is not because, say, top performers tend to have strong brands, that the recommendation follows that companies should invest heavily to build strong brands.

Second, studying what makes companies successful can lead, at best, to some high-level principles but not to specific advice that explains how to translate the high-level principles into an actionable data-driven decision-making framework. Many executives we worked with feel that experts who coach them often leave the more difficult yet most important work to them (or to another consulting company, for that matter). Without substantial industry or consulting experience, even the brightest minds may just have too little information about what happens in the real world to make theories operational and generalizable. That is quite apparent from the frustration that more experienced MBA students have when a professor sometimes hand-waves their challenging questions away through a "let us not get bogged down in operational details."

The preceding statements are based on the comparison that one of this book's authors can make between his experience today versus his experience as a quintessential business school professor some 25 years ago. Daniel started his career in academics as a young business school professor teaching in the MBA and EMBA programs at a respectable business school. The most distressing questions he could get from students were those that tried to apply the theories in the real world, that is, the "how do you apply this in day-to-day business?" questions. In fact, he decided to leave the business school environment precisely because he felt that he did not know much about real-world decisions (not more or less than his colleagues, but in any event, not sufficiently much). The reason was quite obvious: as with many of the new PhD graduates (in his case from an Economics Department), he joined the business school faculty and taught managerial economics and business strategy without ever having been inside a company, let alone worked for a company (other than some summer job as a waiter). What did he know about *doing* strategy? The answer is: nothing. He knew strategy from reading articles and books about strategy. And guess who wrote those articles and books? In many cases, people just like him who had never actually done any strategy.

Admittedly, we are a tad unfair here. Many professors go out of their way to understand and even experience the real-world challenges of strategic decision-making. Yet the bottom line remains the same. The business literature authored by some academics has one enormous drawback: it is not very practical, as it has no real-world experience component; that is, about what works and what does not work in *doing* things. And it is a fundamentally different thing to do things than to talk about things.

It is this understanding that led Daniel to leave teaching business for the management consulting environment. He did so in the hope to learn what really matters, to experience what can and cannot be applied, and eventually to return to business school teaching, this time as an experienced businessman. Admittedly, consulting is still not quite about doing, but surely a lot more driven by solving real business problems operationally than by finding anecdotal examples to prove some theory.

Now, some 25 years after having taught his first classes in managerial economics and business strategy at the business school, and after a 20-year career in management consulting, the author is teaching again. There is just one fundamental difference between now and then: the teacher now knows what can and cannot be used in the real world. And his back-of-the-envelope estimation thereof is startling: of the content material taught in his first course in managerial economics, he estimates that about half was of very limited, if any, use. Things like mathematical production functions, quantitative straight-line demand/supply curves and elasticity exercises (where do the figures come from?) are all a sheer waste of time that confuse rather than enrich the MBA student's experience. They do not help her make better business decisions, which she will only realize years after having left the program.

The other half of the concepts that he taught initially are useful and have validity (e.g., marginal analysis, company demand analysis and price optimization, some of the game-theoretic concepts, etc.) but only if they are made operational and adapted to the real world. For example, it is not sufficient to show how to derive, say, the profit-maximizing price from a given mathematical demand curve. In fact, that is the easy part. What is needed is an operational guideline as to how to gather the data to create a real demand curve in the first place, for example for, say, a cement company in Poland that wants to optimize its prices for different grades of cement.

The same applies to the usefulness of some of the materials taught in traditional MBA–level strategy courses. While courses get continually updated, it is remarkable that many of the business school concepts and cases on strategy relate to the exceptions rather than the rules. The basic objective of strategy, it is often said, is to obtain sustainable competitive advantage, whereas in the real world such advantage is more often than not transient.[9] Admittedly, it is possible to find business school cases that illustrate how companies have established such sustainable advantage for the foreseeable time. And while such cases are quite tough to find in the real world, they are still popular in business school. In fact, cases of prolonged sustainable competitive advantage are so difficult to find that many MBA–level strategy course syllabi often stick to these 10-year old cases rather than substituting them with newer ones that should be more appealing to students.

If cases that exemplify how to reach the ultimate objective of strategy, i.e., sustainable competitive advantage, are so hard to come by, one may wonder about the generalizability of the takeaways from strategy classes that emphasize sustainable competitive advantage. What can an executive of a chlorine or PVC manufacturing company learn from such special cases? And what are the takeaways of such cases for the medical device company that manufactures stents and that was once the leader in the industry but now faces tremendous competition from imitators? Or for the supplier of mass-produced bearings to passenger car manufacturers?

None of the preceding is a problem for instructors whose objective is to teach a great entertaining class with hand-picked examples of successful companies. But in view of the anecdotal or even exceptional nature of these carefully selected examples, it is a serious problem for the practitioner (say, an executive at the PVC company) who goes back home after having attended the executive program and wonders why she cannot obtain some sort of sustainable competitive advantage in her business.

We may be shooting ourselves in the foot by providing the following example, as we are sure you will wonder how generalizable it is. Still, without making any claim of generalizability, we mention it, for whatever it is worth. One of our former colleagues who joined the consulting world at the end of a successful career, in which he had headed numerous businesses in the chemical and pharmaceutical industry, attended one of the most respected (and most expensive!) short-term executive (non-degree) programs in the US. When we asked him afterwards what he had learned, he uttered: "It was a great show . . . but I didn't learn anything new to make better decisions."

By now, you have understood, dear reader, that in this business strategy book we follow a totally different approach. We do not go for non-generalizable principles such as sustainable competitive advantage. Instead, we make six promises that should make it worthwhile digging into this book, whether you are a business strategy practitioner or a business school professor who wants to know more about strategy in the real world.

▶ PROMISE #1: A PRACTICAL ACTION-ORIENTED APPROACH, BASED UPON DOING RATHER THAN OBSERVING

One of the reasons why we felt it was worth coming up with the 40,248th (whatever, it is just a guess) book on business strategy is precisely that we are convinced that there is a need for practical approaches that work because they are based on *doing* real-world strategy rather than *observing* successful strategies. Observing a success does not guarantee being able to replicate it. More precisely, writing or teaching about one's observations is not even close to a guarantee that what is being observed is practically applicable in different settings. This book provides a way of thinking through common problems in business unit and marketing strategy, and then practically tackling them.

That is not to say that we will not use a conceptual framework and will just talk from experience. To the contrary, we do have a rigorous economics-based and customer-centric framework, about which we will talk more later. The key difference with academic approaches is that our framework has been applied, made operational and improved over the years, based on doing real-world strategy projects.

Where do our claims of sufficient experience come from? We have jointly about 50 years of management consulting experience. The nature of the job of the management consultant is precisely this: to come up with solutions that work and that improve the performance of the client company.

Admittedly, many people are a bit skeptical about whether management consultants actually do value-added things. Indeed, using an economist's term, barriers to entry in the consulting industry are zero. Anyone can call himself a consultant and sell air. And it is true that you can fool some clients some time, but if you do so, you will not stay in business for this total of 50 years. Clients are not stupid, and consultants who play what economists call an end game (promise, make money but fail to offer clients a return on their consulting investment, then run) will rarely have repeat clients. We are pretty convinced that a long consulting life is only the prerogative of those who deliver value in the profession.

▶ PROMISE #2: A GENERALIZABLE RATHER THAN AN ANECDOTAL HERO-BASED APPROACH

Another reason to write this book was to tackle the non-generalizability of the theories in many strategy textbooks. As an example, the small-town pre-emption model of Walmart led to years of sustainable competitive advantage for the company, but how applicable is it to, say, a small PVC company making plastic pipes?[10] Or what is the takeaway of all the management books on customer value, on how to be a customer value leader, on capitalizing on the brand and so on, for companies that operate in markets where very little customer or brand value exists?

Take the example of a small company making pentanes. What pentanes really are does not matter, but we tell you for the record: pentanes are oil derivatives that are used as blowing agents in the production of foam. Experience in this and many other industries suggests that it would obviously be awesome if this company could become a customer value leader and capitalize on the brand as an asset. But for now, the hard fact is: pentane customers do not care about the brand, as pentanes are pentanes are pentanes, and the brand per se does not matter. So, what should companies do in a market like this where the brand value is negligible? What should they do if they cannot find customer value? What are the hands-on recommendations then for these middle-of-the-road companies operating in these conveniently forgotten markets?

Or are these PVC or pentane companies better off with the Blue Ocean Strategy® concept? Blue Ocean Strategy® is imperatively about increasing value and decreasing costs, and about discovering oceans of uncontested market space. All the rest is bad (red ocean) strategy. Well, we would like to suggest something: try to talk this way to the General Manager or Marketing Director of a PVC company or of the pentanes producer and see what happens. Our best guess is that your meeting will not last 15 minutes because the theory is so constraining and inapplicable to their world.

In this book, we do not come up with such grand yet rarely applicable theories. Instead we do try to get across a number of practically applicable principles that are generalizable to different settings, even to the PVC or pentane companies that would not know where to find a Blue Ocean® or how to increase the value of the brand. We can make this claim because the management consultant's life is quite a bit less dazzling than the strategy professor's. The latter has all the leeway to select the strategy problems and cases that he is interested in, and not to cover the real-world situations where the theory is harder to apply, like the strategy problem of the PVC company (we doubt that many business cases have been written about this). The management consultant, to the contrary, is faced with a company problem, and has to come up with a solution to that problem, whether the specific company problem is conducive to being tackled with her theoretical principles or not. Observations from hero companies, or theories built around these, are only coincidentally applicable.

In addition, the management consultant does not necessarily focus on a select club of Fortune 500 or other top-performing clients, but also on a wide and diverse range of smaller middle-of-the-road clients, most of whom cannot claim to be the leader in their field. As a consequence, the takeaways from her inside experience are, in our view, a lot richer and more generally applicable than those derived solely from Fortune 500 companies that are studied from the outside.

▶ PROMISE #3: A TOTALLY CUSTOMERS-CENTRIC APPROACH

CustomerS-centric sounds like poor English, but the extra S serves an important purpose. There are plenty of textbooks from influential authors that claim companies to be innovative if they truly focus on *the* customer first, and have what is called an "outside-in" approach. Put simply, "outside-in" means standing in the customer's shoes and viewing everything the company does through the customer's eyes.[11] These authors substantiate the claim of the importance of outside-in analysis by their findings from studies of successful companies like J&J, Walmart, P&G, Apple, Ikea and Amazon, as these have focused on "creating and keeping customers." These companies, they say, were successful because they were customer value leaders or innovators, capitalized on the customer as an asset, and capitalized on the brand as an asset. Compare that, they say, to the companies that were in the Fortune 500 top 25 at the beginning of the century but have lagged behind because they focused on intense budget-cutting more than on customer value.

We fully agree that an external focus on customer value should often, yet not always, be the starting point of many strategic analyses. The limits of cost cutting are well understood, as it may very well cut the roots of the value created and communicated to customers. And the effect hereof may only surface much later than when the cost-cutting exercise took place. Or it may not even surface at all, as the causality between the cost cutting and the deterioration of future performance may not be that evident, given the many other external market conditions affecting a company's profitability.

That being said, one key question pops up when talking about the value of a customer-focused approach: who is after all that notable customer whose needs these top-performing companies are supposed to identify and cater to? What is this customer's willingness-to-pay (this is what customer value is, right?)? And what price do we need to charge to capture some of that value and translate it into profits? Most fundamentally, does it really make any sense at all to focus on "the customer"? Or conversely, is an approach that focuses on *differences* between customers not a whole lot more useful and meaningful?

At least, the fact that customers differ from each other forms the basics of microeconomics. Remember the demand curve from your boring economics courses? It is downward sloping precisely *because* customers differ. Customers all have a different willingness-to-pay for a given product, which is why more is sold at low prices (e.g., for a specific model and trim, say a Mercedes-Benz 350 Coupe) than at high prices.[12] Not because "the customer" buys more of them, but because at lower prices *some* customers who would otherwise have bought another vehicle (whatever that best alternative model may be, such as a Lexus 400, a BMW 540i or what have you) are now switching to this particular Mercedes-Benz model.

The understanding of these differences in customer value is key. And let us keep things simple and to the point: customer value is indeed the willingness-to-pay of a customer for a particular product or service. More precisely, it is the maximum amount of money that the customer wants to pay for that product or service, given his perceived alternatives on the market. In that sense, there is no single customer value but many, many different customer values that differ across customers.

We can hear your reaction: dear authors, you are not entirely fair, because most marketing or business strategists do recognize that there are groups of customers who attach a similar value to a given product, as well as other groups who attach a totally different value to that same product – after all, that is why the term "customer segment" exists. Okay, that is a fair reaction, but we also question whether customer segments are really as clearly defined as they appear in marketing textbooks. If you have ever been in customer segmentation exercises, you know what we mean: there are so many ways in which you can cluster that customer base, and come up with different segments, and hope to somehow have found a set of customers with similar preferences or willingness-to-pay.

Let us assume for a moment that a priori segmentation makes sense, and that we agree upon a segment, say, the segment of high-end luxury sedan buyers. We are sure that at this stage some of you already disagree with the definition of the segment. But since we are the writers and you are the reader, we will have to ask you to bear with us for a moment, and to assume that high-end luxury sedan buyers is a meaningful segment. Does it then make sense to talk about a segment-specific customer value, i.e., the willingness-to-pay of the high-end luxury sedan customer? If it did, then the following would be observed: if the price tag on that Mercedes-Benz 350 Coupe (say $60,000) were to be above the specific customer value of the high-end luxury sedan segment, then obviously, no customer in the segment would buy the vehicle; conversely, if the price were lower than that customer value, say $59,500, they would all buy. This is what economists call an infinite price elasticity: with small drops in price, the amount purchased is the entire market population.

This is not what is being observed. The fact is that price elasticities are not near infinite, whether one considers the total market or a specific segment thereof. The reason is that customer value differences exist across individual customers, whatever segment one may take. What is observed is that when the price drops to $59,500 (everything else constant of course), usually more people buy these models, in line with microeconomics demand theory. And if the price drops even more, even more people buy. While these increases in volume are represented as linear in standard economics textbooks, in reality they are not linear. There are, for instance, some psychological levels below which a proportionately larger number of customers start to buy.

In this book, we do provide an approach to strategy that is hyper-customerS-centric. We will highlight the importance of understanding and measuring differences in customer preferences and willingness-to-pay rather than accurately understanding averages. This is not a small but a fundamentally different way of thinking about customers. It fundamentally affects the information we need to gather to take the right actions required to improve the effectiveness of a business strategy.

▶ PROMISE #4: AN EVIDENCE-BASED REALISTIC MANAGERIAL ECONOMICS APPROACH

We are pretty convinced that some of our readers may frown on the "economics" part in this promise, while welcoming the "evidence-based" dimension. Rest assured, we will not draw demand/supply curves (well, we will just draw a very few, in Chapter 3, but we hope you will like these). More importantly, we will not make a number of assumptions that economists typically make but which, in our project experience, are simplifications that do not hold in the real world. What we do take from economics, however, is the logic that pretty much every customer decision is based upon trade-offs or, more precisely, implicitly evaluates the marginal (or incremental, if you prefer) benefits associated with a particular decision, and the marginal opportunity cost of that decision. Our way of thinking is economic, but the assumptions are not. A few examples illustrate the point.

For one thing, we do not assume the law of decreasing marginal satisfaction (utility) that is so standard in any (non-behavioral) microeconomics or managerial economics textbook.[13] That law states that the extra satisfaction that a customer obtains from increasing the consumption of a particular good or service decreases as the level of consumption increases.

The typical example given in undergraduate lectures is that when a customer has to make a choice between apples and oranges, she may initially be indifferent between one apple and one orange: she may be willing to take one apple at the expense of the orange and vice versa. However, when she already has, say, ten apples and no oranges, that is no longer the case. She would be willing to give up, say, five apples to get one orange: the marginal value of the apple is so low that one extra apple is in fact only worth about a fifth of an orange (not sure that we can cut oranges in five equally sized pieces, but you get the point).

We do not make such assumption because our experience shows that it is not always correct. As an example, one of our clients had the technical capabilities to launch a new non-latex medical glove with one important feature, particularly for surgeons: it had the potential to increase the physician's protection against HIV, measured by the probability that the physician would not get infected, should both the patient be infected with the HIV virus and the physician perforate his glove. One of the things we were asked to do was to assess the extra willingness-to-pay of the economic decision-maker in the hospital for increases in the protection against HIV, knowing that achieving certain further improvements beyond particular levels of protection was technically difficult and thus costly.[14] If we had assumed the law of decreasing marginal utility, an increase in the protection against HIV from, say, 10% to 20% would be more valuable than an increase from 40% to 50%, which in turn would be more valuable than the increase in protection from 90% to 100%.

It turned out from our research that this was not the case for our sample. For many surgeons, the willingness-to-pay for an increase in protection from 90% to 100% was much higher than for any other increase, including the increase in protection from 0% to 90%. That is, the surgeons did not behave according to the "law" of decreasing marginal satisfaction. This understanding was critical for the project because it turned out that the medical glove company could not technically achieve the improvement from 90% to 100% (this would require steel or similar gloves, at the expense of any minimum requirement on glove flexibility). In fact, at the technically maximum achievable protection levels, the company could not command a significant increase in price relative to competitors. As a consequence, the launch project had to be put to a halt, which for sure was not fun to hear but allowed the company to save millions of dollars in otherwise wasted further R&D and launch expenditures.

As another example of our economic way of thinking, we will also use, whenever appropriate, some game-theoretic concepts. If that sounds totally scary, rest assured we will stick strictly to a real-world approach. Brandenburger, Nalebuff and others have made attempts at popularizing game theory as a useful tool for managerial decision-making, and many game-theoretic managerial books are filled with fascinating anecdotal examples that are worth thinking through.[15] But at the end of the day, game-theoretic approaches to strategy turn out to be another hype that died out, as these approaches suffer significantly from the problem mentioned before: they take one important dimension of strategy, i.e., anticipating and influencing competitor reactions, out of proportion, thereby ending up with non-generalizability. For instance, they cannot be applied in very aggressive markets where everyone correctly ignores everyone else's moves.

In addition, even when applicable, i.e., in concentrated markets, the key issue with game-theoretic approaches is, in our view, that they assume that all players play the same game and know that the other players do the same. For example, players are assumed to be hyperrational, which leads to very perverse conclusions that simply do not match reality. Besides, it is often assumed that a player's competitor is maximizing profit and that that competitor believes that the other players are maximizing profit as well. In fact, most experiments fail to confirm the predictions of the theory, as people just do not behave the way they are supposed to.

This is a pattern we also observed when doing game-theoretic simulations at clients in concentrated industries, where the theory is supposed to be applicable.[16] Game theory predicts that, when a game (say, a pricing game) is repeated a finite number of times (say, 10 times), companies would behave aggressively (e.g., charge a low price) from the very beginning. When placing managers in such simulated decision-making setting, we find that most of them are mostly much nicer than the theory predicts. They only tend to become aggressive toward the end of the game (say, around game 7 or 8). Some managers do behave aggressively from the beginning, but for other reasons than those expressed by the theory (that is, backward induction). In the words of the CEO of a food company: "I will charge a low price to play it safe and test the market; if others are non-aggressive, I will also be non-aggressive." This reasoning is totally at odds with game-theoretic predictions in finite games.

Unlike game-theoretic approaches, we do not assume hyperrationality. As a result, we do not use the well-known Nash Equilibrium concept, the one that gets you a Nobel Prize. We surely do not assume that managers maximize profits in addition to thinking about their competitors as profit-maximizers. We have seen too often that this is not the case and that other things, like ego, size or even presence in allegedly prestigious markets do matter, especially for privately owned client companies.

If we neither want to assume the law of decreasing marginal satisfaction nor the assumption of hyperrationality and the profit-maximization objective of our competitors, which dimension of managerial economics do we retain then? Let us say that we use the marginal way of thinking and associated concepts, but do not use the stringent theoretical assumptions. For example, as we already explained, we do use the demand curve concept, which illustrates that when price increases beyond certain levels, at some point volumes sold will decline. But we do not draw a straight downward-sloping line representing a curve relating price to quantity, as evidence shows that the relationship is not necessarily linear. The nature of the relationship can be driven by many factors that differ across industries.

In the cement industry, for example, ex-works prices can often be increased without loss of customers, until a certain point when a particular customer (the one nearest to the competitor) starts to switch. At that point a small price increase will lead to a loss of a volume equivalent to the volume size of that customer. Further small price hikes may not lead to a loss of additional customers until again a critical point is reached where another customer finds it more attractive to buy from his best alternative competitor. If the

cement company continues to raise prices even further, eventually its clos-
est customer or, more precisely, the customer furthest away to the competitive alternative, will also switch. In this market, the demand curve thus
has the shape of a staircase. Microeconomics and managerial economics
textbooks often make you believe that the relationship is either linear or log-
linear (do not look it up it if this sounds like gibberish to you). The reality
says that it is neither.

We do not want to go through the details of what demand curves look like
in various industries. We do want to make a much more general point here:
the most important element that we pick up from managerial economics
and related fields, such as decision analysis, is that when defining strategy, a company should always gather evidence on customer preferences,
as defined before, rather than making too rigid assumptions on what these
preferences should be like (sometimes in-depth understanding may be too
costly from a practical perspective, and later in this book we will provide
you with examples on how to design strategy when this is the case). From
its understanding of these customer preferences, the company should try
to influence customer choices (for instance, by adding or removing features
or services) in a way that is beneficial for itself, in view of what it wants to
maximize (say, profits), and taking into consideration competitor responses
to its actions.[17]

The managerial economic thinking underlying this is that, as a company, we
agree on an objective to maximize (e.g., profits), define some choice variables (say, product features, service levels, etc.) that have a certain incremental cost (development and marginal production or service cost) and
incremental benefits (say, revenues). These revenues are not assumed but
are the outcome of customers making choices, namely their total purchases
made at given price levels, given their best alternatives. At certain prices,
some customers will buy from us while others will not. Some of the customers who hesitate somewhat between our product (or base service) and their
best alternative may actually decide to switch to our product if we increase
certain service levels that these customers value, while not charging them
the full amount of that value. Some others will still refrain from switching. Whether it is worth it to introduce or improve this service level, and
what price to charge for it, depends on our business objectives, the cost of
development, the marginal cost of production or servicing, the influence on
customer choices at alternative price levels, and on competitors' willingness
and ability to emulate our service levels. In short, we try to take actions

that influence customer choices in such a way as to maximize our business objectives, keeping competitor responses in mind.

This is totally different from approaches to strategy that start with the definition of a specific numeric objective, such as: we want to achieve 20% market share in the next three years. Stretched targets like these may be the outcome of a visioning workshop, where they tend to be backed up by plenty of ayes, such as: "We know the target is ambitious but it provides the necessary creative tension between our current reality of 5% and what we want to achieve." Once such ambition has been established, adherents of this approach to strategy then do a gap analysis between the current reality and the ambition (it surely sounds scientific) and, finally, identify the complementary resources and capabilities to fill the gap. Facilitators of visioning workshops emphasize the importance of creating the vision unconstrained by current reality, as that is said to be a condition for maximizing creativity.

Economic thinking again allows to figure out the three issues with this type of commonly used approach: (1) the lack of generalizability, (2) the lack of foundation for profit maximization, and (3) the inconsistency with customers' pursuit of their own satisfaction.

The approach is non-generalizable, simply because of the finite nature of the market, or because of the fact that there is only 100% in 100%. One of the authors once challenged a facilitator of a visioning workshop who firmly believed in the visioning approach, saying that heroic ambitions are necessary to make change happen (we do not disagree with that in its own right) and to achieve things that other companies or individuals would think are impossible. Crossing the Atlantic by plane was one of his favorite examples, pointing out the heroic and ambition-driven achievement of Charles A. Lindbergh, who on May 20–21, 1927 flew the *Spirit of St. Louis* between New York and Paris covering 3600 nautical miles (6700 km). What the facilitator failed to tell us – and perhaps did not know – is that a few days earlier (on May 8–9, 1927), another Charles (Charles Nungesser) and François Coli had attempted to cross the Atlantic in a biplane *L'Oiseau Blanc* ("The White Bird") but were lost.[18] The moral of the story is that failures and downside risks should also be considered when doing a visioning exercise so that a more accurate assessment of particular ambitions can be made.

We pointed this out during the workshop but the facilitator was not amused, as he wanted to come up with stretched ambitions for the company. While the company had less than 5% market share at the time, the facilitator asked his audience: "Why don't you have the ambition to have 20% market share? What makes you think that you should not go for it? If you really believe in it, it is possible, just like Lindbergh really believed in his ability to cross the Atlantic and made it possible." (We have a tendency to believe that Lindbergh made it because he had a better plane than his predecessors, and that his beliefs are of a distant secondary importance). Someone in the audience then asked a question that alluded to the lack of generalizability of the approach: "What if our five competitors have the same ambition?" The facilitator, apparently not a math graduate, replied: "Well, if they all really believe in it, they can do it." Case closed.

The lack of foundation for company profit maximization is the second issue we have with a pure vision-based approach. In almost every dimension of strategy (with the exception of some tacit collusive strategies) it is the case that, because of the existence of markets, if everyone can do it, you cannot make money at it.[19] Well, everyone can basically come up with a stretched vision, but there is no reason whatsoever why added value would be created in realizing the stretched vision. In fact, when the ambition is far removed from the current reality, this is unlikely to be the case, as resources will have to be purchased at market price, and little or possibly even no value will be created in the acquisition of such resources.

Finally, the vision-based approach is not consistent with customers maximizing their own satisfaction. That a company may have an ambition to have 20% market share is one thing. But why would that be realistic? It assumes that 20% of the customers will buy (assuming, for simplicity, equal volumes per customer). Often this assumption is not validated – after all it is just a vision, or a wish. And if wishes were horses . . . then beggars would ride. The problem is that it assumes that customers are French geese that can be force-fed, or in this case, forced to buy your product or service. This is not the case, because it is the customer who decides whether to buy or not to buy, based upon her preferences, switching costs (from her best alternative), budget and the like. All you can do is to influence that choice, to try to make her select your product, but not force her to buy the product. You can only make it appetizing, but cannot force her to eat. Our approach to strategy precisely constitutes an understanding of how customers differ in their preferences and choices, how we can influence these choices in our favor (given our predetermined objective) and what is worth our while, given these choices and the associated costs and benefits of influencing customers' choices.

▶ PROMISE #5: A FOCUS ON COMMON PRINCIPLES RATHER THAN COMMON TRUTHS

The promise to focus on common principles rather than common truths in fact follows from promise #4, but we still like to mention it separately. Analyzing strategic and tactical decision-making problems using tools of managerial economics, whereby we agree upon the objective to be maximized (profits, revenues, etc.), upon the choices we can make (our degrees of freedom in decision-making) and upon the constraints that we need to work with (e.g., global headquarters may impose a minimum level of advertising for a product even though the national marketing and sales unit may not find this optimal from the national perspective alone), leads to some startling conclusions that are at odds with some common truths that appear time after time in the more simplistic business literature.

One of these common truths is to focus (in the sense of investing) on your most profitable customers. This kind of categorical statement may sound appealing and sensible, but it is not. It does not matter how profitable your customer is today, but how much less profitable that customer would be if we spend fewer resources on him relative to another, currently less profitable customer. Spending these same resources on this second customer is a wise move if, as a result, the incremental profits generated at this second customer are larger than the profits lost due to a reduction of the resources spent on the first customer. It does not matter whether a customer is profitable; what matters is the marginal profitability of a customer related to an increase or decrease in investments in that customer. If at all possible, all customers should be about equally profitable at the margin. And, by the way, if the statement to focus on the most profitable customers were true, one should never develop a new customer, as this is initially always unprofitable.

The same holds for products. Some managers like to keep things simple and do enjoy decision rules like: focus on your most profitable products. Surely that is an easy decision, but it is equally unfounded. In fact, the same principle applies here: we should focus on those products where the incremental profitability of our investments is the highest, not those who generate the highest profits. Going by the "focus on your most profitable products" rule would imply that a sales director never invests in new products as these are initially less profitable than the company's older cash-cow products.

One of our clients, a national sales division of a global pharmaceutical company, was faced with such painful decisions. The most important quarterly investment decision was: which products should it put in what was called positions 1, 2 and 3, respectively? That is, which three prescription drugs out of its broader portfolio should the pharmaceutical company's sales representatives promote to influence the physician to prescribe these products, or do so more frequently? Typically, for that company and in this specific geographic market, the product in position 1 was promoted during 6 to 7 minutes of the sales rep's 15-minute visit to the physician's office, the product in position 2 was promoted during 4 to 5 minutes, and the third product was only briefly talked about at the end, time permitting.

The General Manager of the national sales division insisted that a particular product, a well-known painkiller (we do in fact disguise the therapeutic category of the product) was put in position 1, and if that were not possible, that it was at least included in the three products for promotion by the salesforce. The reason: the painkiller was the division's most profitable product out of 20+ products in the portfolio, and the General Manager obviously was afraid of losing the profit streams.

Was the painkiller *incrementally* their most profitable product? Not at all. In fact, for a product that had been around for 25 years, doctors either did or did not prescribe it. It was either, as they say, "in the doctor's pen" or it was not. This implies that promotion probably only influenced less than 3% of the doctors visited, namely the new MDs that joined the profession. And many of these already knew about the product from their time in med school. Hence the marginal loss of stopping the promotion of this product altogether was likely to be very small, and surely much smaller than the marginal gain of promoting the most promising, currently unprofitable new product. The company eventually ended up flipping back and forth, putting the painkiller in first and then again in third position, even though the evidence clearly supported one conclusion: do not promote it.

At a more general level, the point is clear: simple rules usually do not pan out due to a lack of underlying logic. But simple principles do exist. Here it is about assessing the highest incremental gains or losses associated with promoting customers or products and allocating resources where this incremental gain is the largest.

The same logic applies when it comes to launching aggressive low-price fighting brands. An often-heard concern is to make sure that there is no cannibalization of the flagship brand, as that is where all the money is. The implication hereof is that fighting brands should be designed in such a way as to minimize cannibalization. We do not believe that minimizing cannibalization is a correct objective, as that may lead to the development of a totally different product altogether (and defeat the purpose of the launch of the fighting brand, to begin with). Leaving everything else constant, the addition of features to the fighting brand (something that obviously increases cannibalization) makes sense as long as the incremental profits from doing so exceed the incremental losses at the flagship brand, as in that case total profits increase.

We are pretty certain that you have a burning question on your mind: how do we get that information about incremental gains or losses? We will give you insights in this process throughout the book. Sometimes it is not even worth it to figure this out since, you guessed it, the marginal benefit of doing so is less than the marginal cost. But that does not imply that we should therefore revert to simple rules like the preceding. It is then better to make an educated guess about these incremental gains and losses, maximally supported by evidence, rather than to ignore them and fall back on what we may call simplistic rules. Due to their lack of behavioral foundation, there is no reason whatsoever that simplistic rules will improve company performance.

▶ PROMISE #6: A TOTALLY OPEN AND TRANSPARENT POSTURE

The five foregoing promises all derive, one way or the other, from our intent to bring a pragmatic managerial economics perspective to strategy design. This sixth and final promise is of a slightly different nature, as it derives from the disappointment we very often feel when reading business books. We do not know about you, dear reader, but many business books leave us frustrated. While everything sounds very promising in the first chapter, the promises do not materialize, and in fact we often feel that the authors wasted quite a bit of our time. Surely, we learned something, but the takeaway is often too little compared to the (ahem) marginal opportunity cost of reading the book.

Our irritation is greatest with the obfuscation strategy that some business books appear to follow. Having read, say, 100 pages of a book whose authors invariably claim to be specialists in their field, we expect to get to the core of the matter on page 101, and finally find some practical advice about how to apply the high-level concepts that the authors have been expounding. Unfortunately, the buck stops at page 101, with the authors stating that such "technical details" are beyond the scope of the book. Is it not quite ironic that a book that expands, say, on the worth of a customer value strategy would not manage to explain how to actually measure customer value? When this happens, we certainly feel taken for a ride.

In this book, we will be totally open and transparent. We will explain step by step how to develop quantitative evidence in support of business strategy decisions such as how to enter this new market that is already being served by strong incumbents; how to defend our position against aggressive new entrants; or how to sustain margins when price is the only thing our customers seem to care about.

While taking you through our logic, we will use mundane real-world examples, as this book addresses managers of the, so to speak, 99% of companies that are not part of this exclusive club of hero companies with solidly differentiating capabilities (think of Google, Apple, Amazon and the likes today). The reality of most companies is that they cannot identify markets where they can establish long-term sustainable competitive advantage, they cannot identify Blue Oceans®, they cannot pre-empt others, and they cannot be protected from competition and the like. That is why this book reaches out to managers who have had it with management books filled with bright color pictures of distant stars. It reaches out to managers who are after a book with principles and methods for making better real-world strategy decisions, even in the absence of superior capabilities or sustainable competitive advantage.

Let us be clear, though. This is not an easy book. From time to time it will put your brains to test. To put it differently, dear reader, it is not the kind of book that you read cursorily at the beach or in the airport lounge when waiting for your delayed flight. But who says that strategy, or management for that matter, is an easy affair? In any case, we do hope that the promises we made in this first chapter will make reading this book worth your time and effort. We surely do not want you to have ex post regret.

▶ STRUCTURE OF THE BOOK

The book is organized as follows. In Chapter 2, we review an efficient end-to-end process for making business strategy decisions, starting with "Grand Strategy" and leading to "Operational Strategy." While all subsequent chapters of this book are about Operational Strategy, we find it crucial to explain the differences and links between Grand Strategy and Operational Strategy first. In fact, Grand Strategy and Operational Strategy are just two high-contrast archetypes that we are introducing for didactic purposes, in the same way that Richard Thaler and Cass Sunstein make the distinction between Econs and Humans in their book *Nudge*, and Daniel Kahneman between System 1 and System 2 in his book *Thinking, Fast and Slow*.[20]

Our starting point is that a company's business strategy ultimately is about determining product (or service and solution)-market combinations (PMCs) with which it can earn a sustainable, or, at least, as-long-as-possible economic profit. Operational Strategy serves to identify and assess such specific PMCs based on empirical customer evidence and pragmatic managerial economics tools. But a company cannot afford the time and resources required to do a sequential, exhaustive, quantified, evidence-based assessment of every imaginable PMC. It needs an efficient mechanism to funnel, screen and filter potential business opportunities that constantly pop up. Grand Strategy relates to such a funnel process. Grand Strategy uses traditional strategy notions (that is, industry attractiveness, competitive advantage, and the like) to assess the merits of business opportunities in a quick-and-dirty way: some will easily be discarded as non-attractive and/or non-feasible; others may appear to be both attractive and feasible, at least at first sight. Grand Strategy thus leads to *hypotheses* about the moves a company could make to attain an as-long-as-possible competitive advantage. Operational Strategy relates to the subsequent deep dive, leading to either the confirmation, adaptation, detailing or possibly rejection of the Grand Strategy hypotheses and of the strategic options that a priori appeared the most attractive and feasible.

In other words, in Chapter 2 we show that Grand Strategy should be the start of an end-to-end process that closes with Operational Strategy. We find that at many companies Grand Strategy and Operational Strategy, if done at all, are disjointed. In addition, the conceptual foundations for Grand Strategy are often weak, as we have started explaining in this introductory chapter. Crafting Grand Strategy is overhyped, while the real proof of the pudding is in the design of Operational Strategy – this is where the numbers kick in, top and bottom line. What we are saying then is that Grand Strategy is fine as long as it is used as a smart lead-in to Operational Strategy.

Chapters 3 through 6 are all about Operational Strategy. They focus on understanding the real commercial potential of various selected strategic options in an empirical and maximally customerS-centric manner: how to determine which strategic option to select, and how to adapt or fine-tune it for maximum commercial potential?

This is the really tough part. We are not in Dreamland here, but in the hard, daily reality that most companies are faced with. Grand Strategy will have indicated the option or options with the hypothesized largest commercial potential, for instance, entry in an adjacent geographic market. Unfortunately, most new markets are already cluttered with products and services from incumbent players, and it is terribly difficult to find differentiating value, especially as a latecomer. Operational Strategy is then very important because it allows us to figure out, given our capabilities and constraints, how to obtain a sustainable or, more realistically, an as-long-as-possible competitive advantage.

It is about getting an in-depth understanding of customers' behavior, their switching costs and their hidden unmet needs. When talking about unmet needs, we do not mean grand needs style iPod, iPad or iPid (whatever that may be), which, in a sense, are the easy ones. It is more difficult to be successful in markets where few unmet needs exist or are known. Often these needs are hidden in the pain points that customers have in working with their current suppliers. The challenge is, first, to get to know these pain points, and then to do a better job than competitors in a way that is difficult for them to imitate, so as to make at least some customers switch. Think, for instance, about launching a new vehicle in an already cluttered competitive environment, or about entering into hard-to-differentiate markets such as payroll services or medical peripherals.

In Chapter 3 we explain the general way of thinking when doing Operational Strategy, that is, how we measure all things that matter in forecasting customer choices and hence our revenues and margins, such as customers' must-haves, willingness-to-pay, willingness-to-buy and switching value.

Once we have explained the foundations of Operational Strategy, we enter Part 2 of the book. It consists of three chapters, each of which deals with one specific application of the Operational Strategy way of thinking. Based on our experience, we feel that these three applications represent the vast majority of basic Operational Strategy choices that business managers face in the real world.

First, in Chapter 4, we explore how to address the problem of entry into a new market. That is, how do we apply and tailor the framework and measuring tools described in Chapter 3 to launch a new product, service or solution into a new or adjacent market, and how does this culminate in adapting or fine-tuning the Grand Strategy hypothesis about the best launch strategy? We also show how we derive the revenue, profit and cash flow forecasts from such exercise, in a totally customerS-centric manner.

In Chapter 5 we look at a defense strategy problem. More specifically, we first explain how to approach the problem of adapting the product or service offering, and possibly its price, when faced with a new aggressive entrant. Second, we look at the other option in defense against a new (often low-priced) competitor, namely the launch of a fighting brand. We approach both problems yet again by using the way of thinking and measuring tools explained in Chapter 3.

In Chapter 6, we look at the worst of all possible situations – call it the antipode of the iPads of this world: what to do when competing in a very competitive market, where customers seem to care about price only, and facing hyper-aggressive competitors. If strategy is indeed about improving profits, how can we do so when we actually have zero competitive advantage? We keep on applying the economic and customerS-centric way of thinking from Chapter 3, and propose a logical framework to still improve margins when little customer value or willingness-to-pay actually exist.

Finally, in Chapter 7, we summarize the conclusions from our exploration of Operational Strategy. We present the seven core ideas to remember when doing Operational Strategy in your own company's real world. We hope you will find all chapters of this book quite interesting, as they are the missing link between the hopes of an ambitious vision and the hard reality of customers' choices and competitors' reactions.

▶ NOTES

1 See, for example, Martin Reeves, George Stalk and Filippo Scognamiglio Pasini, "BCG Classics Revisited: The Experience Curve," *BCG Perspectives* (May 28,

2013). Pankaj Ghemawat, one of Michael Porter's followers at Harvard at the time, offers a specific critique of BCG's experience curve concept as a foundation for strategy: Pankaj Ghemawat, "Building Strategy on the Experience Curve," *Harvard Business Review* (March–April 1985): 143–149.

2 See, for instance, Geoffrey James, World's Worst Management Fads, www.inc.com/geoffrey-james/worlds-worst-management-fads.html, published online May 2013.

3 See, for example, Michael E. Porter, *Competitive Strategy* (New York: Free Press, 1980), and countless other references.

4 C.K. Prahalad and Gary Hamel, "The Core Competence of the Corporation," *Harvard Business Review* (May–June 1990): 79–91.

5 David Collis and Cynthia A. Montgomery, "Competing on Resources: Strategy in the 1990s," *Harvard Business Review* (July–August 1995): 118–128.

6 Jim Collins and Jerry I. Porras, *Built to Last: Successful Habits of Visionary Companies* (New York: HarperBusiness, 1994).

7 W. Chan Kim and Renée Mauborgne, *Blue Ocean Strategy* (Boston: Harvard Business Review Press, 2005).

8 Alan Lewis and Dan McKone, *Edge Strategy: A New Mindset for Profitable Growth* (Boston: Harvard Business Review Press, 2016).

9 See, for example, Rita Gunther McGrath, *The End of Competitive Advantage: How to Keep Your Strategy Moving as Fast as Your Business* (Boston: Harvard Business Review Press, 2013).

10 Walmart's initial strategy in discount retailing consisted of establishing stores in small towns and remote areas in the southwestern United States. These towns were too small to support more than one discount retailer. Being a first mover in these towns, Walmart pre-empted entry by others and obtained a lasting advantage that allowed it to raise prices in these areas relative to the competitive cities without inducing entry by newcomers or established competitors (see Pankaj Ghemawat, "Wal-Mart Stores' Discount Operations," Case Study 9-387-018 [Boston: Harvard Business School, 1986]).

11 George S. Day and Christine Moorman, *Strategy from the Outside In* (New York: McGraw-Hill, 2010).

12 For those who never took any economics courses or simply forgot: a downward-sloping demand curve means that for a given good, more is being sold at lower prices, everything else constant.

13 The difference between a microeconomics and a managerial economics textbook is that the latter tries to make the reader believe that the textbook concepts are applied in the real world, which cannot be further removed from the truth; a microeconomics textbook justifiably does not make such claims.

14 The economic decision-maker varied from hospital to hospital, depending on whether it is physician-led (where usually a key opinion leader has plenty of influence on the purchasing decision and where price thus plays a less important role) or admin-led. So, salespeople had to make sure not to bark up the wrong tree.

15 Adam M. Brandenburger and Barry J. Nalebuff, "The Right Game: Use Game Theory to Shape Strategy," *Harvard Business Review* (July–August 1995): 57–71. See also the same authors' book *Co-opetition* (New York: Currency Doubleday, 1996), and Avinash K. Dixit and Barry J. Nalebuff, *The Art of Strategy: A Game Theorist's Guide to Success in Business and Life* (New York: W. W. Norton & Company, 2008).

16 See, for example, Bernard Guerrien, "Can We Expect Anything from Game Theory?" in *A Guide to What's Wrong with Economics*, ed. Edward Fullbrook (London and New York: Anthem Press, 2004), 198–209.

17 See, for example, Peter Wakker and Daniel Deneffe, "Eliciting von Neumann-Morgenstern Utilities When Probabilities Are Distorted or Unknown," *Management Science* 42 (1996): 1131–1150.

18 See http://en.wikipedia.org/wiki/Transatlantic_flight

19 This is of course not new. See, for example, Sharon M. Oster, *Modern Competitive Analysis* (New York: Oxford University Press, 1999).

20 Richard Thaler and Cass Sunstein, *Nudge: Improving Decisions About Health, Wealth, and Happiness* (London: Penguin Books, 2009). Daniel Kahneman, *Thinking, Fast and Slow* (London: Penguin Books, 2011).

2

Grand Strategy as a lead-in to Operational Strategy

The term "strategy" has an enticing ring to it. It brings to mind images of managers who rise above the daily mêlée and use their great wisdom to make decisions that have a profound impact on the course of their company, if not of history. More often than not, though, it turns out that having to revert to the use of the word "strategy" is an attempt to cover up deep hesitation or even desperation.

When a company announces that it is "investigating strategic options," it often means it is put with its back against the wall by investors who have run out of patience and are seeking to carve up the company. When a manager presents a new business proposal as a "strategic investment," most likely she reckons there is a fair chance the initiative will never make money. When the title on someone's business card reads "Senior Vice President Strategy," you may be dealing with a manager who did not quite make it higher up in the executive hierarchy. Finally, when a consultant calls himself a "strategy consultant," it may simply be a cover to extract higher fees for his services.

Be assured: neither hesitation nor desperation are the reason for us using the word "strategy" in the title or elsewhere in this book. We use the word as a reference to an end-to-end process to make better, solidly founded decisions to improve a company's performance. Furthermore, throughout this book we will keep on referring to what we call Grand Strategy and Operational Strategy, and to the fundamental distinction between these two concepts. That distinction is needed, not to create yet another disguised strategy fad, but to capture why business strategies often fail, and to understand what needs to be done to improve the effectiveness of strategy design. We explain this later.

It is fashionable these days to put the blame for the failure of a strategy on its poor execution or delivery rather than on flaws in its very design. As a matter of fact, strategy consultants often use this excuse to hold their clients accountable for a strategic recommendation not delivering the promised results. We are convinced that the failure of many business strategies is simply due to their flawed design. These design flaws occur whenever companies limit themselves to formulating wishes, ambitions, intentions or plans on the basis of senior executives' gut feel, pet ideas, infatuation with the latest management fad, opportunism to getting the budget approved or "we-need-to-communicate-something" needs. They simply don't take the time prior to implementation to rigorously assess the feasibility and effectiveness of their strategic choices and their financial effects.

To dramatically improve their chances of success, companies must understand that it is not their internal wishes or desires that will make or break a company's strategy but that it is ultimately customers' decisions to buy or not to buy its products or services that matters. Hence companies should base their strategic decisions on rigorous logic and real evidence drawn from potential customers who, in economists' terms, are maximizing their utility, and in layman's terms are just looking for the best deal. It is what these customers can be predicted to buy and, in particular, whether and how many of them will switch from their best alternative option to any of the company's proposed strategic offerings, that ultimately determines the success of a strategy.

That is why we make the distinction between Grand Strategy and Operational Strategy. Grand Strategy leads to intentions and hypotheses about the moves the company could make to attempt to attain a sustainable competitive advantage or, more realistically, an as-long-as-possible competitive advantage. Operational Strategy, then, tests these selected possibilities in depth, thus either confirming, detailing, adapting or rejecting the Grand Strategy hypotheses. Any such adaptation (of product or service features, price levels, target segments and the like) is based upon an evidence-based understanding of the various options that are needed and feasible to increase the percentage of potential customers that can be predicted to switch to the company's adapted new offerings. It is this understanding that ultimately should culminate in reliable estimates of attainable volumes at different price levels and hence revenue forecasts.

Many companies today do Grand Strategy some way or the other; very few do Operational Strategy. We are not advocating the abandonment of Grand Strategy. Quite to the contrary, we are saying that strategy formulation should be an end-to-end process, starting with Grand Strategy and leading to Operational Strategy.

In this chapter we will first elaborate on the meaning of Grand Strategy. Then we will further clarify why an end-to-end process covering both Grand Strategy and Operational Strategy is required. Next, we will describe an effective and efficient way of running the Grand Strategy part of the process, as a lead-in to Operational Strategy. Afterwards, we will demonstrate the merits of Grand Strategy other than being a required lead-in to Operational Strategy. And finally, we will illustrate the various concepts with a case example called Payroll Inc. The subsequent chapters of this book will be all about Operational Strategy.

One word of caution about this chapter on what we call Grand Strategy. Grand Strategy is an umbrella term for gazillions of quite similar approaches to strategy that companies, consultants and academics are already applying or advocating today. We are not bringing anything fundamentally new in this chapter. Many readers will be familiar with one or the other notion. The purpose of this chapter is to enable our diverse readers, from whatever "segment" they may be, to assess how their way of designing strategy fits with the end-to-end process (Grand Strategy + Operational Strategy) that we are advocating: what to keep, what to change, and how to connect to Operational Strategy.

▶ THE MEANING OF GRAND STRATEGY

Dear reader, did you ever dare to ask a company's boss whether he has a strategy? Asking the question is almost as insulting as enquiring whether he showered that morning. In any case it is very likely that the answer will be: "Of course we do have a strategy."

With that affirmative answer he may refer to a recent strategy exercise that resulted in a number of choices about "where to compete" and "how to compete", and in business goals to be achieved in 3 to 5 years' time. Or in the absence of such an explicit exercise, he may point to the fact that his managers are thinking all the time about where to spot a market opportunity, how to persuade customers, and how to beat competitors.

Those arguments are perfectly reasonable. The Oxford Dictionaries Online defines strategy as "a plan of action designed to achieve a long-term or overall aim", which is a shorthand version of Chandler's 1962 definition of strategy as "the determination of the basic long-term goals and objectives of an enterprise, and the adoption of courses of action and the allocation of resources for carrying out these goals."[1]

In fact, there is academically little disagreement about the meaning of business strategy. First, it is generally agreed that business strategy is about answering the following questions:

▶ Where to compete (in which product/service/solutions-market combinations);

▶ How to compete in these markets (with which specific products, services or solutions, at what price, and targeted to what segments);

▶ Which assets and capabilities to deploy or acquire to do so.

Second, the objective of such a strategy is to improve the company's profit performance in a way that the profit improvement is sustainable over time, which in reality boils down to "as-long-as-possible." Third, the "where to compete" and "how to compete" choices must be based on a combination of:

▶ The attractiveness of the markets in which the company could compete – everything else constant, the more attractive, the higher the average profitability of the players in that market;

▶ The company's assets and capabilities – the more the assets and capabilities can create competitive advantage in certain markets, the more a company does better than average;

▶   The barriers to imitation – the less the willingness and ability of competitors to imitate, the higher the sustainability of superior profits that are generated.

Hence, and fourth, strategy formulation requires an external analysis, an internal analysis and an analysis of imitation capabilities of existing or potential competitors.

When push comes to shove, those four points explain the essence of business strategy, whatever the wordings and fads put forward by managers, consultants and academics. For example, BCG uses the questions "where to play" and "how to win" to refer to the notions of where and how to compete, respectively.[2] In an article that received the McKinsey Award for best HBR article of the year, Professor David Collis and the late Michael Rukstad of Harvard Business School use "scope" and "advantage," respectively.[3]

More generally, a number of business books written several decades ago are still reasonably relevant to current business practice.[4] Michael Porter's statement, "In essence, the job of the strategist is to understand and cope with competition," is still very true, even if provokingly contested by INSEAD Professors Chan Kim and Renée Mauborgne, who proclaim "Don't compete with rivals, make them irrelevant."[5,6] Richard Rumelt, Professor at UCLA, provides a more secular description: "Strategy is not your aspirations. Strategy is concerned with how you will arrange your actions and resources to punch through the challenges you face."[7] Gary Pisano, Professor at Harvard Business School, offers a variation on the same tune: "A strategy is nothing more than a commitment to a pattern of behavior intended to help win a competition."[8] In our view, Constantinos Markides, Professor at the London Business School, puts it in the most down-to-earth way: "Business strategy is all about making difficult choices: Who will be your target customers? What will you offer them? How will you do it? The goal for every company should be to answer these questions differently from its competitors – and thus stake out a unique strategic position."[9] Lawrence Freedman, Professor of War Studies at King's College London, takes an alluring beyond-business view, arguing that strategy is about "employing whatever resources are available to achieve the best outcome in situations that are both dynamic and contested."[10]

In the following paragraphs we will explain how these elegant statements can be translated into a practical way of working. We will give a short refresher of the traditional strategy matrix and illustrate its use with an example. We will also point to the differences and links between strategy, vision, values and mission. As we have already cautioned earlier in this chapter: depending on your background and experience, you may already be familiar with some of these concepts, in which case we ask you to bear with us for a bit.

The strategy matrix: concept

A business strategy formulates choices, first about "where to compete." These are often expressed in terms of the product-market combinations that the company and its business units will focus on. A product is broadly defined here as a physical product (e.g., a car), a service (e.g., a rental car) or a solution (e.g., a mobility promise). A market can be defined by a combination of geography (e.g., the world or, say, sub-Saharan Africa), customer group (e.g., all customers or, say, private households) and application (e.g., all applications or, say, home-to-work commuting). From the description of the product and market follows the depth of the company's vertical integration (e.g., catalytic converter and/or exhaust system and/or assembled car).

A business strategy also includes the choices about "how to compete," that is about the specific products, services or solutions that the company will offer, at what price and targeted to what segments. These choices are informed by both external and internal considerations. The external considerations derive from an understanding of (1) how many customers there are in the targeted market, (2) how customers in these markets look at the company and its products, services or solutions and thus consider buying these rather than choosing another alternative, and (3) how customers differ in the way they look at these products, services or solutions. Factors that may impact customers' perception and willingness-to-buy are the company's brand, visible product attributes (e.g., look-and-feel), customer benefits (e.g., safety performance), price (e.g., total cost of ownership per mile) and any possible switching costs (from their current best alternative).

The internal considerations relate to the company's assets and capabilities. The focus is hereby on assets and capabilities that competitors find hard to imitate, at least temporarily (e.g., proprietary intellectual property, an exclusive partnership, a dense distribution network, a trusted brand). Some of these assets may already exist within the company, while others may need acquiring or developing (e.g., through a joint venture for engine development).

Both the "where to compete" and "how to compete" choices must be based upon a combination of the company's distinctive capabilities and assets, and the attractiveness of the markets in which the company could deploy these capabilities and assets. Market attractiveness is a relevant aspect, as it refers to two external factors, namely (1) the size and growth of the market, and (2) the extent to which, on average, prices can be elevated above cost in that market. A company's distinctive capabilities and assets are also a relevant aspect, as they determine the extent to which a particular company can do better or worse than the market average in meeting the needs of some customer groups, and thus the extent to which it can create a wedge between willingness-to-pay and the cost of meeting these needs.

In order to guide the discussions about these choices and to document their results, strategy practitioners are fond of using matrices. Anybody who has been to business school or has worked with strategy consultants knows, possibly to his chagrin, that matrices are the staple of Grand Strategy practitioners. Generally speaking, a matrix is a chart portraying the position of a portfolio of objects being analyzed – be they business units, companies, competitors, industries, customer segments, projects, research areas, etc. – in two dimensions that are considered to be of relevance for the strategic decisions to be made with regard to the portfolio of objects. For example, if we were to analyze a portfolio of proposed R&D projects, each project would be represented by a bubble, the size of which is proportional to the project's budget; we could then plot each R&D project in a two-dimensional field, based upon the assessment of its technical feasibility (horizontal axis) and the market potential of its targeted outcome (vertical axis); the resulting plot could inform an intelligent debate about priorities and the optimization of the portfolio.

To refresh the memory specifically about strategy matrices, let us review three of the better-known vintage matrices.[11] First comes BCG's growth-share matrix. It visualizes the relative market share enjoyed by a business unit (horizontal axis) and the growth rate of the market in which the business unit is operating (vertical axis).[12] Implicitly, the relative market share is supposed to capture the capability dimension, as a high market share is a one-dimensional indicator of the extent to which the company is able to meet customer needs. Similarly, the growth rate is a one-dimensional indicator of market attractiveness. Each business unit is represented by a circle, the area of which is proportional to business unit sales. Plotting all the company's business units in this grid could inform executives about cash allocation decisions. For example, a business unit with a high relative market share in a slow-growing market is considered to be a cash cow whose cash should be re-invested in other business units or corporate projects, or be used to reimburse investors.

The GE-McKinsey matrix plots the business units on two similar yet more broadly defined axes: the attractiveness of the industry to which the business unit belongs (horizontal axis) and the competitive strength of the business unit (vertical axis), which McKinsey & Co. is happy to interchange with "competitive advantage" or "competitive position."[13] As McKinsey & Co. emphasizes, the position of a business unit in the grid is just the starting point of an analysis of the most appropriate investment choice for it, such as "grow" or "exit."

Arthur D. Little's life-cycle approach is the third classic, even if largely forgotten by now. In this approach, business units are plotted in a grid showing the life-cycle stage of the industry to which the business unit belongs (horizontal axis) and the competitive position of the business unit (vertical axis). Again, the position of the business unit should suggest some strategic choice, such as "prove viability" or "selective development."

Rest assured that we will not explain the umpteen other matrices that have sprung from the imagination of strategy practitioners ever since. Extensive literature exists on the subject. Heroic ideological debates have raged about the finer merits and gross shortcomings of one or the other matrix. But while they do come in different shapes and forms, at the end of the day almost all of them boil down to the same two dimensions: "attractiveness" and "advantage" (or, occasionally, "fit" as a generic shorthand). They suggest that a company's choice of action should depend, on the one hand, on the intrinsic attractiveness of any arena in which it may choose to play; and, on the other hand, on how well its particular capabilities fit in: do they allow the company to create a competitive advantage in the arena concerned, and hence do better than average? In addition, the matrix should be used not only to plot today's position but also the future position (typically 3 to 5 years from now), assuming current planned investments. It is obviously the latter that is more important for making investment reallocations.

Furthermore, the matrix does not only analyze the expected attractiveness and future competitive position of the company's current businesses. More importantly, it is also used to assess the desirability of *new* areas of business, and is then populated with bubbles that represent the company's potential future businesses for which no bubbles exist. In the latter case, attractiveness refers to the future attractiveness of the market at the time of potential entry, and advantage relates to the company's future presumed potential competitive position.

As an aside, we should add an important warning here, even though we know that many strategy academics will frown at it: a company does not want competitive advantage per se – it wants to maximize commercial returns, usually in the form of profits. In that sense, competitive advantage is about creating a wedge between a customer's willingness-to-pay for a company's offering and the cost of doing so. In other words, competitive advantage is a relative concept that captures how the company is performing and, roughly, how profitable the company is relative to the other players in the same industry. A particular profit level can be achieved by riding the wave of a relatively profitable industry, without necessarily being a top performer, or by creating a competitive advantage in an otherwise low-profit industry or, finally, by being a relative underperformer in an utterly profitable industry. Obviously, the best of both worlds is to have a competitive advantage in a highly profitable industry, but the questions are usually about what to do when one does not have this luxury.

The attractiveness-advantage type of matrix neatly captures key concepts of two time-honored schools of thought about strategic management and integrates them into a simple and intuitive framework that managers find appealing and useful.[14] The attractiveness dimension dovetails with the school that teaches that strategy should primarily be designed based on an understanding of the structural characteristics of industries and competitors' presumed strategies. The advantage dimension dovetails with the school that teaches that strategy should primarily be designed based on the extent to which a company's specific resources, competences and management capabilities can be leveraged to create competitive advantage in different markets.

More recent constructs, such as Tod Zenger's foresight/insight/cross-sight theory, Christopher Bingham et al.'s position/leverage/opportunity framework and Arnoldo Hax's Delta model by and large fit into that mold.[15,16,17] So do some other approaches that correctly point out that a matrix is a static picture of reduced relevance in an increasingly turbulent business environment, and that thus a dynamic framework is called for. While the traditional matrix can also show some dynamics (e.g., plotting both current and future positions), more dynamic frameworks such as scenario analysis explicitly capture uncertainties: scenarios are narratives that visualize multiple plausible futures in which the company might compete.[18] Play-scripting is another one: a play-script is a narrative that involves the company and all other organizations connected to it, and that describes the changing roles each of these play.[19] These dynamic frameworks may indeed generate a movie rather than a picture, but a movie after all is a rapid sequence of pictures, and each of the pictures is still a two-dimensional frame of attractiveness and advantage.

The strategy matrix: example

To illustrate the idea, let us do a thought exercise related to a non-profit organization. Imagine that you are in charge of a youngsters' organization, and that you need to select some performing art or sport at which this group of, say, fifty kids should excel, so as to be able to perform for an audience on a regular basis. Your ideas about interesting domains run very broadly, and you could imagine the kids to become ballet dancers, circus artists, hockey players, wrestlers, basketball players . . . you name it. But you have to make choices, because you will need to recruit a trainer, spend time on promoting the group, etc. Therefore, as a Grand Strategist, you would proceed in four steps, with the first two steps running pretty much in parallel and/or iteratively.

As your goal is to excel, the first step is to look into the kids' talents. That in itself allows you to filter out those domains that are in any event ruled out due to the kids' inherent capabilities, and to creatively think through all domains at which they could possibly excel. To take an extreme example, imagine that most of the kids fall below the growth curve, and that upon reflection of what they are really good at, you conclude that they are particularly creative, borderline hilarious, when quarreling with each other. What does this accomplish? It helps at identifying domains beyond the ones that you may have been thinking of initially, such as activities where small size or low weight is an asset, not a liability. For instance, trick riding, which is about performing stunts while riding a horse, may not have been in your initial list but may be added upon reflection of the kids' specific "weakness," i.e., their small size. Alternatively, improvisational theater may not have come up in your initial list of domains either, but does come up when deeply reflecting upon the kids' capabilities.

This way of working also allows you to be efficient at identifying possible domains. For instance, in this case there is no point in spending time identifying the local neighborhood's interest in high jump, basketball or volleyball exhibition games, whatever the neighborhood may be willing to pay to attend such events.

After having narrowed down your list of domains based on your understanding of the kids' capabilities, you are ready for the second step. You would think about how easy it will be to attract an audience for any specific domain, not just once, but time and again. How big an audience you can attract and how much you could charge for an entrance ticket will depend on the size and the possibly latent interests of the population in the neighborhood. It will also depend on whether other groups are already active in the domain; whether your audience would compare the others' performance with what you have in mind; how your performance would be different from the others'; and how the others might react once you enter the field. Of course, you would also think about the potential growth of the size of the audience over time.

In the third step, for each of the retained domains, you would dig deeper into your kids' talents and at the diversity therein. You would consider how well their physical, intellectual, artistic and psychological abilities would allow them to excel in each of the retained domains. You earmark one sub-group as the creative actors, the others as the ballet dancers, and yet another group as the trick riders, etc. The creative actors sub-group, for example, may already form a dream team, pretty much ready to perform on stage. But the trick riders sub-group may have the advantage of being tiny and able to keep their balance, while only a few of them have actually ridden horses. They are not quite fit for a performance at this stage, unless you invest a lot of time and effort at raising or honing their horseback riding skills.

Finally, holding your breath, you would draw an attractiveness-advantage matrix (see Figure 2.1). You would use your best judgment in plotting each sub-group and throw in some back-of-the-envelope financials on top. Then, you would present the matrix to the kids' parents for approval. You would recommend going for improvisational theater and wrestling, and, ultimately, forget about trick riding.

Sounds artificial, if not ridiculously childish? Maybe it does. But what we have just described is the essence of Grand Strategy. Basically, we are saying

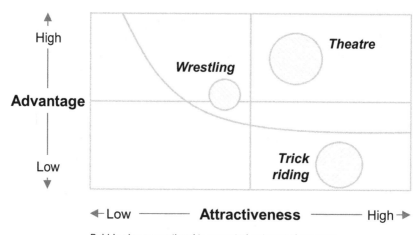

Bubble size proportional to expected net annual revenue

FIGURE 2.1 Example of attractiveness-advantage matrix

that we will go for what we are good at and for which we can create some lasting interest, while spending our money wisely.

That being said, we should realize that the recommendations are still at the level of hypotheses. We have relied upon assumptions about the neighborhood's preferences. We have no evidence from the field that our hypotheses are right. For example, we have not gone out to put representative people in choice situations in order to test which audiences would be attracted by which specific offerings relative to the many other ways in which they could spend their leisure time. But at this Grand Strategy stage of the strategy process, that is fine. The validation and adaption of the hypotheses and the detailing of the choices will be part of the Operational Strategy stage, which we will cover from Chapter 3 onward.

The example also points to the weakness of the so-called SWOT (Strengths-Weaknesses-Opportunities-Threats) tool loved by – forgive our arrogance – amateur strategists. A SWOT analysis would have pigeonholed the kids' small size as a weakness, whereas in reality it is an asset that at least a priori forms the basis for a viable offering. Similarly, SWOT categorizes an external trend as either an opportunity or a threat, but the meaning of an external trend for a company depends on how it deals with the trend. For example, a declining birth rate at first sight may spell disaster for any retail chain active in baby clothing; but it may be an opportunity to have parents and grandparents spend more on the fewer kids they have. Likewise, SWOT assumes that stronger is always better, but when it comes to a competence that is a must-have yet without scope for differentiation, "good enough" is better than "best," lest resources are wasted. For example, a retail chain may have a great secure online payment system, but there is no point in investing in a level of security that exceeds industry standards as it may not have any effect on customer choices. Let's summarize by saying that the SWOT tool is so fundamentally flawed that we will not spend any more time explaining it.

The link with mission, values and vision

The strategy matrix, and other more dynamic tools such as play-scripting that emphasize agility, help to think about and visualize "where to compete" and "how to compete" choices on the basis of market attractiveness and the company's potential competitive advantage. These choices constitute what we call a Grand Strategy.

You may wonder, dear reader, how the other popular concepts of "mission," "values" and "vision" fit into this picture. It suffices to read the statements of a couple of companies to see that these terms are often used interchangeably. For example, what one company calls a vision, is called a mission by another one. The confusion does not matter too much, as long as the content is meaningful to the people concerned. That being said, most professionals would use the definitions in the paragraphs that follow, or at least something that closely resembles them.

Let us start with mission. A company's mission is a statement of purpose. It makes the company's raison d'être explicit. The link with Grand Strategy is that it ultimately constrains the choices about where and how to compete. P&G, for example, refers to its mission as Our Purpose, which reads as follows (at least at the time of this writing):

> We will provide branded products and services of superior quality and value that improve the lives of the world's consumers, now and for generations to come. As a result, consumers will reward us with leadership sales, profit and value creation, allowing our people, our shareholders and the communities in which we live and work to prosper.

Walmart's evolved from the lyrical "To give ordinary folk the chance to buy the same thing as rich people" to the more prosaic "Saving people money so they can live better," but the essence has not changed. Facebook states that the most important thing it can do is "to develop the social infrastructure to give people the power to build a global community that works for all of us."[20] The International Diabetes Federation, to take a non-profit organization, has an even more precise and concise statement: "To promote diabetes care, prevention and a cure worldwide."

Companies bother about mission statements because meaningful choices about where and how to compete can only be made at the level of the company's business units: after all, a business unit by definition is a part of the company's activities for which a strategy can be developed independently of the other business units. Furthermore, these choices are subject to regular updates, say once every three years. The company may also decide to create new business units or eliminate existing ones. Therefore, the business unit level choices at most companies are embedded, implicitly or explicitly, in some more overarching, unifying and enduring guidelines at corporate level that set the (sometimes fuzzy or permeable) boundaries for what the company as a whole will and will not strive to do (e.g., a passenger car manufacturer choosing to stay out of the commercial vehicles business).

A company's values are a statement of behavior. They serve as the internal compass that should guide the actions of all its employees. They prescribe the desired attitudes and character of the organization. P&G states that "Our Values reflect the behaviors that shape the tone of how we work with each other and with our partners," and has grouped them under the headings of Integrity, Leadership, Ownership, Passion for Winning, and Trust.

A company's vision is a statement of aspiration. It sets the goals the company wants to achieve at some (defined or uncertain) point in time. It describes the kind of organization it wants to become. Volkswagen Group in 2011 defined

> four goals that are intended to make Volkswagen the most successful and fascinating automaker in the world by 2018: leading in customer satisfaction and quality; Volkswagen Group profit before tax margin > 8%; volumes > 10 million units p.a.; top employer.

The International Diabetes Federation simply states that its vision is "Living in a world without diabetes."

A company's mission and values clearly fall outside the scope of what we call Grand Strategy. They provide the context and boundaries within which Grand Strategy choices must be made. These choices must stay true to the company's mission and values.

The distinction is less clear cut for the company's vision. The vision describes the company's longer-term goals and aspired future state. The strategy describes the choices and associated concrete steps the company anticipates to take to get from its current state to the aspired state (e.g., an R&D project, a new product line, the set-up of a foreign subsidiary, an acquisition, a stock-market listing, the creation of an online distribution channel, etc.). Hence, a company's vision and strategy are designed iteratively. The company's over-all goals, if intended to be attainable, should be the consolidated outcome of a series of strategic choices. Conversely, the company's vision may contain some non-economic goals (that is, environmental, social or governance goals such as being among the Ten Best Employers in the country) to be taken into account when making strategic choices.

▶ GRAND STRATEGY AND OPERATIONAL STRATEGY AS AN END-TO-END PROCESS

A company needs both Grand Strategy and Operational Strategy and should closely link them. Operational Strategy should be preceded by Grand Strategy, and Grand Strategy should be followed by Operational Strategy. In the following paragraphs we will explain why that is the case. We will also explain why this book focuses on Operational Strategy.

Why Operational Strategy should be preceded by Grand Strategy

A company's business strategy is ultimately about determining product-market combinations (PMCs) with which it can earn a sustainable, or, at least, as-long-as-possible economic profit. It involves making two choices simultaneously and iteratively: determining the company's offering (i.e., different sets of product/service features and prices) and selecting customer segments (i.e., groups of customers with sufficiently homogenous willingness-to-pay). Which of these PMCs could provide a sustainable profit in essence depends on three factors: trends and opportunities existing in the outside world, the distinctive assets and capabilities the company can bring to bear, and barriers to imitation and retaliation by potential competitors.

Operational Strategy tools – which we will explain in-depth in the subsequent chapters – serve to identify and assess a company's potential in specific PMCs. There are countless existing and novel opportunities (products, services or solutions), each covering numerous stages of the industry value chain (e.g., from raw materials to distribution) and various geographic and customer segments. Ideally one would like to perform an in-depth assessment of both the attractiveness of each potential market and the company's ability to create sustainable competitive advantage in each of these markets, culminating in a business plan with evidence-based financial forecasts. In practice such a sequential, exhaustive, quantified, evidence-based assessment is impossible to do for each imaginable opportunity because of the time and investment required. At the same time, arbitrarily limiting the number of opportunities to be investigated is equally problematic because of the risk that creative out-of-the-box opportunities are overlooked.

Hence, a company needs an efficient mechanism to funnel, screen and filter potential opportunities that pop up. It should be able to make well-founded decisions in an efficient manner about the types of opportunities that are worth taking through an in-depth assessment. As a consequence, a company needs a funnel process by which it first sets an (inspirational) ambition level for the overarching goals it wants to achieve at some distant future point in time (this is its "vision"); then establishes some a priori boundaries (albeit permeable) of the types of businesses it will and will not consider; then captures insights from diverse internal and external sources to generate (sometimes wild) business ideas and opportunities; and finally deploys some quick-and-dirty methods to screen the business ideas and opportunities (for example through a strategy matrix), and formulate hypotheses about which of these remaining opportunities appear sufficiently promising to subject them to an in-depth assessment.

Grand Strategy is such a funnel process. It is used to develop high-level changes in the company's overall direction and focus. Operational Strategy is about the subsequent in-depth assessments, leading to either the confirmation and detailing, the adaptation or the rejection of the Grand Strategy hypotheses. Operational strategy makes sure that the Grand Strategy changes do not stay as just high-level semi-finished wishes, but convert into operationally detailed and evidence-based choices leading to commercial improvements; or, worst case, it reveals that the suggested direction needs to be revisited.

A company cannot do Operational Strategy in a void without the direction, focus and creative stimulus provided by Grand Strategy. Conversely, senior executives should not consider their job done when they have designed the company Grand Strategy, leaving Operational Strategy to lower-level managers in the field. They should go down all the way into Operational Strategy, because it may tell them that the intent and directional choices that resulted from their Grand Strategy exercise turn out to be wrong: their wishes about the sales and profit potential of their hypothesized offerings just do not, or at least not sufficiently correspond to what customers would actually buy. They should thoroughly understand why they may have to backtrack on decisions made earlier and change course.

For example, when toying with a strategy matrix, say in preparation of a Grand Strategy off-site, executive teams tend to use a merely qualitative low-medium-high scale to plot the positions of the company's existing businesses and new opportunities onto that matrix. They are unlikely to show great interest in backing up the positions in the matrix with reams of hard figures, as they reckon that the illusory precision is not worth the effort. Is this a bad attitude? Not necessarily, as long as the participants in the off-site realize that the resulting Grand Strategy statements are just qualitative hypotheses, and as long as they are willing to follow on with Operational Strategy to either confirm, detail, adapt or reject the hypotheses. In other words, Grand Strategy is fine as long as it is the start of an end-to-end process that closes with Operational Strategy.

Like the coned beam of a flashlight in the dark, Grand Strategy illuminates the boundaries of a supposedly safe way forward. The further out, the wider the angle and the lower the visibility. As one moves forward, one distinguishes more clearly the specific obstacles that emerge from the dark, at which point one devises an Operational Strategy to dodge them. But sometimes during this imaginary journey in the dark, one may be confronted with an insurmountable obstacle (say, a deep ravine) or a path too risky to follow (say, crowded with wild animals). At such points, courage should prevail over doggedness, and one should turn the flashlight sideways or even backtrack. The same applies to business decisions: if the outcome of the Operational Strategy exercise reveals that there are too many insurmountable obstacles or risks, one should be ready to revise or relinquish the hypothesis and intent formulated in the Grand Strategy exercise.

For example, one of our clients, call it BandCo, was a medical supplies company whose product range included safety devices to identify and trace patients in hospitals. It had embarked on a Grand Strategy to become a leading supplier of a broader range of medical supplies (medical aprons, medical labels, syringes, surgical sutures and the like). To that end, it had even acquired a company (BibCo) in its largest geographical market, knowing that BibCo was dominant in one of these supposedly complementary areas, including medical bibs and aprons. The Grand Strategy was in fact so engrained in the company that it had changed its name from BandCo to BandCo BibCo. The question now was about how to operationalize the strategy of expansion into these complementary medical supplies in other geographic markets where BibCo had not been present previously. In the Operational Strategy phase, it unfortunately turned out that the maximum potential to grow share profitably in the bib and apron market in these other geographic markets was limited and surely not worth the required investments to do so. As a result, the company did abandon its efforts and, later on, inconspicuously dropped BibCo from its corporate name, reverting back to the original BandCo name.

Why Grand Strategy should be followed by Operational Strategy

As is also clear from the preceding BandCo example, Grand Strategy alone is not fit for concrete strategic decisions that translate into specific investments and expectations of return for which specific managers are likely to be held accountable sooner rather than later. When that is at stake, Grand Strategy should retire and free up space for Operational Strategy. Managers need skills in Operational Strategy when they irrevocably commit millions of dollars and a bucketful of career prospects. It is in such critical moments that they wish they had something more robust than Grand Strategy, namely a precise and evidence-based documentation supporting the desirability and feasibility of the specific strategic choice.

One of the most devastating facts demonstrating the inappropriateness of relying on industry averages for concrete strategic decisions is a finding by Marakon Associates on differences in company profitability, as reported by Pankaj Ghemawat and Jan Rivkin.[21] Comparing the profitability of businesses, they report that only 10 to 20% of the variation in profitability is explained by differences in average industry profitability. Within-industry effects explain 30 to 45%, and effects that fluctuate from year to year account for the remaining variation. L.G. Thomas and Richard D'Aveni not only have confirmed these findings but also point out that the relative importance of the latter two factors, i.e., within-industry effects and the volatility of temporary performance, has increased over time.[22] That is, (guesstimated) average attractiveness matters in making strategic decisions about which markets to compete in . . . but not very much.

What matters more is how well a company performs or is expected to perform within an industry. And that requires that a company knows how and where its specific capabilities can be leveraged to profitably come up with products, services or solutions that, everything else constant, a sufficiently large number of customers would want to buy at a price that significantly exceeds costs. To estimate this, it is critical to understand individual customer preferences and whether some of these customers' preferences can be triggered or developed to induce them to buy the company's (new) products or services. That is the essence of Operational Strategy: understanding potential customer choices on the basis of in-depth evidence unknown even to those customers, rather than on what the executives think customers are likely to choose or, even worse, should choose. Customers' choices ultimately determine what the company's competitive position and surely the company's revenues will be. Operational Strategy thus substitutes accurate evidence for Grand Strategy hypotheses that build on existing data of average market profitability and on gut feel about the competitive position, revenues and margins that the company is assumed to be able to achieve in a market.

Operational Strategy provides evidence-based answers to a number of questions: what investments are needed to convince an individual customer to consider abandoning her best alternative option (which could be her current supplier, another supplier or simply "nothing") and buy your company's products or services instead? How many customers will switch, given their differences in preferences? And how does this investment compare to the benefits your company gets from those customers switching?

We do hope that you will agree with us that these are the key questions that need to be answered before committing resources. In the chapters that follow, we will provide a pragmatic step-by-step approach to handling such assessments. For now, do not get worried if you do not quite see yet how you could answer these questions in practice.[23]

Clearly, Grand Strategy and Operational Strategy are not two different worlds in two different time zones populated by different tribes. Grand

Strategy and Operational Strategy, while being distinct, feed on each other, and involve the same managers. Grand Strategy is a statement of intent. It is based upon presumed customer needs and upon the presumed relevance of the company's capabilities. The accountability for its realization is safely distant, both time-wise and person-wise. Operational Strategy, on the other hand, implies an irrevocable commitment of resources; it is based upon evidence of likely customer behavior and upon specific actions through which the company's proven capabilities are deployed; and it translates into time-bound budgets and budget assumptions for which specific managers will be held accountable.

To clarify the difference between Grand Strategy and Operational Strategy in yet another way, let us consider two fairly recent studies that purport to explain, once and for all, what makes a company truly exceptional. The first study, by consultants at Deloitte, claims to have identified, on the basis of a statistical study of thousands of US.-traded companies, two foundational concepts on which companies have built greatness over many years.[24] First, "compete on differentiators other than price," such as brand, style or reliability. Second, "prioritize increasing revenue over reducing costs," through either higher prices or greater volume.

We respect others' views, but Deloitte's definitely is not ours. We find that it is utterly risky to work with general rules based upon "on average" results. In strategy, averages never matter. It is the specific situation that does. That the greatest companies have strong brands, stylish products and so on is no surprise. But it does not mean that as a general rule one should invest in, say, a brand. For example, the brand value for base or intermediate chemical products is often less than 1% of the price. So why should a base or intermediate chemical company want to invest in the brand when the return is so small? It is almost a recipe for financial failure.

Should one have higher prices then? Compared to what? Tell this story to the low-cost airlines and they'd send you into orbit if they could. In their very case and given their very target segment, higher prices are a recipe for failure, as most of the people in that segment only care about one thing: the lowest price. In this case, lower prices *up to a point* will lead to higher revenues, even though this may not be the case in many other situations.[25] Following general rules when such rules are simply not generalizable or applicable can just kill a business.

The key questions are: in my very business, is there a willingness-to-pay for brand? By how many customers? When is brand not important? When is it worth investing in differentiators and the like? And when do these so-called differentiators differentiate insufficiently, relative to a customer's willingness-to-pay for these differentiators? In the latter case, differentiation is again not worth the effort, as more value can be offered to the customer by precisely eliminating the pseudo-differentiating elements, and possibly even give some of the cost savings back to the customer through lower prices or other benefits.

Again, in strategy there are no general rules that one should follow, nor benchmarks, to use a scientific-sounding term. Benchmarks are important for operational excellence to answer questions such as "how many hours should a salesperson spend at the client in the fine chemical industry?" They are meaningless, even dangerous in strategy. Cross-industry comparisons of the preceding type do not address the industry-specific issues. And intra-industry comparisons or benchmarks ignore one fundamental thing: strategy is not about doing the same thing, but about doing things differently. There are no general strategies (low cost versus differentiation) that always work, just as there are no general strategies that always work in chess-games. In fact, when playing against a star chess player, one may have just one chance out of 1000 to win the game. When doing the same as the champion, chances are zero.

In strategy, the crux of the matter is to understand what customers are willing to pay for, if anything, relative to the cost of offering the product, service or differentiator, and make decisions accordingly. It is to understand what specific differences in the company's offering at which price do make a sufficient number of customers switch to its offering so that it maximizes profits, given the development and marginal cost of supplying the offering, and given competitors' ability and willingness to emulate the company's strategy. Answering these questions based upon real customer-driven data is the heart of Operational Strategy.

The second study, by consultants at McKinsey & Co., aims at distilling, from a study of nearly 3000 global companies, generalizable lessons about what it takes to win consistently.[26] Their advice to companies that are in the elite, i.e., have sustained the highest economic profit over more than a decade, is as follows: "If you're in the elite, 'use it or lose it.' . . . Really know the formula that got you there and vigilantly watch for signs of change. You can't rest on your laurels." We cannot argue with that wise counsel, but the real question is how one gets in the elite, and how one stays there. Our answer is to go beyond Grand Strategy into Operational Strategy.

Why this book focuses on Operational Strategy

While Grand Strategy and Operational Strategy are equally needed, all of the following chapters of this book are devoted to the latter. We find that crafting Grand Strategy is overhyped while the real proof of the pudding is in the design of Operational Strategy – this is where actual decisions and commitments are made, and the numbers kick in, top and bottom line.

Grand Strategy is not only overhyped but its conceptual foundations are often weak. Consultants often facilitate Grand Strategy projects to get excitement, alignment and stretched ambitions. As we said in Chapter 1, there is absolutely zero foundation for the belief that a stretched ambition is a guarantee for success. It has to be able to pass the test of market economics: if strategy were so easy as setting an ambition, understanding the gap, and then filling the gap, then everybody would scramble to fill that very gap. But if everybody can do it, and there are markets out there, you will not make money at it, while making money is ultimately the goal of strategy. There has to be a solid economic foundation, even if only in hypothetical terms, for this stretched ambition to create value.

We can only speculate why Grand Strategy is overhyped. Maybe it helps to think about the "I don't sell perfume, I sell hope" saying, which is varyingly attributed to Coco Chanel, Charles Revlon and Helena Rubinstein. While perfumes are expensive both to market and to buy, these grand products are supposed to make you feel good. And if the commercials are to be believed, they even make people in the street turn their heads.

One of the reasons why Grand Strategy may be akin to perfume is that some not-so-solid consultants can package the process well, for example by referring to the miraculous achievements of hero companies, as discussed in Chapter 1. Such projects presumably are easier to sell than projects that start from the hard, not-so-pleasant reality of a company struggling to enter a new market staunchly defended by incumbents, or to ward off an aggressive entrant, or to find a way to differentiate its offerings to customers who mostly care about price.

Grand Strategy visioning exercises may be fun too. But they are often quite unfounded, as participants are supposed to look into what they want to be, both for themselves and for the company, rather than what they can be, given their capabilities. Guess what? Such poorly conceived visioning workshops may take two days, but they pretty much invariably end up with the same outcome: "We want to be number one." They rarely, if ever, conclude with "we want to be the fourth largest player in the industry," for instance.

So, yes, Grand Strategy smells great, just like perfume. But as we do not like to admit but all know: if you don't look that great, perfume will not help – it may make things worse. Analogously, going for an unfounded Grand Strategy goal independent of the company's current capabilities and market reality is worse than doing business as usual.

Operational Strategy, by way of contrast, is akin to medicine. If well designed, well prescribed and well administered, it relieves pain, cures diseases and strengthens the body. That is why we would rather focus on Operational Strategy, in spite of Coco Chanel's insistence that "une femme sans parfum est une femme sans avenir" ("a woman without perfume is a woman without a future"). We believe that a woman (or a man, for that matter) who stays in shape without perfume (or cologne) has a better future than a coach potato drenched in various fragrances.

▶ GOOD PRACTICE FOR THE GRAND STRATEGY DESIGN PROCESS

A company not only needs both Grand Strategy and Operational Strategy, it should also closely link the two, as we have just explained. If Grand Strategy is done as a lead-in to Operational Strategy in an end-to-end process – with senior executives being involved in both – the strategy process will be both more effective (i.e., leading to evidence-based choices that generate economic profit) and more efficient (i.e., not wasting time on seeking in-depth evidence for unpromising choices that could have been discarded up front). Of course, that benefit will be achieved only if the Grand Strategy process itself is designed well. A Grand Strategy process is well-designed if it is fit for purpose, efficient and open to out-of-the-box opportunities, and embedded in daily life.

A fit for purpose process

A company's executive team does Grand Strategy implicitly all the time, certainly in turbulent and fast-changing environments requiring responses on the spot. Executives constantly think of threats to the profitability of the business, and consequently also think about opportunities to counter these threats. But sometimes they want to go through an explicit Grand Strategy exercise. There is no one-size-fits-all design for such an explicit exercise. The design may range from a one-off study outsourced to a strategy consultant, to a series of visioning workshops in which a broad selection of senior managers participates. Which design is chosen depends on three factors: the specific circumstances that triggered the need for the explicit Grand Strategy exercise; the nature of the strategic issues to be addressed; and the company's maturity in terms of strategic thinking. Let us have a look at these three factors.

The trigger of the explicit Grand Strategy exercise

Generally speaking, there are two circumstances that may lead to the conclusion that it is time for an explicit Grand Strategy exercise. One is externally driven and the other is internally-driven.

The externally driven occasion relates to many a CEO's ever-present angst that some major opportunities, i.e., things with a long-term impact or being out of the ordinary, get ignored in day-to-day business discussions or in the annual budgeting exercises. An explicit Grand Strategy exercise may allow the executive team to systematically connect the dots, perform an inside-out reflection starting from the company's capabilities, and generate ideas for (radically) new business opportunities, i.e., solutions for particular market needs. They can then also make a high-level evaluation of these solutions based on the attractiveness of the market and the company's ability to have a favorable position in it. In short it allows the team, by and large, to assess how well the company's solutions would meet customer needs relative to other solutions.

The internally driven occasion relates to many a CEO's constant quest to leverage the collective intelligence and strengthen the cohesion of her executive team: confront each executive with the others' ideas; crystallize their shared experiences into a coherent view; and condense their combined intuition into a meaningful statement of choices about which opportunities to pursue and how do to so.

The specific triggers that lead to the conclusion that the time has come for a Grand Strategy exercise can be quite diverse. One situation is when a new CEO comes on board and seeks a way to confirm and commit to the company's future direction, scope and overall goals together with her executive team. For example, at a materials manufacturing company, the Chief Financial Officer was appointed to be the new CEO, and soon after decided to bring his executive team together for a two-day off-site visioning session. While the company was doing very well and the outcome of the process did not include any radical changes to the company's strategy, the exercise enabled the CEO to make his mark and strengthen the bonds within his new team.

In other situations, some strategic questions may have been swirling around for quite a while within the executive team, without ever getting a clear, conclusive and shared answer, prompting the CEO to do an exercise to settle these questions "once and for all." For example, at a financial services company active in Europe and Asia, one of the pet ideas of some senior executives was that the company should enter Africa rather soon. While that and other similar issues did not require urgent resolution, the CEO finally decided to have a two-day off-site with his entire team to identify all these lingering strategic issues and collectively agree on the directional choices for each of them.

In still other situations, the company may have emerged successfully from a traumatic event that had required everybody to focus on the short term, and is then seeking to establish some longer-term strategic directions. In one specific case, a truck company came out of bankruptcy through the injection of fresh capital and a partial change of the senior management team. One year after the crisis and rebirth, the company's business was stable again, prompting the CEO to launch a three-month strategic exercise to outline the direction for the next five years.

Yet another trigger could be external events that catch the management team unaware and confront it with some basic soul-searching questions about its scope, direction and focus. Examples of such external events can be a failed takeover bid and break-up attempt of the company; a public castigation of the company by a non-governmental organization, pressure group or activist investor; or a major unexpected move by a competitor affecting the prevailing equilibria in the industry – think about Mittal Steel's unheard-of but successful bid for Arcelor in 2006, which created a firm more than three times bigger than its nearest rival in the steel industry. Or imagine the introspections occurring in the automotive industry in the early 1990s when Nicolas Hayek, the then-CEO of the Swatch Group, launched his ideas for the ultra-urban car eventually called Smart.

Finally, the annual budgeting exercise may also trigger a Grand Strategy initiative. The budgeting exercise may show (again) that continuing on the business-as-usual path is leading to declining revenue and/or profit growth rates, prompting the CEO to ask her team to do a systematic in-depth search for (radically) new growth opportunities. For example, a manufacturer of nonwoven materials for technical textiles decided to launch an ideation project to think through how it could identify and capitalize on new areas for growth. Ideation is the creative process of generating and elaborating new ideas. In this specific case, the unmet need was identified quickly: it related to soccer fields in areas where water is in short supply and a need exists for an alternative for standard rubber-filled artificial turf fields that are too hot to play on. The ideation sessions focused on how to meet that need, given the company's current capabilities and the complementary capabilities it could acquire.

The nature of the strategic issues

The second factor influencing the design of the Grand Strategy process is the nature of the strategic issues to be addressed. For example, if the issue is about identifying specific new potential areas for growth starting from the current technology portfolio, then it makes sense to set up a multi-disciplinary project team using ideation techniques and making proposals to the company's executive team. If the issue is about establishing strategic principles that can guide the company in initiating or responding to potential long-term corporate-level partnerships, then a one-day closed-doors off-site with the executive team may be more appropriate. Likewise, if the issue centers around setting priorities between ten alternative product-market combinations, then it makes perfect sense to work explicitly with attractiveness-advantage matrices. Finally, if the issue centers around the company's potential responses to alternative M&A scenarios that could materialize within its industry, then a well-prepared, structured and intelligent debate may suffice.

The maturity of the executive team

The third factor influencing the design of the Grand Strategy process is the maturity of the company's executive team in terms of strategic thinking.

Some companies have an extremely entrepreneurial, operational and pragmatic culture where decisions are made instinctively on-the-spot, driven by a fast trial-and-error philosophy rather than by thoughtful upfront considerations of core capabilities, competitive intensity and other strategy jargon. At such low-maturity companies (which nonetheless can be very successful), one would use other steps and tools than at companies dominated by brainy MBAs (let alone former strategy consultants) that have a tradition of going through formal strategic planning. For example, at a low-maturity company, it may be counterproductive if not outright dangerous to hold just a two-day visioning off-site out of the blue. By lack of a shared strategy vocabulary, frame of reference and joint travelling experience, the hyped off-site may derail into a sterile show-and-tell contest, a souped-up budgeting exercise, an entertaining pie-in-the-sky daytrip, or some other happening without much positive impact.

An efficient process

To make the Grand Strategy process efficient, we generally advocate the so-called inside-out approach. When looking for new paths for growth, a company should ask first what it is particularly good at, either in terms of capabilities (say, inventory management) or in terms of the functional properties of its current products (say, fire-resistance). It should then think through the markets in which these capabilities (or competences, what's in a name?) can be set to use, or brainstorm about the new product applications made possible by these functional properties.

This inside-out approach is the opposite of the outside-in approach of markets-first capabilities-second. The inside-out approach tends to be more efficient because it filters out ideas for opportunities for which the company lacks the capabilities. It can of course acquire some capabilities, but if it has to acquire *all* capabilities to get the job done, it will not make much money, as in well-functioning markets the value will be totally provided by the current owner of the capabilities. In other words, the inside-out approach prevents wasting time on the in-depth exploration of seemingly wonderful market opportunities that the company could not deliver profitably.

We recall a case in which a client of ours was a proud producer of a basic ingredient that was claimed to have some health benefits in a number of markets: nutraceuticals, nutricosmetics, cosmeceuticals and sports nutrition.

Specific submarkets included skin care, nail care, joint health, health nutrition, wound healing and a number of others. The company wanted to investigate its potential to enter different stages of the value chain and different regions in the world for each of these submarkets. To that purpose, it started a Grand Strategy exercise outside-in: analyzing the attractiveness of the market and the presence of competitors in each of these combinations of submarket, value chain stage and region. With eight submarkets, five value chain stages and five regions, we were talking about two hundred possible markets to analyze! Half a year later, the analyst in charge of this research was still doing market attractiveness analysis. When asked what one concludes from a market being attractive, the analyst was dead silent, as most attractive markets were indeed terribly difficult to enter and would require this company to acquire all relevant capabilities.

The key question is of course not to figure out whether these markets are attractive. By that argument, one can find many more attractive markets: how about the market for products that can make you live forever? Or, more seriously, how about the fragrance market? Or, to take an exaggerated case to make the point, how about the market for aircraft manufacturing? These markets are on average attractive to a great extent because they are protected by barriers that are terribly difficult to overcome. And they are difficult to enter because they benefit from a first-mover brand advantage that latecomers lack (fragrance industry), or they require much specific knowledge and a capability that latecomers may not have (aircraft manufacturing).

So, when looking for growth opportunities, rather than performing an analysis of possible markets, it makes a lot more sense to first analyze what the company is capable of doing or what benefits it can produce first, and then filter out what markets it would consider based upon this understanding. This allows one to understand which firm-specific barriers the company can overcome that others may not be able to do. Going back to the preceding example, if the company's basic ingredient is not shown to have much effectiveness in bone health, then why bother analyzing the 25 combinations of value chain stages and geographic combinations associated with the bone health application?

A process leading to out-of-the-box opportunities

In addition to being efficient, the inside-out approach has the advantage of stimulating totally out-of- the-box ideas that may be overlooked otherwise.

Far-sightedness and peripheral vision are not frivolous qualities. Quite to the contrary, a company's capability of sensing, interpreting, and acting on weak signals about opportunities and threats emerging from changes in technology and consumer tastes is critical.[27] Day and Schoemaker's research in fact shows that less than 20% of firms have developed such peripheral vision in sufficient capacity to remain competitive. The concepts of "marketing myopia" (the phenomenon that a company withers because it concentrates on selling its current products while ignoring its customers' shifting needs) and "the innovator's dilemma" (the phenomenon that a leading company is so good at something that it continues putting all its efforts into perfecting it, but fatally ignores or denies the emergence of a disruptive technology or innovation) reinforce this view.[28,29] More recently, attention has gone also to "big-bang disrupters" (the idea that entire product lines are being wiped out in a very short period of time by game-changing innovations) and "transient advantage" (the idea that companies in high-velocity industries should focus on a portfolio of transient advantages instead of a sustainable competitive advantage).[30,31]

Opening the mind to new paths for growth in new markets currently not served or envisaged is especially important when current markets commoditize and the company is not the low-cost player. Inside-out creative thinking reduces the risk of being totally constrained by one's current industry blindness or by ideas for growth generated by people who tend to focus on the current business or anything adjacent to it. The ideas for these potential future businesses can be gathered by asking managers for ideas obtained from open-minded customers, suppliers and other sources with which they interact on a daily basis. Alternatively, structured ideation sessions can be organized in order to increase the chances of generating out-of-the-box ideas that may be totally unrelated to the company's current markets but at the same time feasible for the company.

Inside-out thinking does not mean that one should spend endless workshops on identifying current capabilities, and only think through customer needs and market potential much later on in the process. To the contrary, Grand Strategy truly calls for an analysis of both internal capabilities and external needs and markets, in an iterative way. Any good executive is able to do the two in rapid succession. It is the equivalent of the debate by innovation scholars about the distinction between "technology-push" and "market-pull." At the end of the day, successful innovation results from an interlocking push-pull process.

An example of successful inside-out approach to strategy is that of a manufacturer of extruded polystyrene foam. This company was totally focused on cost cutting, as its customers used the material in commodity applications such as packaging and insulation. Ideas of current customers, management and staff were focused on only one thing: how to cut costs further. In fact, marketing was pretty much non-existing in this company. Such cost cutting was necessary as, barring some specific logistical services, the company's customers only wanted one thing: the lowest possible price. A Grand Strategy reflection changed things dramatically. The company started digging into the physical properties of the material, which can be summarized as: (1) having a high strength-to-weight ratio, (2) having hydrophobic properties and preventing water penetration, (3) being cost effective and easy to use, and (4) being virtually permanent/non-degradable. Understanding these physical properties and totally forgetting about current applications, the company started to get involved in a number of ideation sessions in which five hundred new ideas were generated in 20 new applications, including many creative ones (how about floating oil rigs?), which were filtered for feasibility. Eventually, the market potential for 30 new business opportunities was analyzed. That is, the market attractiveness of these new applications was analyzed in combination with the ability of the company to position itself favorably in this market: does it meet a need better or at a lower cost than existing applications; or even better, does it meet an unmet need that is, by definition, not met by others? Eventually this process led to a more than twofold increase in the value of the company's innovation pipeline (these are the company's words, not the consultant's).

A similar exercise took place at a manufacturer of glass beads used in horizontal road markings to reflect the light beam from car headlights and thus provide extra safety at a low cost to night drivers. When the road markings business came under pressure and margins plunged, the company made a conscious effort to analyze the functional properties of the beads and identify new areas for growth based on identifying applications for combinations of these properties. It turns out that with some minor modifications, the beads can be used in totally different applications. To name a few: fine beads can be used as a filtration compound instead of sand; ultrafine beads can be used as an additive in premium coatings to make them more abrasion-resistant; and beads can also be used in the surface treatment of stainless-steel products.

A way of thinking embedded in daily life

Our description of the Grand Strategy process so far has assumed the reliance on explicit exercises (e.g., a visioning off-site or an ideation session) and formal tools (e.g., a strategy matrix). We should add, though, that when facing strategic decisions, what matters is not so much the explicit exercises and formal tools as the mindset being created, i.e., being aware that any decision to commit resources to a business initiative should be tested, first, against the company's distinctive capabilities, and, second, the attractiveness of the markets in which it could deploy these capabilities. This awareness should be present all the time, i.e., not just at the formal obligatory annual reviews of company strategy, and should permeate all management levels, i.e., not just the top executive layer.

In view of the turbulent environments in which companies operate, it is of high importance for a company to be capable of formulating robust answers and making good decisions at various levels within the organization on an ongoing basis. This is in line with John Roberts' view that the most that can be done by top management is the setting of broad strategic direction or intent. Specific strategic choices, he says, are likely to emerge from a multitude of decisions taken throughout the organization.[32] Similarly and within the same context, Eric Van den Steen defines strategy as the "smallest set of choices to optimally guide the other choices," meaning that it should provide managers and employees with just enough of the full picture to help them align their decisions on these strategic choices, and thus ensure overall consistency, while allowing flexibility and evolution over time.[33] In that sense, top management needs to establish a company-wide strategy capability.

▶ THE MERITS OF GRAND STRATEGY

Earlier in this chapter we have explained the importance of Grand Strategy as a lead-in to Operational Strategy in an end-to-end process. First, Grand Strategy acts as a funnel, discarding business opportunities that are shown to be insufficiently promising to be worth taking through an in-depth assessment in the subsequent Operational Strategy. Second, Grand Strategy feeds the business opportunities funnel with out-of-the-box ideas and reduces the likelihood that totally new fountains of growth are overlooked by Operational Strategy.

While the lead-in role of Grand Strategy is the main reason for doing Grand Strategy, there are four other merits of doing Grand Strategy, even in isolation from Operational Strategy. Grand Strategy can be a powerful tool to help company executives orient, bond, inspire and explain. In what follows, we will clarify each of these four merits.

The orientation power of Grand Strategy

Going through a Grand Strategy formulation process can enable the executive team of a company to make or confirm some fundamental long-term directional choices for the company. This may occur, for example, through a well-prepared off-site in which the team develops a "Vision 2025." The outcome of such off-sites does not imply any immediate (financial) commitments for which the team members can or will be held accountable in the future, but it provides some boundaries for future strategic discussions and more specific choices that then do lead to commitments and accountability.

For example, one of the outcomes of the visioning process at a European financial services company was the directional choice not to enter the African market, even though a growing number of outside observers were claiming that the African continent would be the next fountain of growth and that the window of opportunity for early movers was closing fast. At a materials manufacturing company, one outcome of the visioning process was the directional choice to double the size of the company within seven years while relying primarily on organic growth.

Outcomes like these are of monumental significance, but we would qualify them as statements of intent rather than strategic decisions. They are based on the educated gut feel of executives who know their business inside out, possibly complemented with some ballpark figures. But they are not based – in fact they neither can nor need be based – on a quantified and field-tested assessment of alternatives that proves ex ante that the chosen alternative is better than any other.

A good example of the orientation power of Grand Strategy relates to PPG, today the world's leading coatings and specialty products company. We have not been part of any Grand Strategy process at PPG, but as observers we find that theirs is a fascinating story. Established in 1883, PPG (Pittsburgh Plate Glass Company) was primarily a diversified glass manufacturer until

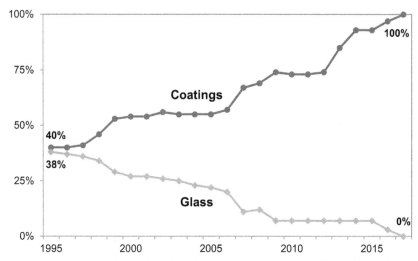

FIGURE 2.2 Evolution of PPG Industries' sales split 1995–2017

about 25 years ago. The company then embarked on a purposeful trans-formation that turned the company, step-by-step, into a focused coatings manufacturer, as Figure 2.2 shows.[34] We can assume that at some point in time the company's executive management team must have crystallized its thinking and confirmed the company's orientation toward coatings. Once management was aligned to follow that course of action, one can imagine that any request for further investments in the legacy glass business was scrutinized very carefully.

More generally, the benefit of Grand Strategy discussions – provided that they do not occur too often – is that they set boundaries "once and for all" (which in practice means for a couple of years) and subsequently, when managing the day-to-day business, avoid wasting time on discussions on topics that have been closed. This brings us to bonding, which is the second merit of Grand Strategy.

The bonding power of Grand Strategy

When senior managers of a company get together and jointly work on the formulation of some fundamental choices, bonds are created. We are not referring to the personal ties that result from socializing and team-building activities that take place at such events. We rather refer to the collective intuition and conscience that form during the process. As everyone is involved in all the discussions during the process of achieving consensus, a common point of reference is created. Whenever one of the executives (involuntarily) puts something up for debate again in the months or years that follow, the others can formulate a gentle yet clear reminder: "Hey John, you were there when we discussed that. Remember? Didn't we all agree that we would stay out of Africa?"

In fact, many CEOs, and newly appointed ones in particular, use the process primarily for that purpose. They seek team confirmation and commitment to ideas that were already taking shape in their heads before. CEOs, when they commit to an explicit Grand Strategy exercise, do not do it just for the fun of it, or because it makes them look visionary in the eyes of others. They often do it because they have to respond to internal pressures that have been building up over months or even years (going back to the same example, some Board members nagging to "do something about Africa – it will be the next fountain of growth!"), which cannot be relieved through a decision by the executive in charge (e.g., "expand the dealer network in Nigeria") or through some end-of-year budget meetings with the management team. At some point, after a multitude of exchanges with colleagues or Board members, the CEO may conclude: "Well, wouldn't it be a good idea to all get together and develop a Vision 2025?".

In other words, the decision to do such an explicit Grand Strategy exercise (in this case, in the form of one or more visioning sessions) does not come out of the blue. Because pressures have been building up, executives are keenly aware of their company's pain points, i.e., the overarching issues where they find it difficult to get to clear and agreed choices and decisions ("Shouldn't we go into Africa now?," "Shouldn't we fundamentally question our partnership strategy?,"). Most of these issues are not urgent, and cannot be answered with a simple "yes" or "no," but they may tend to re-emerge over and over again, indicating it may be time to address them "once and for all."

In our experience, many of the most successful Grand Strategy formulation processes have been those whose outcome was, in a certain sense, most disappointing. They were disappointing in that no radically new choices were made; they only made latent ideas explicit, and clarified and fine-tuned them. But they were successful in the sense that they aligned people around common points of reference that turned out to be of enduring value afterwards.

By the same token, the process is also effective for onboarding new members into the team. Within the scope of a few days, they get fully immersed into the fundamental strategic issues affecting the company. Vice versa, and more cynically, the process can be used to induce recalcitrant team members to isolate themselves and, thus, bind in. Disagreeing about a fundamental point with your CEO in a face-to-face conversation without witnesses is one thing; perpetuating disagreement in front of all your silent, staring colleagues is quite another. One of our former associates, when explaining the power of the process to clients, always referred, possibly with a keen sense of drama, to a visioning session he had facilitated where one of the participating executives had resigned publicly on the spot.

The inspiring power of Grand Strategy

The third benefit of a Grand Strategy process is that it leads to insights, concepts and expressions that the executive team members can use afterwards to communicate with the company's middle managers and other employees in a simple, clear and hopefully inspiring way. Eager junior colleagues in particular do expect their leaders to communicate an inspiring vision of the future that provides strong yet challenging growth prospects to themselves.[35] In addition, it turns out that companies whose leaders articulate a clear purpose and get middle managers' buy-in exhibit superior financial performance.[36] That is where Grand Strategy comes in handy. A Grand Strategy exercise forces the participants to pin down their views about the company's purpose (mission), aspirations (vision), values (behavior) and choices (strategy) in, say, no more than seven points. The communications department will then gratefully wordsmith these into simple and appealing catchphrases that can be used in internal roadshows, newsletters and the like. Because they are simple, the catchphrases lend themselves to memorization and repetition. One of the shortest and most telling catchphrases we know is Nike's "Crush Adidas," which it used in the 1960s as a rallying cry to beat the then-market leader.[37] As any manager knows, repeating a simple message time and again is the only way to make its meaning sink in, that is, embed it firmly in the minds of employees.[38] And that is not as straightforward as it seems; witness the recent research by Timothy Devinney.[39]

The oil and gas company ConocoPhillips, for example, has come up with the acronym SPIRIT to communicate its values, which "set the tone for how we behave." The acronym stands for Safety, People, Integrity, Responsibility,

Innovation and Teamwork. It is tempting to mock such attempts at force-fitting a set of profound values into a single, supposedly spirited catch-term. But the point is that these gimmicks serve as scaffolds for executives building stories that catch people's attention.

The communication efforts in fact go beyond merely the transmission of a message. The purpose of communicating the strategic messages continually is also to tune managers' and employees' brains cognitively to what the company has established to be its future direction. As a consequence, they will be more alert to relevant strategic opportunities and threats. They will pick up and interpret meaningful weak signals amidst all the noise and clutter.[40] They will anticipate specific low-probability yet high-impact events (known as "wild cards").[41] And they will think about making their company more robust in its particular areas of vulnerability (i.e., cope with "black swans").[42] Sharing and repeating the outcome of a Grand Strategy formulation process can be an effective means to that end.

The explanatory power of Grand Strategy

Grand Strategy communications can extend to external audiences who like ambitious concepts and visionary stories. The outcome of the Grand Strategy process can be a powerful tool for company executives to explain their views about the company's functioning and prospects to investors, partners, customers, regulators, the media, the labor market and other external stakeholders. These stakeholders can understand them relatively easily and, equally importantly, gratefully regurgitate them in turn to their clients. For instance, a financial analyst may pick up the company's story from an investor presentation, only to use it in her own pitch to an asset manager, who in turn uses it in her pitch to a financial investor.

All of that suits executives just fine, since Grand Strategy is a subject they can talk to outsiders freely about. Because Grand Strategy is nebulous and distant, the risk that an executive thus leaks valuable information to competitors, reveals insider information or commits to unattainable objectives is small. In addition, Grand Strategy statements are statements of intent rather than strategic decisions. And even if the statements include measurable goals, these are so far out in the future and contingent on so many conditions that they do not really constitute a hard yardstick of accountability.

▶ THE PAYROLL SERVICES CASE EXAMPLE

To clarify what we mean by strategy as an end-to-end process, let us consider the case of Payroll Inc. While Payroll Inc. is a fictitious name, its case is real. We have disguised or tweaked some other names, facts and figures for confidentiality reasons and/or to optimize the didactic value of the story. We will explain the triggers of their decision to start an explicit Grand Strategy exercise, as well as the process eventually leading to an Operational Strategy assessment of one specific business opportunity.

Payroll Inc. is a European provider of outsourced payroll services to small, medium and large-sized companies and public sector organizations, with corporate headquarters in its home market, the Netherlands. It realized a consolidated turnover of €300 million in 2013, following a 15% compound annual growth rate during the 25 preceding years, mostly through organic growth, and with a solid track record of profitability.

With a 20% share of the outsourced payroll services market, Payroll Inc. had become the market leader in its home market. It had also added HR consultancy to its portfolio of services (such as personnel-related tax & legal advice, payroll automation, and HR training courses), which accounted for one-third of consolidated turnover in 2013. More recently, Payroll Inc. also made some first attempts at internationalization by taking over two small payroll services companies in two nearby countries, namely Belgium and Luxembourg.

While Payroll Inc. was doing fine, its CEO and Board of Directors were also wondering about the company's future growth path. Various external and internal trends were feeding their musings. First, they recognized the limited potential for further growth in the company's core business, i.e., payroll services in the home market. The limited growth potential was the result of (1) the stable size of the labor force, which drives the number of monthly pay-slips to be processed, (2) the company's high market share, (3) the futility of share-stealing tactics in a relatively standardized market with limited scope for differentiation, (4) the high level of payroll outsourcing in the home market and (5) the possibility that the government might change regulations that gave the payroll sector a semi-protected status and hence supported its profitability.

Second, the CEO and the Board sensed some important developments in the business landscape. First, the increasing frequency of changes in social legislation and the growing need to invest in expertise and automation stimulated consolidation and raised barriers to entry. Second, the sector attracted the interest from much larger players in adjacent sectors, such as information technology integrators, business process outsourcing service providers and staffing agencies.

The third development was that third parties (investment bankers, etc.) regularly presented Payroll Inc. with opportunities to acquire companies in adjacent business areas. Irrespective of the intrinsic value of the individual acquisition target, the question that came up time and time again was whether Payroll Inc. should even want to be active in the target's business area. For example, one opportunity concerned a company active in leadership training and coaching, a much softer area than automating the processing of pay-slips.

Fourth, Payroll Inc. had a strong team of young, talented middle managers. Providing personal growth prospects was key to retaining them. And finally, as a result of its historic no-dividend policy, Payroll Inc. was sitting on financial reserves worth €400 million, raising the question of how to put it to work more profitably.

All things considered, Payroll Inc.'s CEO and Board started to reflect upon the company's business orientation and the boundaries of its future activities. While pondering these questions, they were sensing the tension created by two opposing forces: their sense of the need to stick to one's knitting on the one hand, and their managers' entrepreneurial urge to explore promising new terrain on the other.

The CEO and his executive team eventually decided to do an explicit strategy exercise. With hindsight, it can be said that the exercise consisted of three distinct phases, spread over two years (see Table 2.1). We would label phase 1 and 2 as being in the realm of Grand Strategy, and phase 3 in that of Operational Strategy. At the outset, they did not plan on going through these three phases. They understood the need for phase 2 and envisaged the nature hereof further to the outcome of phase 1. The same is true for phase 3 versus phase 2.

The design of the process was in line with the strategic maturity of Payroll Inc.'s executive team, which we would rate as fairly high. A number of particulars pointed to its high maturity level. To begin with, the CEO was eager

TABLE 2.1 Phases of end-to-end strategy process at Payroll Inc.

	Phase 1: Global vision	Phase 2: Strategic directions	Phase 3: Market entry plan
Objective	Establish a shared vision of the company's future scope, growth priorities and goals	Validate the international business concept, set market entry priorities, and make financial estimates	Develop a business plan and investment proposal for entry into the German market
Outcome	Vision text, with the decision to launch an internationalization study	Strategic plan with alternative growth scenarios and estimates of cash flows and financing requirements, with the decision to start with entry into the German market	Comprehensive business plan based on a quantitative bottom-up assessment of attainable volumes, prices and margins

to consult Payroll Inc.'s Board of Directors on strategic matters whenever one surfaced. While Payroll Inc. was only a medium-sized company with a local scope, several of its directors were senior-ranking executives from large multinational companies in other sectors such as pharmaceuticals and financial services with a solid tradition of strategic thinking; other directors were professors from business schools. Furthermore, every year Payroll Inc.'s senior executives attended executive education courses at a top US business school. Payroll Inc.'s CEO had the habit of instructing his executive assistant to systematically keep one day a week in his calendar free from operational meetings so that he could devote time to "thinking." And finally, Payroll Inc. was used to working with top-tier strategy consulting firms.

Phase 1: Global vision

Phase 1 was a fairly traditional visioning exercise centered around a two-day off-site with the executive team. With the help of an external facilitator, they prepared the off-site thoroughly through interviews with each member of the executive team and with selected Board members. The interviews were meant to gather views on Payroll Inc.'s real assets and capabilities, on fundamental external trends, uncertainties and threats, and hence on business opportunities Payroll Inc. could pursue. These are in fact the key ingredients of an attractiveness-advantage matrix. The interviews were also used to gather participants' views on key strategic aspects, other than Payroll Inc.'s future services and target markets, that they should clarify during the visioning off-site: the company's future business model, the needed competencies to be developed to be successful in these markets, the partnerships to establish, its overall organization structure, and the financial and non-financial goals to attain. In addition, the interviews allowed the identification of sources of factual intelligence (market analysis reports and competitor profiles) that could be included in a briefing pack for all off-site participants. Finally, the interviewees could also share their expectations about the set-up of the off-site in terms of agenda, deliverables and tone.

The said briefing pack contained pre-reading material, with the objective to give all off-site participants the same perspective on the strategic issues, enable the use of a common language, ground the vision in facts, and open the mind to creative thinking. Specifically the briefing pack contained the following chapters: a structured summary of the interviews held, thereby emphasizing the company's core competencies; factual profiles of the company's current activities in terms of product range and market position; a factual summary of the company's recent financial results and its three-year plan; a simulation of the company's financial firepower, i.e., the funds available for strategic investments given expected free operating cash flows and debt levels; external views on the company as apparent from customer feedback reports; and an external market research report with estimates of market size by segment as well as competitor profiles.

In the six weeks following the off-site, the facilitator drafted a vision text on the basis of the discussions held during the off-site. The annex of the draft included an attractiveness-advantage matrix indicating the position of various ideas for growth opportunities outside the current core business (i.e., outside payroll services in the home market) that they had identified and debated about during the preparatory interviews and/or off-site. Figure 2.3 shows a highly simplified version of the matrix, which synthesizes a number of tentative conclusions, including a rough estimate of future company revenues.

First, the Payroll Inc. executives were fairly confident about the continued potential of the classic HR consultancy business that they had started to develop in the home market in the preceding years. That market was sizeable and growing at a higher rate than the payroll services market, even though

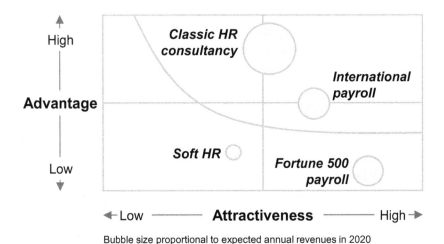

Bubble size proportional to expected annual revenues in 2020

FIGURE 2.3 Attractiveness-advantage matrix with business growth opportunities

in a more volatile way. And its core payroll services business provided Payroll Inc. with both a natural client contact point to offer legal advice and an often exclusive or at least an early view on automation issues at the client.

The soft HR business (leadership training and coaching), however, was deemed a no-go, as the domestic market was fairly small and, even more importantly, Payroll Inc. lacked both the business model and consulting profiles required for this supposedly touchy-feely business. While some executives brought forward arguments about how they could increase market attractiveness, the low-low position in the matrix clearly visualizes the final decision.

The debate about the third opportunity took a bit longer. It concerned the extension of the core payroll services business to the very largest companies, i.e., the subsidiaries of the global Fortune 500 companies in Payroll Inc.'s home market. While this market in itself was fairly attractive in view of the large volume of pay-slips, the Payroll Inc. executives concluded that it would require inordinate amounts of investments to make this business profitable: payroll outsourcing decisions at these companies were made at distant corporate headquarters; the scope of service contracts tended to cover the company's subsidiaries worldwide; and Payroll Inc. would have to displace large established payroll service providers with a global reach and processing centers in low-cost countries. They eventually concluded to drop this opportunity.

The final opportunity was both the most tantalizing and the most enigmatic one. It concerned the full-blown geographic expansion of the core payroll business beyond the home market and the two neighboring countries into the rest of Europe. Sporadic past contacts with payroll service providers in other countries had shown that the payroll outsourcing market in many European countries was far less developed than in the Netherlands. Likewise, very few local providers could match Payroll Inc.'s top-notch quality, even though pay-slip accuracy and timeliness is a must for clients everywhere. In addition, Payroll Inc.'s domestic clients who had subsidiaries in other European countries were increasingly enquiring about pan-European integration of pay-slip processing and payroll-related data. At the same time, Payroll Inc. recognized that social legislation and payroll practices are different in each country, thus preventing a simple copy-paste of its successful home market system. So, they decided to put the bubble in a hypothetical highly attractive and medium-advantage position in the matrix.

All executives provided their comments on the draft through one-to-one discussions. In parallel, the Chief Financial Officer asked one of his staff members to do a number of ad hoc analyses required to put more solid figures onto certain statements. For example, the analyst took some historic sales figures and growth rates for each of the product lines within the classic HR consultancy business to make an estimate of its total expected annual revenues in 2020. Due to lack of easy access to hard data at that time, the possible revenues for the three other opportunities were simply estimated very roughly as a proportion of the classic HR consultancy revenues, and even this was based on the executives' gut feel. Such gut-feel estimate was acceptable for the opportunities they were not going to pursue, but clearly inadequate for international payroll, prompting them into phase 2, as we will see.

Finally, the executive team had a second one-day off-site to review the final version of the vision text, which consisted of seven pages, one for each strategic aspect covered. The paragraph related to the international payroll business is shown in Box 2.1.

At this second off-site the team also decided on the major follow-up actions. One of these was to launch a study to elaborate Payroll Inc.'s internationalization strategy for its payroll services, given the highly hypothetical position

---

BOX 2.1   EXAMPLE OF A VISION TEXT

Business outside the home market

We will offer international payroll services to strengthen the loyalty of our existing customers in the Netherlands and to attract new ones. Our business concept for building our international payroll services business is as follows:

- ▶ Product: offer enriched payroll, i.e., wage calculation accompanied by social-legal advice.

- ▶ Geographic: focus on European Union countries where the foreign subsidiaries of customers from our home market are located (i.e., we follow our customers internationally), thereby aiming for 80% coverage.

- ▶ Customer size: focus on companies having more than 500 employees in our home market and up to 10,000 employees in total.

- ▶ Technology: preferably use our home market interface combined with a wage calculation engine from the target country.

- ▶ Extra option: set up a second home market next to the Netherlands.

- ▶ Rhythm: have the ambition to establish a prominent presence in some 15 countries within the next 5 years.

---

of that opportunity in the matrix. They thus decided to initiate what we have called phase 2. One of the other decisions was to review the internal organizational design of Payroll Inc.'s home market activities. This is not a strategy topic per se, but that is OK: not all outcomes of a Grand Strategy exercise are about choices related to product-market combinations.

Note again that the preceding vision statements are statements of intent, not backed up by much evidence. This is perfectly fine for this phase 1, as the statements are based on the collective wisdom of Payroll Inc.'s highly experienced executive team and have been made explicit through a careful facilitation process. But the hypothetical nature of the statements is borne out by the fact that, as a result of the more detailed findings in phase 2, Payroll Inc. scrapped the statement about setting up a second home market.

Note that the vision resulting from this process is not a one-line catchphrase. It is an unpolished text, for internal use, and as such restricted to Payroll Inc.'s executive team and Board of Directors. Again, this is fine. One-liners such as the ones discussed in the beginning of this chapter when discussing mission and vision may be nice fall-outs from a visioning exercise, but they are not the essence. In addition, they are often so stylized that the people who did not participate in the visioning exercise don't get the full underlying meaning of the one-liners anyway.

Phase 2: Strategic directions

If phase 1 was a fairly traditional visioning exercise conducted by Payroll Inc.'s executive team, then phase 2 was a fairly traditional strategy formulation exercise conducted by a Payroll Inc. project team. The objective of phase 2 was to detail and validate the international payroll opportunity highlighted in Payroll Inc.'s company vision, as established in phase 1. More specifically the project team answered the following questions:

▶ Which service package and technology platform should we offer to customers in foreign countries?

▶ What types of companies should be our target customers (what size, in which industry, . . . within the constraints set by the visioning exercise) and which decision-makers should we target (the Chief Financial Officer, the Chief HR Officer, etc.)?

▶ What international growth model should we adopt: should we follow the company's home country customers as they internationalize; or should we adopt the "oil slick" approach, i.e., spread progressively and concentrically from our home country; or should we copy/paste our home country approach to a second (distant) home market to be built?

▶ In which specific European countries should we establish a presence?

▶ In which specific sequence and at what pace should we enter the prioritized countries?

▶ What drivers have a major impact on investment size, revenues, costs, cash flow and lead-times?

▶ What is the magnitude of the peak investment and minimum time required to break even in any given country?

▶ What are the total financing needs and break-even times in each of three scenarios (fast, medium and slow roll-out across Europe)?

▶ How shall strategy realization be monitored?

▶ What measures should be taken to manage implementation risks and ensure success?

▶ What near-term implementation steps should be taken?

To answer those questions, the Payroll Inc. project team took all the right actions over a five-month period. They conducted some hundred field interviews with potential customers across Europe. They conducted learn-from-good-practice interviews with ten other companies that had gone through a similar internationalization path before. They did desk research on each European country to assess their intrinsic attractiveness to a payroll services provider and their fit with Payroll Inc.'s specific capabilities. They worked out a financial model to simulate the impact of diverse growth scenarios. They had seven workshops to review intermediate results and plan next steps. They regularly briefed Payroll Inc.'s CEO. And they produced a convincing PowerPoint presentation for the Board of Directors, dutifully containing all the right attractiveness-advantage matrices.

A simplified version of one of the matrices is shown in Figure 2.4. It indicates the position of each country in terms of its intrinsic attractiveness and its fit with Payroll Inc.'s specific capabilities, i.e., the extent to which Payroll Inc. could carve out a competitive position in that market. The scale for these two dimensions was quantitative (1 to 5), unlike the qualitative low-to-high scale used in the phase 1 matrix. To score a country's attractiveness, the project team used ten weighted criteria, some of which could be hard-measured (e.g., the size of the labor force working in medium-sized companies), and some of which were qualitative assessments based on desk research and the field interviews (e.g., the complexity of payroll regulations). To assess Payroll Inc.'s potential competitive advantage in a country, the project team used five weighted criteria, such as the extent to which potential customers in the country would be receptive to one of the distinctive features of Payroll Inc.'s service offering. These too were qualitative assessments based on the field interviews.

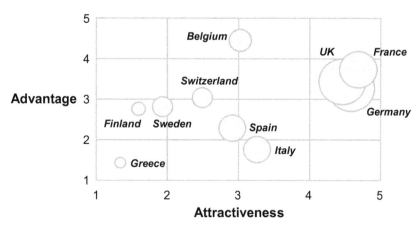

FIGURE 2.4 Attractiveness-advantage matrix with country growth opportunities

While the assessments in phase 2 were much more specific, detailed and numerical than those in phase 1, we would still qualify the work and outcome of this phase as Grand Strategy, and not yet as Operational Strategy. The reason is that the conclusions and decisions were still of a directional nature. They clearly indicated where to go and where not to go, but they were still intentions, hypotheses about what potential features or services (which Payroll Inc. already had in-house or should develop) could make some customers switch, and, ultimately, rough estimates of attainable revenues and profits. The Board did not have to sign off on a specific investment proposal. While a poor-quality study would have put the CEO's credibility at stake, he was not going to be held accountable for specific financial results to be achieved three years down the road.

Again, this was a fine or even desirable outcome of phase 2, because it was not designed to bring hard evidence of how many potential customers, say in Germany, would even consider outsourcing or switching suppliers; what the barriers are for potential customers to switch to the unknown Payroll Inc. from the Netherlands; which of the hypothesized drivers of switching are in fact true differentiators that do make people switch; which of these drivers are just too costly without inducing much switching; and, eventually, how many potential customers switch at what price for which specific offering. Unless these questions were answered reliably, all estimates of potential revenues and margins were, well, very rough hypothetical estimates for which you would not put your career at stake.

Answering these questions was the very purpose of phase 3 of Payroll Inc.'s strategy exercise: to develop a business plan and investment proposal for entry into the German market. It was Operational Strategy at its very best, using rigorous, quantitative demand estimations to make a bottom-up assessment of attainable volumes, prices and margins.

We do not mean to say that phase 2 (or phase 1, for that matter) was superfluous. Quite to the contrary: these phases enabled Payroll Inc.'s executive team to see the growth potential of the international market (outcome of phase 1) and to identify Germany as the most promising country to enter first (outcome of phase 2). They enabled Payroll Inc. to gradually zoom in on the product-market combination (PMC) with the presumably greatest potential, and then to unleash the full power of Operational Strategy on that specific PMC. In other words, Payroll Inc. followed an end-to-end strategy process.

▶ CONCLUSIONS

It is quite likely that phase 1 and phase 2, as described previously for Payroll Inc., one way or the other are similar to strategy exercises that you have gone through at your company. But the real novelty, we dare say, relates to phase 3. In the following chapters, we will explain in depth how such a phase 3 is done. The reason why we nevertheless talked in this chapter about Payroll Inc.'s phase 1 and 2 is to explain the difference between Grand Strategy and Operational Strategy, and to demonstrate that strategy should be an end-to-end process covering both Grand Strategy and Operational Strategy. At many companies, Grand Strategy and Operational Strategy, if done at all, are disjointed.

Adopting the end-to-end philosophy does not necessarily mean that every single time one should go through (the equivalents of) phase 1, phase 2 and phase 3 systematically, explicitly and sequentially. To the contrary, in some circumstances phases 1 and 2 are combined, or one moves straight into phase 3, or one starts with phase 3 and finds that there is again a need for phase 1, etc.

In some situations, one could even pursue a business opportunity without doing an upfront in-depth Operational Strategy assessment like the one Payroll Inc. did in phase 3. After all, senior executives are paid a premium for their ability (i.e., their intelligence and experience) and willingness to take calculated risks (i.e., bearing the personal consequences in case of miscalculation and failure), for their skill at seeing that ability and willingness in others, and for their comfort with doing Operational Strategy cursorily. Nevertheless, when major investments are called for, not doing Operational Strategy explicitly, before pushing the commit button, is like taking off in a hot-air balloon without anticipating where you might land – safely.

▶ NOTES

1 Alfred Chandler, *Strategy and Structure: Chapters in the History of the American Industrial Enterprise* (Cambridge, MA: MIT Press, 1962).

2 Kermit King, Gerry Hansell and Adam Ikdal, "When the Growing Gets Tough, the Tough Get Growing," *BCG Perspectives* (October 29, 2014).

3 David J. Collis and M. G. Rukstad, "Can You Say What Your Strategy Is?" *Harvard Business Review* 86 (April 2008): 82–90.

4 See, for example, Michael E. Porter, *Competitive Strategy* (New York: Free Press, 1980); and Arnoldo C. Hax and Nicolas C. Majluf, *Strategic Management: An Integrated Perspective* (Englewood Cliffs, NJ: Prentice-Hall, 1984). For a more recent textbook, see: Gart Saloner, Andrea Shepard and Joel Podolny, *Strategic Management* (Hoboken, NJ: Wiley, 2001).

5 Michael E. Porter, "The Five Competitive Forces That Shape Strategy," *Harvard Business Review* (January 2008): 78–93.

6 W. Chan Kim and Renée Mauborgne, *Blue Ocean Strategy* (Boston: Harvard Business Review Press, 2005).

7 Richard P. Rumelt, *Good Strategy Bad Strategy: The Difference and Why It Matters* (New York: Crown Business, 2011).

8 Gary P. Pisano, "Creating an R&D Strategy," Working Paper 12-095 (Boston: Harvard Business School, April 24, 2012).

9 Constantinos C. Markides, *All the Right Moves: A Guide to Crafting Breakthrough Strategy* (Boston: Harvard Business Review Press, 1999).

10   Lawrence Freedman, *Strategy: A History* (New York: Oxford University Press, 2013).

11   Arnoldo C. Hax and Nicolas C. Majluf, *Strategic Management: An Integrated Perspective* (Englewood Cliffs, NJ: Prentice-Hall, 1984).

12   Bruce D. Henderson, *The Growth Share Matrix or The Product Portfolio* (Boston, MA: The Boston Consulting Group, Inc., 1973). Relative market share refers to the market share of a company divided by the market share of its largest competitor; if the company is market leader, relative market share can thus exceed 1.

13   Kevin Coyne, "Enduring Ideas: The GE – McKinsey Nine-box Matrix," *McKinsey Quarterly* (September 2008).

14   For a good overview of these schools of thought, see David J. Teece, Gary Pisano and Amy Shuen, "Dynamic Capabilities and Strategic Management," *Strategic Management Journal* 18 (1997): 509–533.

15   Todd R. Zenger, "What Is the Theory of Your Firm?" *Harvard Business Review* (June 2013): 72.

16   Christopher B. Bingham, Kathleen M. Eisenhardt and Nathan R. Furr, "Which Strategy When?" *MIT Sloan Management Review* (Fall 2011): 71–78.

17   Arnoldo C. Hax, *The Delta Model: Reinventing Your Business Strategy* (New York: Springer-Verlag, 2009).

18   Kathleen Wilburn and Ralph Wilburn, "Abbreviated Scenario Thinking," *Business Horizons* 54 (November 2011): 541–550.

19   Michael G. Jacobides, "Strategy Tools for a Shifting Landscape," *Harvard Business Review* (January–February 2010): 76–84.

20   As quoted in George Serafeim, "What Mark Zuckerberg Understands About Corporate Purpose," *Harvard Business Review* (website) (February 22, 2017).

21   Pankaj Ghemawat and Jan W. Rivkin, "Creating Competitive Advantage," Note 9-798-062 (Boston: Harvard Business School, February 25, 2006).

22   L.G. Thomas and Richard D'Aveni, "The Changing Nature of Competition in the US Manufacturing Sector, 1950–2002," *Strategic Organization* 7 (November 2009): 387–431.

23   For a quick answer, see Daniel Deneffe, Julie Vandermeersch and Gregory Venters, "Overcoming the Real Barriers to Entry into Adjacent Markets," *Prism* (first semester 2010): 22–37. We will provide the in-depth answer in Chapter 4.

24 Michael E. Raynor and Mumtaz Ahmed, "Three Rules for Making a Company Truly Great," *Harvard Business Review* (April 2013): 108–117.

25 Depending on elasticities, marginal costs and competitor responses.

26 Chris Bradley, Angus Dawson and Sven Smit, "The Strategic Yardsticks You Can't Afford to Ignore," *McKinsey Quarterly* (October 2013): 8–15.

27 George S. Day and Paul J.H. Schoemaker, *Peripheral Vision: Detecting the Weak Signals That Will Make or Break Your Company* (Boston: Harvard Business Review Press, 2006).

28 Theodore Levitt, "Marketing Myopia," *Harvard Business Review* (July–August 1960): 45–56.

29 Clayton M. Christensen, *The Innovator's Dilemma: When New Technologies Cause Great Firms to Fail* (Boston: Harvard Business School Press, 2007).

30 Larry Downes and Paul F. Nunes, "Big-Bang Disruption," *Harvard Business Review* (March 2013): 44–56.

31 Rita Gunther McGrath, *The End of Competitive Advantage: How to Keep Your Strategy Moving as Fast as Your Business* (Boston: Harvard Business Review Press, 2013).

32 D. John Roberts, *The Modern Firm: Organizational Design for Performance and Growth* (New York: Oxford University Press, 2004).

33 Eric Van den Steen, "Strategy and the Strategist: How It Matters Who Develops the Strategy," *Management Science* 64 (October 2018): 4533–4551. See also Eric Van den Steen, "A Formal Theory of Strategy," *Management Science* 63 (August 2017): 2616–2636.

34 Based upon the authors' analysis of figures drawn from the annual reports of PPG Industries.

35 James M. Kouzes and Barry Z. Posner, "To Lead, Create a Shared Vision," *Harvard Business Review* (January 2009): 20–21.

36 Claudine Madras Gartenberg, Andrea Prat and George Serafeim, "Corporate Purpose and Financial Performance," Columbia Business School Research Paper No. 16–69 (June 30, 2016).

37 Jim Collins and Jerry I. Porras, "Building Your Company's Vision," *Harvard Business Review* (September 1996): 65–77.

38 Charles Galunic and Immanuel Hermreck, "How to Help Employees 'Get' Strategy," *Harvard Business Review* (December 2012): 24.

39 Timothy Devinney, "All Talk, No Action: Why Company Strategy Often Falls on Deaf Ears," *The Conversation* (March 26, 2013).

40 Paul J.H. Schoemaker and George S. Day, "How to Make Sense of Weak Signals," *MIT Sloan Management Review* (Spring 2009): 81–89.

41 Paul Saffo, "Six Rules for Effective Forecasting," *Harvard Business Review* (July 2007): 121–131.

42 Nassim Nicholas Taleb, *The Black Swan: The Impact of the Highly Improbable* (London: Penguin Books, 2007).

3

The foundations of Operational Strategy

As the previous chapter clarified, Grand Strategy is in fact a statement of intent rather than a set of strategic decisions. The strategic directions included in the statement of intent reflect the educated, structured gut feel of executives who hypothesize internally that a particular decision (e.g., entering a new market) would benefit the company commercially, whichever way defined (e.g., as higher revenues and net profit).

In some way or another, these hypotheses are based on some form of (high-level) internal and external analysis. The internal analysis highlights the company's unique strengths in terms of assets and capabilities relative to competitors. These can of course be virtually nil at many middle-of-the-road companies.[1] The external analysis typically includes, in the first place, an assessment of the market (its size, growth and attractiveness) and of competitors, and possibly in second place, some understanding of customer needs or unmet needs in these markets.

The external market and competitor analyses undertaken in a Grand Strategy exercise typically go into quite some detail. It is easy to put some fresh analyst (with or without an MBA degree) to work and ask her to find out everything about the external market that the company considers entering into in the future. An (overly) detailed analysis of competitive intensity, market size and growth, market attractiveness and competitor profiling is often the outcome hereof (especially if the analyst holds an MBA) because it is easy and quick to obtain: there is simply plenty of information available about markets and competitors through commercial market research reports, annual reports, press announcements, investor presentations and the like.

But customer analyses in the affected markets are less detailed, and, surprisingly, often even absent. That is, we have seen plenty of cases where the Grand Strategy has been disproportionately influenced by the vision of where the company wants to go, backed up with some market and competitor analysis. The ballpark revenue forecasts that these strategic directions are supposed to generate, though, are never (we repeat: never) driven by an analysis of customer choices. Often, these revenue forecasts are driven by what is needed to convince oneself that the business case for the selected strategy appears positive. They are typically constructed at the very end of the Grand Strategy meetings, where the participants simply make assumptions about the share of total market revenues that the company will obtain, often in sheer hockey-stick mode. But since these revenue forecasts have no behavioral foundation based on customer choices, they are unlikely to be of much value, let alone unbiased.

That customer choices are typically ignored in the Grand Strategy scheme of things is on the one hand totally disconcerting – to say the least – but on the other hand understandable.

The disconcerting dimension stems from the mere observation from any Managerial/Microeconomics 101 course that revenues equal price times quantity sold at that price. That quantity sold consists of the number of customers who choose to buy one or more units of the product at this price, given all the available competitive alternatives (including the alternative not to buy).

The understandable dimension relates to the fact that this information is not easy and surely not quick to obtain, in sharp contrast to higher level market and competitor information. One would need to know what choices customers who are looking for the best deal would make under the hypothesis that the company has pursued its Grand Strategy and launched one or more products or services in this market. While Grand Strategy off-sites are typically prepared by analysts and sometimes supported by consultants, that preparation does not include rigorous potential customer choice analysis. And customers are typically not invited to off-sites – understandably so.

In view of the money at stake, such behavioral foundation for revenue (and hence also profit) forecasts based on customer choices is desperately needed when making a strategic business decision such as entry into a new geographic market. In that case, there is a need to validate the implicit hypothesis that a sufficient number of customers in the targeted market will voluntarily want to buy the company's products, services or solutions at prices that are assumed in these forecasts. And a seasoned executive's wish about revenues, and implicitly about the behavior of customers, or at least a fair portion of them, may very well not coincide with how customers will really act when faced with many alternative options. There is in fact a fair amount of evidence that gut feel may not be a good predictor of future outcomes.[2]

It is primarily the lack of behavioral customer foundation of these revenue forecasts, and the possibly significant difference between gut feel and actual future revenues, that necessitate the testing, adaptation and operational-ization of the Grand Strategy, no matter how adamant management may be about "this new strategy being a necessary next step in our company's growth – a strategy that will benefit all of our stakeholders, first of all our customers, but also our employees, investors, . . ." Please fill out the dots. While assessments of costs related to a future strategy also have their share of inaccuracies, the major inaccuracies and uncertainties are not here, but on the revenue side.

Therefore, after the Grand Strategy direction-setting, it is essential to clarify two things. First, is the hypothesis that emerged from the Grand Strategy correct, that is, would the particular strategic direction generate sufficient commercial return, however measured (such as ROI, at least x% EBIT as of year 4, etc.)? Second, if the hypothesis is correct, what would operationally be the best product and price positioning strategy within the general direc-tion of the Grand Strategy to obtain the highest possible commercial return, and ideally achieve an as-long-as-possible competitive advantage?

To show the importance of testing the revenue forecast as a driver of the profit forecasts, let us go back to our medical glove example from Chapter 1. Top management at the company concerned was so much in love with their ability to produce the superior glove (90% HIV-proof) that they wanted to launch it ASAP, and, as their Grand Strategy said, of course value price their gem. Putting themselves in the shoes of some of their customers, they were convinced of a particular "reasonable price" at which "most customers" would buy their product. That price was ten times higher than the current latex gloves available on the market.

The disheartening reality obtained from testing the hypothesis operationally, however, was that very few customer segments cared at all about the superior benefits of the glove (dermatologists do not bathe in blood) and were not willing to pay the targeted price. In fact, for reasons explained in Chapter 1, it turned out that the commercially most appropriate price, given the willingness-to-pay of customers and the distribution of that willingness-to-pay across customers, was just a few cents above the price of current alternative gloves. Consequently, the Grand Strategy hypothesis was rejected and the project was abandoned.

That outcome was an inconvenient truth but, as with global warming, it is better to know it than to ignore it. In this very case, the knowledge of the expected commercial failure of the product at the hypothesized price saved the company millions of dollars in further R&D and launch expenditures.

The preceding example shows that the resources invested in operationalizing the strategy, that is, in testing the Grand Strategy hypothesis in a fact-based manner, pays off handsomely, even when the test results indicate that the hypothesis was wrong. R&D and launch expenditures are typical examples of totally sunk costs: you cannot recover them once incurred. When the hypothesis is rejected, the return does not come in the form of incremental revenues but in the form of savings.

Once the Grand Strategy hypothesis of a commercially viable strategy has been confirmed, we can proceed with operationalizing the strategy.[3] That essentially means that we determine, on the basis of facts, the 4Ps of the marketing mix (that is, price, product, promotion and place), knowing that these do make all the difference.

In the given medical glove case, the confirmation of the Grand Strategy hypothesis (in this case: the negative confirmation, i.e., the rejection) gave a quantified forecast of future revenues, capital expenditures, operating expenses, EBIT and cash outflows (the financial plan, that is). If the project had not been discontinued, then the further operationalization would have clarified which specific glove to launch (what features, to which customer segments, with what unique selling proposition (USP), and at what price), and what resources would have been needed to make this happen.

In this chapter, we will explain, in quite some painstaking detail, the behavioral framework that underpins our way of operationalizing a Grand Strategy outcome. We will first explain the types of Grand Strategy outcomes we want to test in Operational Strategy. Then, we will clarify the behavioral assumptions that we make when doing such testing. Next, we describe the rigorous process used to measure willingness-to-pay and willingness-to-buy. Finally, we take a simple case example to explain in depth how our method works in practice.

▶ TYPES OF GRAND STRATEGY OUTCOMES TO BE TESTED IN OPERATIONAL STRATEGY

Let us use a simplified but concrete example and go through three distinct types of decisions and uncertainties that can come out of a Grand Strategy exercise. We go back to the Payroll Inc. example of Chapter 2. Payroll Inc. is a payroll services company that currently is the market leader in the Netherlands, and is considering international expansion, given the limited growth prospects in its home market. Therefore, it undertakes a Grand Strategy exercise, focusing on the question whether to internationalize or not, and if so, in which country.[4] By and large, the outcome of the Grand Strategy exercise can relate to three possible cases, two of which would need further testing in Operational Strategy:

- ▶ Case 1: We do not want to internationalize.

- ▶ Case 2: We consider internationalizing into one specific market, say, neighboring Germany.

- ▶ Case 3: We consider internationalizing and have a number of options (say two, to keep things simple), but have no idea as to which one is most viable:

    - ▶ Option 1: entry into Germany.

    - ▶ Option 2: entry into Belgium.

Case 1: Do not internationalize

The Grand Strategy exercise simply reveals, for instance, that margins are razor-thin in the markets for which Payroll Inc. might have the capabilities required to enter, and that there are no possible niche strategies available to them that would allow the company to obtain much higher margins than the current ones. The research performed by the company's analysts shows that those markets are simply too close to competition policymakers' ideal market structure: perfect competition.[5] The analysts may have recorded that many companies entered and exited markets with pretty much the same service offering, and that their employer, Payroll Inc., is actually not even a low-cost player at home. With this info, the outcome from the Grand Strategy exercise should be: do not internationalize.

In this case, the implications are that the payroll services company should not bother, through an Operational Strategy process, to dig further and try to find out whether the decision – which actually is a hypothesis – is really correct. It is very likely to be correct, and there is just no point in spending tons of internal and possibly external resources to find out how much value the company would be destroying should it internationalize anyhow.

Oddly enough, in our experience, many companies then still want to do a detailed analysis of the viability of entering in some markets. In one of our entry projects, our client, an ingredients producer, considered moving downstream into food processing, simply because "margins are much higher there than in the ingredients market" ("Question: why would that be?" Well, what about: "Because entry is so darn difficult."). It was pretty clear from the onset that this company had no unique capabilities to offer product or service features that may make customers in the processed foods market switch and that are difficult to imitate. It just turned out that managers focused excessively on market attractiveness, at the expense of competitive advantage considerations. In a situation where it is a priori difficult to identify what may make customers switch, doing a detailed customer choice analysis is often meaningless. The only option would then be to undercut, which in turn is only viable when the entering company has a significantly lower cost position than incumbent players, so that incumbents can be reasonably assumed not to follow the price cut, a heroic assumption in this very case.

Case 2: Internationalize into one specific market

Imagine that Payroll Inc. concluded from the Grand Strategy exercise that it would consider internationalizing by moving into neighboring Germany. In that case, we do have implications for operationalizing the strategy. In fact, the two key questions to answer are:

1. Is entry into neighboring Germany commercially viable?

2. If so, how will the company compete, that is, what product/service will it offer, what is its USP, what price should it charge, and what are the capital expenditures and operating expenses needed to enter successfully?

Case 3: Internationalize into a still-to-be-defined market

A third possible outcome of the Grand Strategy exercise is that Payroll Inc. concluded that it would internationalize but did not quite know which markets to enter, debating between option 1 (Germany) and option 2 (Belgium). The company just did not have enough information about which entry strategy would be most profitable. The two key questions to be tested in Operational Strategy are now:

1. Which entry strategy is commercially most sensible: entry into Germany or entry into Belgium, knowing that the outcome of Operational Strategy could still be the rejection of both and thus ending up not internationalizing?

2. For the selected market (if any), how will the company compete, that is, what product/service will it offer, what is its USP, what price should it charge, and what are the capital expenditures and operating expenses needed to enter successfully?

It turns out that the approach needed to make the right customerS-centric decision in case 3 is intrinsically the same as in case 2, but requires analyzing two markets (Germany and Belgium) as opposed to one (Germany). In case 3, at the end of the day, the selection about option 1 versus option 2 depends on how commercially attractive both options are relative to each other, whatever the commercial measure may be. Therefore, in the following sections of this chapter, we will focus on the approach needed in case 2. Once that is clear, it is easy to understand how to operationalize the strategy when faced with two or more options. Generally speaking, it is important to keep the number of high-level options limited, as it takes time and money to work out the commercial return for each of them.

▶ BEHAVIORAL ASSUMPTIONS WHEN TESTING GRAND STRATEGY OUTCOMES

In this section, we will clarify the behavioral assumptions that we make when testing a Grand Strategy hypothesis. Recall that we want to decide two things. First, whether a particular hypothesized, and at this stage ill-defined, strategic move (in the case of Payroll Inc., entry into Germany) is commercially desirable. And second, if that move is indeed commercially desirable, how we operationalize it, and how we define in detail what to do: what product/service to offer, what is the USP, what price to charge, and what are the investments needed to enter successfully.

We also want to do so in a totally customerS-centric way, based upon an understanding of how customers would respond to our decisions. The overall approach, and for us the only meaningful approach to any strategic problem, starts from understanding how customers would respond to various offerings that we can offer at various prices. Further, since customers differ, it is critical to understand how customers differ in their responses to our offerings.

We make two basic behavioral assumptions. Assumption 1 is that customers, when making choices between alternatives, look for the best deal. Assumption 2 is that customer preferences differ across customers, even within so-called segments, if these exist at all. The key thing about our assumptions is that they are minimalistic: they just make explicit what we all know about customers. These assumptions are such a real description of customer behavior and choices that they are hard to disagree with.

We do not use any other assumption or statement about customers, and surely none that falls in the hero strategy category. Rather, we draw the following implication from our assumptions: a potential customer will buy a new offering (product, service or solution) only if the monetary value that he attaches to this offering (i.e., his willingness-to-pay) minus its price is positive and exceeds:

(1) the monetary value that he attaches to his best alternative (which may be the current offering from his current supplier, the offering from another

supplier, or simply "nothing" if currently he is not buying any comparable offering), MINUS

(2) the price of that best alternative, PLUS

(3) the switching costs, if any, of moving from that best alternative to that new offering.

That implication applies both to truly innovative offerings that create new markets (where the best alternative is by definition "nothing") and to offerings that are differentiated in existing markets.

Assumption 1 basically tells us the following: if a customer is faced with a choice between two or more offerings, he will pick the offering that gives him the largest difference between his willingness-to-pay (his monetary value) and the price he has to pay for that specific offering, provided that difference is positive. It that difference is negative, the customer will simply not buy. We call this difference the deal value. This is the same as what economists call consumer surplus, but that is less telling.[6] Often the best of all available alternatives coincides with the current offering, as this is the revealed preference of the customer.

Assumption 1 is not only critical but also truly real because it is exactly what customers do. For example, imagine you want to buy a new TV because yours broke down. You are kind of happy that it did, so that you can finally replace that still-functioning yet boxy TV set of yours. You walk into an electronics store (bricks-and-mortar or online) and look at the various models. The hottest one at the time of this writing is the latest OLED model (Organic Light Emitting Diode, just in case you did not know), launched by company TVcompA, with a price tag of $9000. You do not want to pay that much for a TV, even though you do have the budget – you'd rather use the money toward a new car to replace your 2002 clunker. The absolute maximum you want to pay for a TV is in fact $5000 (that is, if you are totally excited about the product). In the below-$5000 range you see an appealing 55" UHD TV (this you obviously know: Ultra High Definition . . . well, we did not), also from TVcompA, but it carries a price tag of $3400. Walking or scrolling down, you also see an appealing LCD TV (now this, we will not explain) from a less well-known brand: TVcompB. The price tag is $800 (you guessed it, it is really $799.99).

Now you are really in doubt about which model to buy. On the one hand, the UHD TV offers four times better resolution than conventional LCD models. On the other hand, you cannot really see the difference with the naked eye. But you can tell your friends that the screen resolution is better and make them feel ignorant when talking about UHD. What a joy life can be! It takes you a long time to make up your mind, and eventually you swallow your pride, give up on the "almost latest technology" and end up buying TVcompB's product. This means, by what economists call revealed preference, that TVcompB's product in fact offered a better deal than TVcompA's. More precisely: the difference between your willingness-to-pay for the UHD TV from TVcompA (say, $3500) and the $3400 price tag on the TVcompA TV must have been smaller than the difference between your willingness-to-pay for TVcompB's product (say, $1000) and its $800 price tag. Customers may not even know or be able to express that willingness-to-pay, but unless they are plain stupid, that is what they do. We do not assume that they are plain stupid.

Sometimes, choices are extremely difficult. Even for basic grocery store products, say a cleaning product, a customer sometimes finds himself waffling for five minutes to make a choice between the branded product and the store brand. In that case, it somehow must mean that his deal value is roughly the same for both products. When they are exactly the same, he may actually get irritated, as this means that he is truly indifferent between the two products, and hence it takes a long time to choose, simply because he cannot. In that situation, he would rather have someone else choose for him. In reality it means that it does not matter what he picks.

Let us continue with the second of our two assumptions. Assumption 2 says that preferences differ across customers, even within so-called segments, if such segments exist at all. This does not need much explaining, as we discussed that observation in Chapter 1. The point is: you may select TVcompB's product, but someone walking in the store may pick the UHD from TVcompA without any hesitation, and a third person may want the OLED model. Note that all three customers may be very well off, live in similar areas, and all have college degrees. That is, they may be in the same "segment" (determined by income levels, education, etc.). The problem is that belonging to a segment may really not explain much other than that they are likely to need to own a TV, and even that is not a certainty.[7]

It may sound counter to many marketing assumptions, but belonging to a particular customer segment (a group of customers with assumedly similar preferences related to observable characteristics such as income, demographics and the like) in many cases explains very little about customer choices. A customer-specific analysis of choices at different price levels (that infamous downward-sloping demand curve that we referred to earlier on) may be much more critical than trying to force customers into certain groups. The group effect just does not explain enough in the variation of choices at different price levels. At least for the choices of TV it does not.

We now return to our example of Payroll Inc., the payroll services company that is headquartered in the Netherlands and considering moving into Germany further to an explicit Grand Strategy exercise. Imagine that, say, a German consulting company that currently outsources its payroll processing to a local German company called Lohn Inc. is a potential customer for Payroll Inc. The consulting company pays a particular price, say €100,000 a year, to have its payroll processed by Lohn Inc. Processing the payroll is a rather complex activity, as some employees have rather complicated legal situations: some are employed in two or more regions; others just got married or divorced, possibly in a foreign country, thereby changing their residency status; etc. All of this surely does not facilitate the task of the payroll company, which has to provide the right services and make sure that every employee obtains the pay-slip with the correct amount given her legal situation, at the right time and at the right place (an agreed-upon address, usually the home address or the office mailbox).

Imagine now that the consulting company is reasonably satisfied with the services of Lohn Inc. and values those at €140,000 (if it values them less than €100,000, then the consulting company better stop consulting activities toward its clients). In other words, €140,000 is the maximum amount that the consulting company wants to pay to stay with Lohn Inc. This amount is perhaps not explicitly known by the consulting company, but implicitly it is: it is the price at which it would stop buying services from Lohn Inc. The consulting company thus has a deal value (the value of the deal with Lohn Inc.) of €140,000 − €100,000 = €40,000.

Imagine now that Payroll Inc. would supply exactly the same services, with exactly the same brand reputation as Lohn Inc. (lots of assumptions, we know, but they are necessary to make a point). Then, if the price of Payroll Inc. is just 1% below the price of Lohn Inc. (that is, €99,000), would the consulting company switch? If there are no switching costs, which are the sum of the monetary and non-monetary costs (or explicit and implicit costs, if you prefer) of switching from one's current position (in this case, the current supplier Lohn Inc.), the answer is yes. Why? Because we assume that customers are looking for the best deal. That is, they are looking for the biggest gap between their willingness-to-pay and the price to pay. And, under the preceding assumptions, Payroll Inc. offers a bigger deal value (€41,000) than the €40,000 offered by Lohn Inc.[8]

Conversely, imagine that Payroll Inc. offers more benefits to the consulting company than Lohn Inc., and that these services are worth €1000 (they have some value, we just do not know to what it relates). Now, even if Payroll Inc. offers the same price of €100,000, and if the switching costs are zero, then the consulting company will switch to Payroll Inc. (assuming no other company in the market offers a better deal value).

As far as switching costs are concerned, the reality is of course different from the assumption of zero switching costs made earlier. Whether we are business-to-business (B2B) or business-to-consumer (B2C) customers, we do not switch so easily, for the simple reason that switching costs do exist. Recall our definition of switching costs: the monetary and non-monetary costs associated with moving from one's current position to another supplier. As consumers, we know what those look like. One of the authors has been stuck for years with the same electricity provider, even though he knows that there are cheaper and equally reliable suppliers around. Why is that so? He is put off by the hassle of cancelling the plan with the current provider, filling out new forms, sending in paper forms with a handwritten signature, cancelling the bank direct bill payments, setting up a new one with the new provider, etc. Come to think of it, this is the same reason why he is with the same bank that charges an arm and a leg on a monthly basis and that, at the end of the day, is not any better than the other banks.

Generally, in the case of imperfect information, customers may be risk-averse and not want to switch overnight from one supplier to another. In the preceding B2B payroll services example, the customer (in this case the HR manager of the consulting company in Germany) may want to "see if it works," and work with the two suppliers in parallel for a month or two. Whether or not the new supplier charges for these two trial months (or simply charges a small fee), there is a cost associated with this. Non-monetary switching costs for the HR manager include the learning costs of moving from one supplier to the other, and the fact that it will take her a lot of time and effort to make the point to top management. The higher value she would receive from switching suppliers may be smaller than all of these internal costs, and switching will not take place.

In reality things are even more complex. In our experience (and we presume in yours), willingness-to-pay varies considerably across customers, but so do switching costs. We are sure that you know people who switch for very small price differences and have few switching costs, or at least seem to enjoy the process of looking for the best deal without calling this a cost.

The preceding has critical implications for the understanding of the revenue potential of a growth strategy. We would ideally need to know the distribution of the net willingness-to-pay of potential customers for any product or service that we launch, whereby net willingness-to-pay is the difference between a customer's willingness-to-pay minus switching costs. In fact, this distribution of net willingness-to-pay is what economists would call the firm-specific demand curve that relates the price of a particular product, service or solution to the volume that would be purchased at that price.

For readers who did take some course in microeconomics or managerial economics, forgive us if this calls to mind bad memories of demand (and supply) graphs that as a student you may have so despised, especially since you probably had no clue where they came from (neither did the professor), why they were drawn linearly (neither did the professor), and why price was on the vertical axis and volume on the horizontal axis (the professor is likely to have known, as it is rooted in economic history). The latter seems totally counterintuitive, as we really are interested in knowing how much volume would be purchased at what price, thus with price being the independent variable and volume the dependent variable. The standard textbook has the variables reversed, as illustrated in Figure 3.1.

We can answer some of the questions any economics student must have asked when seeing this demand graph. Let us start with the question about the choice of axes. Price is the dependent variable in the graph because the British economist Alfred Marshall messed it up. He was the one who started to popularize (well, what's in a word) the graphical analysis of economic relationships in 1890, in his textbook *Principles of Economics*. In addition, he did so in a counterintuitive way by sticking price on the vertical axis. We assume that he was probably totally unaware that in doing so he was going to agonize millions of economics students ever since. In any event, since it was the leading textbook in England for many years, it became the standard, and other textbooks simply copied the concept.

Price

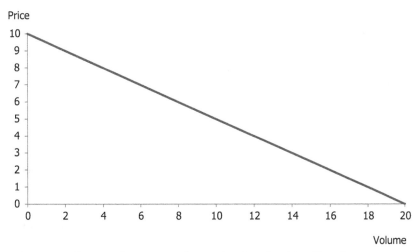

FIGURE 3.1 Demand curve as shown in standard textbooks

Price

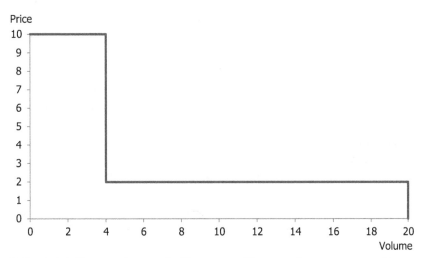

FIGURE 3.2 Demand curve in the case of two customer segments

The second question is: why is the demand curve linear? There is no reason for this. It is just an assumption, and not a good one at that, as the reality can be totally different, as we started to explain in Chapter 1. If there are two clear customer segments for a given product or service (those who value the product or service and those who do not really value it much), then the demand curve would look something like the curve in Figure 3.2. Some customers (the price-insensitive segment, so to speak) are willing to pay a high price (up to $10) for the specific product, whereas others (the price-sensitive segment, so to speak) are willing to pay no more than $2.

There are numerous marketing articles written about the two types of segments, as if the distribution of willingness-to-pay across customers is binary. There is no a priori reason for this. In fact, based upon our extensive experience in assessing willingness-to-pay, we neither observe the linear nor the segmented curve.

The point is that it is very important to understand and estimate this distribution, rather than to assume it, or, even worse, to work with some sort of average willingness-to-pay ("customer value") of the market or of an assumed segment. This is the case because a same average may lead to totally different managerial decisions. Let us take an example of two scenarios to illustrate our point. In both scenarios, there are just 400 potential customers for a particular product (a widget, we guess), the average willingness-to-pay is €4.5, and the average cost to produce the product is €1. The difference between the two scenarios lies in the distribution of willingness-to-pay, as shown in Table 3.1. In scenario 1 we have a small very price-insensitive segment and a large very price-sensitive segment. In scenario 2, to the contrary, we have two equally sized segments that do not differ that much in willingness-to-pay; the one segment is just a bit more price-sensitive than the other.

What is the implication for setting prices and for forecasting revenues and margins? In scenario 1, pricing on the basis of averages would make you conclude to price just below the average (at, say, €4.4), as is illustrated in Figure 3.3. Doing so would give you revenues of €440 and a margin of €340, as only the customers with a willingness-to-pay of €12 would buy the product. Customers with a willingness-to-pay of €2 would not buy.

Taking into consideration the distribution of willingness-to-pay, the conclusion changes dramatically. You would either charge a price of €12 (in which

TABLE 3.1 Differences in willingness-to-pay

Scenario 1		
Type of customers	*Number of customers*	*Willingness-to-pay*
Price-insensitive	100	12
Price-sensitive	300	2
Scenario 2		
Type of customers	*Number of customers*	*Willingness-to-pay*
Somewhat price-insensitive	200	5
Somewhat price-sensitive	200	4

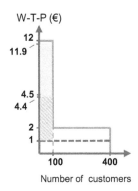

Using average willingness-to-pay:
- **Average W-T-P** = ((12x1)+(2x3))/4 = € **4.5**
- **Optimal price** = € **4.4**
- **Revenue** = 4.4 x 100 = € **440**
- **Margin** = (4.4 – 1) x 100 = € **340**

Using distributional information:
- **Optimal price** = € **11.9**
- **Revenue** = 11.9 x 100 = € **1190**
- **Margin** = (11.9 – 1) x 100 = € **1090**

W-T-P = Willingness-to-pay

 = Real W-T-P distribution   = Margin using average W-T-P

 = Unit cost   = Margin using distributional information

FIGURE 3.3 Revenues and margins in scenario 1

case only 100 customers would buy) or €2, in which case everyone would buy. In this case, the highest revenues are obtained when the price is €12 (or just below, say, €11.9). The attainable revenues are then €1190 and the corresponding margin is €1090.

That is, under this scenario, setting the price for this specific product based on the distribution of willingness-to-pay generates close to three times as much revenue and margin as setting the price on the basis of some average willingness-to-pay. On a more general level, both revenues and margins (and their forecasts) can be significantly higher when understanding the *distribution* of willingness-to-pay values, that is, the differences between potential customers. Hence, when setting up a business plan in an empirical customerS-centric way, we must take this into consideration.

In scenario 2 (see Figure 3.4), pricing on the basis of the average willingness-to-pay generates revenues of €880 and margins of €680. When taking the distribution of willingness-to-pay into consideration, prices are best set at €3.9 rather than €4.9 (and definitely not €11.9), leading to revenues of €1560 and margins of €1160.

In reality, of course, there is less discontinuity between the segments, and some customers just happen to be somewhere in between. In fact, we try

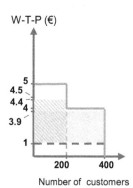

Using average willingness-to-pay:
- **Average W-T-P** = ((5x2)+(4x2))/4 = **€ 4.5**
- **Optimal price** = **€ 4.4**
- **Revenue** = 4.4 x 200 = **€ 880**
- **Margin** = (4.4 – 1) x 200 = **€ 680**

Using distributional information:
- **Optimal price** = **€ 3.9**
- **Revenue** = 3.9 x 400 = **€ 1560**
- **Margin** = (3.9 – 1) x 400 = **€ 1160**

W-T-P = Willingness-to-pay

⟋ = Real W-T-P distribution

⟋ = Unit cost

▨ = Margin using average W-T-P

☐ = Margin using distributional information

FIGURE 3.4 Revenues and margins in scenario 2

to illustrate two general points. The first point is that the distribution of customers' willingness-to-pay (the shape of the demand curve) is totally critical to optimize prices and maximize profits, which in turn is so critical to have a realistic business plan. Different distributions can lead to totally different optimal prices (€11.9 versus €3.9 in the preceding example) for any new product, and thus to different volumes and, most importantly, different revenues (€1190 versus €1560). If only some average willingness-to-pay (or so-called "customer value") is measured, then revenues and profits are much lower.

This first point also has an implication on the product development process. A company first needs to know the distribution of value across customers, and hence the product's optimal price, before developing it. Often, the opposite is done, where price is determined at the very last moment, for instance through pricing clinics.

The second point is that the distribution of willingness-to-pay cannot be imposed or assumed. But that is exactly what happens when managers talk about segments, which, supposedly, are customers with similar preferences. Even if one segments down to a fine level of detail, it still does not make sense to talk about representative customers within each segment, i.e., to assume that all customers within the segment pretty much all have the same willingness-to-pay. Unless, of course, each customer becomes a segment in its own right, which defeats the purpose of segmentation to begin with.

Assuming that a segmentation can get you homogeneous groups of customers is an illusion. It would require that a given combination of values for certain types of segmentation variables (age, income level, region, etc. in a B2C environment; type of application, customer relationship, customer size, etc. in a B2B environment) would fully explain the willingness-to-pay of all customers who fit within the given range. This is surely not the case. Even worse, segmentation workshops (we have gone through a fair amount of these) often end up in endless discussions as to which customers belong to what segments, and some customers are then painstakingly attached to a particular segment. Often the segmentation is reviewed after a while, because segmentation is said to be a learning process, or because segmentation is said to be dynamic by definition, or any other reason that can be invented to deny that it is just impossible to predict the preferences of customers based upon two or three variables, each having two or three distinct ranges (e.g., a segment could be something like "25 to 35 year old dual-income consumers in metro areas" or "large-sized customers in Southern California having more than 50% of their output in high-tech applications").

The point is: if a segmentation is meaningful, it can at best reduce the variance of the willingness-to-pay of customers within the segment, but not the need to understand that distribution, which is critical for operationalizing a strategy. Of course, once the Operational Strategy has been established and choices have been made (e.g., about the price to charge for the new product), so-called sales segments can be defined to allocate the salespeople to particular groups of customers, as a function of their affinity, experience, contacts, etc.

▶ THE CORE CONCEPTS OF WILLINGNESS-TO-PAY AND WILLINGNESS-TO-BUY

You may argue that this type of thinking is all nice and, ahem, theoretical: what is the point of all this thinking if we cannot measure the core of the idea, that is, the monetary value of the willingness-to-pay for a product, and the distribution thereof across potential customers? In this section, we will demonstrate that it is possible to measure willingness-to-pay and to infer willingness-to-buy. Willingness-to-pay is the monetary value that a specific (potential) customer attaches to a particular product, service feature or improvement thereof. Willingness-to-buy indicates whether a specific (potential) customer will or will not buy a product, service feature or improvement thereof at a specific price.

Once we know the willingness-to-pay and willingness-to-buy of a specific (potential) customer, we can derive the firm-specific demand curve for a particular product or service (that is, how much volume would the company sell at different prices) by aggregating the outcomes of the individual decisions of different potential customers in the market. In Chapter 4 we will discuss this demand curve when the strategy is to enter a new market ("growth strategy"). In Chapter 5 we will discuss the same when the strategy is to adapt the product or service in an existing market in response to new entrants ("defense strategy"). In Chapter 6 we will discuss what to do when price is the only thing that customers care about ("zero competitive advantage").

In the current chapter, we continue to focus on understanding increases and decreases in value or willingness-to-pay and the effects on willingness-to-buy at the individual customer level. We infer these through a sophisticated indirect interview method from a sample of customers. For good reasons explained later, we never ask direct questions about willingness-to-pay or willingness-to-buy. Our method for discovering this information is both theoretically sound and field-tested. It is theoretically sound in that it is built upon a minimum number of reasonable behavioral assumptions that you, dear reader, can evaluate, as we have no black box; it does not impose any additional assumptions, as other methods implicitly or explicitly do. In addition, its foundations have been tested in experimental settings and have received wide academic acceptance.[9] Furthermore, the method is widely accepted by clients where we have applied it. Interviewed managers who have been through the method typically feel very satisfied in that they understand their own preferences better.

The goal of the method is to be able to forecast with the highest possible degree of accuracy the choices made by an individual customer. Imagine we are a manufacturer of industrial pumps.[10] All we want to forecast is whether a given customer from a sample of customers will buy *any* pump with any combination of features and price. If we know this for all subjects in the sample, then we obviously have gold if not platinum information, provided the sample is representative of the population. In that case, we do in fact have the information about the company-specific demand curve for *any* type of pump that it could possibly launch. And, yes, this is *the* most important information that a company could probably wish to have.

Obviously, we cannot just ask these individuals which pump they would buy at what price, and this for two reasons. The first reason is that, even with a limited number of features with many possible values, there are simply an infinite number of questions to ask. For example, a warranty can vary anywhere from the customer's minimum requirement to, say, 120 months, and mean time between failure can vary from the customer's minimum requirement (say, 1000 hours) to whatever is technically feasible (say, 3000 hours). Now just combine these two features and add various price points, and the interviews per customer would last for days, even if one can adapt the questions as a function of previous answers. Imagine now five or six features. . .

Our method *can* deal with this important issue in a conceptually sound way, that is, without imposing *any* major assumptions. In that, it differs from other approaches, even choice-based ones, such as many types of "conjoint analysis." Faced with the fact that only a limited number of choice questions can be asked to a given individual (given the infinite number of combinations), these methods necessarily need to define specific levels of the attributes up front. That makes sense for what are naturally discrete features (three different colors for instance; or 0–1 variables, such as "with or without a warning light") but it is more difficult for continuous variables such as mean time between failure (MTBF), warranty and price, to name a few. These methods must specify specific levels (e.g., MTBF of 1000, 2000 and 3000 hours, warranty of 6, 12 and 24 months, and a price of $4000, $5000 and $6000) whereas these levels may not be the critical switching values for the customer. Our method, by way of contrast, does make it possible to understand willingness-to-pay and willingness-to-buy for *all* levels of the continuous variable. It does so through the use of indifference analysis rather than choice analysis, ratings or rankings.

In addition, our method overcomes numerous other limitations of conjoint analysis. For one thing, all forms of conjoint analysis record customers' responses (be they choices, ratings or rankings) and then process them by means of some type of regression analysis to infer the impact of the levels of the attributes on customers' "utility." In its most commonly used form (adaptive), choice-based conjoint analysis asks which packages a customer prefers (when faced with, say, three different options). This implies that choice-based conjoint analysis can say that one package is preferred over another *but not by how much* and not in relation to a customer's best alternative. Our method, by way of contrast, *accurately* determines *how much more* one package is worth than another (in terms of willingness-to-pay) and whether it would be purchased *relative to the customer's best alternative*. This is truly the only relevant comparison for a customer in his decision-making.

Further, our method accurately determines the difference in value between that best alternative and a proposed offering of our company, and can thus find out what improvement is necessary, at the individual customer level, to make that customer switch. In doing so, it picks up *all* relevant differences between a proposed offering and the customer's best alternative. This is relevant and can be huge, as it covers *all* tangible and intangible differences with the best alternative: past experience with the salesperson of an existing supplier (if that is the customer's best alternative), differences in look and feel, differences in features between the best alternative and a proposed offering that were not covered by the interview questions, to name a few very critical elements.

That points to two fundamental shortcomings of conjoint analysis. First, it does not make the key comparison that the customer makes, that is, with the customer's best alternative (it is often made with the "none of these" option). Second, conjoint analysis assesses the preferences only for the included features. It does not measure the sum of the value of the measurable and non-measurable non-included features relative to the best alternative, while ultimately this is key to a customer.

Further, for the more technical reader, note that any type of regression analysis *must* assume a specific functional form between the choices, ratings or rankings made and the levels of the attributes of the product (that can be linear regression, logit, Hierarchical Bayesian, etc.). If this a priori functional form does not correspond to the true (but unknown) form of customer preferences, then this will lead to estimation bias. Our method, by way of contrast, does not use *any* regression analysis and, hence, will not have such bias.

Finally, in many forms of conjoint analysis, specific modeling assumptions are being made about, for instance, the individual utilities in relation to that of the population. For example, in the most advanced forms of Hierarchical

Bayesian estimation, the distribution of willingness-to-pay is assumed to be normally distributed around the average willingness-to-pay in the population, thus explicitly making an assumption about the shape of the demand curve.[11] In latent class estimation, customers are assigned to a particular segment and their willingness-to-pay is assumed to be the same as average willingness-to-pay of that segment. In addition, in many conjoint estimation methods, customer responses of all interviewed customers or of supposed "segments" are stacked on top of each other to estimate, by means of regression analysis, the biggest influencers of some *average* preferences.[12] We argued before that working with average preferences or average willingness-to-pay is not very useful for better decision-making. Our method does not work with averages or imposes restrictions across individuals. It *infers* the demand curve and does not make any assumption about that shape for reasons that we explained earlier in the chapter.

The second reason why we cannot ask customers whether they would or would not buy a specific product at a specific price, or what their willingness-to-pay would be for a specific product, is that such question gives totally biased results, especially in B2B markets. This phenomenon is well-documented in the literature on the subject. As Nagle et al. put it, "the results of such studies are at best useless and are potentially highly misleading."[13] One might as well not ask such questions, as they are a pure waste of time. An interview with a shrewd purchaser in B2B markets will obviously not lead to his true willingness-to-pay, as he is likely and justifiably afraid that, should he reveal it, it is likely that the seller will use that information against him in the form of higher prices. In B2C markets, direct consumer interviews may even lead to the opposite effect: in an attempt not to appear cheap, customers may reveal a higher price than they are really willing to pay.

How do we proceed then without making any of these assumptions? We will infer customers' preferences and forecast their choices, making three minimalistic assumptions that are standard (and sensible) in preference theory.

Assumption 1: Completeness

The completeness assumption simply means that for any two choices (say two different pumps in this case, pump A and pump B, each with different feature levels), the customer either prefers A to B, or she prefers B to A, or she is indifferent between A and B (i.e., she cannot choose or does not care which one she gets). The completeness assumption simply says that individuals cannot say that they do not know. They either prefer one over the other or are indifferent (if they say that they are on the fence, this is pretty much another way of saying that they are indifferent, even though some scholars will debate that not knowing which of two options to select is equivalent to being indifferent between the two options).[14]

Assumption 2: Transitivity

The transitivity assumption means that if a customer prefers A to B and B to C, then the customer will prefer A to C. Also, if the customer is indifferent between A and B and indifferent between B and C, then the customers is indifferent between A and C. Transitivity of preferences is a fundamental principle shared by most major contemporary models of decision making.[15] For example, if an individual who is faced with the choice between an apple (A) and a banana (B), picks the apple, and when faced with the choice between a banana and cherries (C), picks the banana, then it is pretty reasonable to conclude that (under the same circumstances), when faced with the choice between an apple (A) and cherries (C), he would pick the apple (that is, we do not need to ask the question about his choices between apple and cherries, as we infer it from his preferences of A over B and of B over C).

Assumption 3: Additivity of preferences

The additivity assumption means that the increase in satisfaction associated with an improvement in one feature does not depend on the level of the other features. Even though the additivity assumption does not always hold, it is quite standard in preference analysis, provided of course one does not split up complementary features. To say it in layman's terms and with a concrete example: it does not make any sense to infer an individual's utility improvement associated with an increase in the number of left shoes, as the utility increase depends totally on the number of right shoes; it is the number of pairs of shoes that improves utility, and they should be treated as one.

While the first two assumptions are reasonable (though are occasionally violated in reality, as we are not all super-rational beings, witness all of the advances made in behavioral economics), the third assumption needs to be tested per feature. If that assumption is not correct, then two dependent features will have to be treated as one. In the remainder of the explanation, and for simplicity's sake (it is hard enough as it is), we will assume that the additivity assumption for all features has been tested with the interviewees and is satisfied.

We will now explain how our trade-off method uses these assumptions to extract customer preferences. Through this method it can be predicted whether a particular individual would buy a specific proposed product or service with a set of features or benefits that a company is offering (as opposed to his best alternative offering, which could also be "nothing"). If the answer to this is negative (that is, the customer prefers his best alternative), then we need to understand "by how much" he prefers his best alternative. We call that the switching value: it is the deal value for the best alternative minus the deal value of what we propose plus the switching costs, if any, from the best alternative. If the difference is zero, the customer is indifferent between his best alternative and switching to our offering. We then also need to understand from the customer's preferences what the increase in willingness-to-pay is for our proposed product if we were to improve the product or add extra features within our capabilities: if this increase in willingness-to-pay eventually bridges the switching value gap, the customer will select our improved product or service. Note that a decrease in price is also an option, as is a combination of a price decrease and an increase in willingness-to-pay, as long as the gap is being closed.

Gaining this understanding requires a complicated, tricky and time-consuming process of one-on-one interviews. Whether these interviews are physically face-to-face or web-enabled depends on whether the look-and-feel elements do or do not matter. But the interviews definitely cannot happen by means of short phone calls or by letting people fill out online questionnaires. There are two reasons for this.

First, people do not necessarily know their preferences, and definitely not for new products or services, which are the most exciting ones in strategy design. We need to extract them, in fact craft them, as they are about things that people cannot express. As you will see in the following case example, the questions that the interviewee needs to answer demand his fullest attention. Hence, we need to make sure that all of the interviewee's attention is focused on extracting his preferences, and that the interviewer in fact helps the interviewee at crafting those preferences. This cannot be done through a 15-minute call or a stand-alone questionnaire.

Second, when using a 15-minute call or a stand-alone questionnaire, one does not control the circumstances in which the interviewee is answering the phone or filling out the questionnaire. It is no secret that the effect of external stimuli can significantly affect the answers provided. If the interviewee is, say, a Duke Blue Devils basketball fan, and is answering the questions (either over the phone or via a questionnaire) while watching the Blue Devils trailing against their worst enemy (UNC), then one can pretty much be guaranteed that this will negatively affect his willingness-to-pay (however measured) for additional features, since at that time nothing matters, so to speak. One just does not know (and does not want to know) what people are doing at the other end of the line.

Many people, typically those who are not too versed in statistics or econometrics, believe that these effects will cancel out when taking a large sample. While the large sample reduces the variance in the answers, there is no reason that it will reduce the bias. In other words, the large sample will simply lead to what we call "accurately inaccurate" results, which is a pretty cold comfort and useless for our purpose.

In the next section, we will take a very simplified case example of the manufacturer of industrial pumps to explain how we used the interview process to go to the heart of the matter. We will do two things. First, we want to understand how the willingness-to-pay of a potential customer changes with changes in the levels of some features that the manufacturer could technically offer. Second, we want to understand the switching value for that individual between a specific offering and his best alternative. It is this combination of information that will allow us to predict whether a specific potential customer will buy *any* specific industrial pump.

The case relates to a B2B business and a "search good," which are goods that have attributes that can be evaluated prior to purchase or consumption. In the case of a pump, a potential customer can assess its benefits based on the levels of the product features (e.g., efficiency, warranty and the like). The method has to be slightly adapted in the case of "experience goods," which are goods that can be accurately evaluated only after they have been purchased and experienced. Many B2C products (such as chocolate bars and drinks) and services fall into this category. We will explain how to adapt the method to experience goods or hybrid goods (search and experience, such as hotels) at the end of this chapter.

For now, dear reader, it is critically important to bear with us and focus your attention on the specific case of industrial pumps and its underlying logic rather than asking the question *at this stage* as to how this approach would apply to other types of products. The better you understand the logic through this specific case, the easier it will be for you to understand how to apply it elsewhere.

▶ THE INDUSTRIAL PUMP CASE EXAMPLE

In this section, we will first address how we measure changes in willingness-to-pay as a function of changes in benefits associated with any product and service features. Then we will show how we measure the switching value. It is the combination of the understanding of switching value and willingness-to-pay for changes in the offering that will allow us to infer willingness-to-buy at different price levels.

Eliciting willingness-to-pay

The specific example is based on a real case. As part of its Grand Strategy, our client, a manufacturing company, was considering entering into the industrial pumps market. To understand its market potential and eventually revenue and margin forecasts, it had to understand potential customers' preferences. We explain the preference elicitation interview process in the following. We will move into the more practical issues (sample size, incentives to participate and the like) when digging into specific cases in subsequent chapters.

The potential customers are those customers who consider buying one or more pumps in the coming year, mostly to cool down a nuclear power station. We interview a sample of potential customers with the sole goal of understanding their preferences. Hence, we need to put a given customer at ease and explain to her that there is no right or wrong answer, but that the only goal is to understand what she values. A pump has a number of product level features (such as efficiency and mean time between failure) and service level features (such as warranty and delivery time of spare parts). For a number of these features, a particular customer has minimum requirements: if these requirements are not met, she will never buy this particular pump. We ask the customer what these requirements are, and, if necessary, reformulate the question to make sure she understands. Another way of putting it is that these are the must-haves that must be satisfied, as without them, she would never buy the pump, *even if it were free*. So, imagine for now that we have figured out (through such interactive interviewing) that the customer's minimum requirements for a particular pump are as described in Table 3.2.

That is, this individual has expressed that she will never buy a pump that requires external cooling before it heats up to 80°C. Or she will never buy a pump with a delivery time of 10 weeks. Generally, unless a pump satisfies *all* of the individual's minimum requirements, then no increase above these minimum levels in *any* feature will command any willingness-to-pay: the customer just does not want the pump. Period.

For those features for which more is better (e.g., warranty, efficiency) we have to ask this customer what the minimum level of the feature is. That is, below this level she would never buy the pump, whatever the other features. For those features for which less is more (e.g., delivery time, price) we have to ask this customer the level for this feature above which she would never buy the pump. Since we are reiterating to the customer that all we want is to understand her needs and preferences, she has no incentive to lie about her minimum requirements, with the possible exception of the feature "highest price above which she would never buy." We can infer from the discussion on price later on that even if she does lie and provides a somewhat lower value, it does not affect the accuracy of our willingness-to-pay elicitation method.

TABLE 3.2 Customer's minimum requirements for selected features

Product and service level features	*Minimum requirement*
Efficiency	50%
Mean time between failure (MTBF)	1000 hours
Warranty	0 months
Delivery time of pump	8 weeks (max)
Delivery time of spare parts	48 hours (max)
Price	$5000 (max)
No external cooling required below a temperature of	80°C

The pump of course has other features than the must-haves (e.g., speed, look-and-feel, brand, or a specific noise reduction feature that other pumps do not have), but let us say for simplicity that this specific individual has no specific minimum requirements on these other features. That is, she would consider buying a pump without, for instance, the noise reduction feature, provided the deal value of that pump is higher than the deal value of a pump with the noise reduction feature.

What we want to know is how to accurately measure this individual's willingness-to-pay for two types of things: for improvements in the feature levels above the individual's minimum requirements, and for totally new features altogether added to the product or service that provide a specific benefit. But which features do we throw into the preference elicitation process? In reality, we should only measure improvements in feature levels or benefits from additional features that possibly satisfy a customer's unmet need, that are "important" to her, and, if included, may bring more value than her best alternative.

Identifying or hypothesizing at a high level what could meet unmet needs does not take place in Operational Strategy. It took place already during the Grand Strategy process, and is in fact something that a company is continuously aiming to discover, either through an explicit exercise (ethnographic interviewing, participant and non-participant observation, focus groups and the like) or through day-to-day Grand Strategy. As we have seen in Chapter 2, Grand Strategy ultimately leads to hypotheses about promising strategic options that should enable the company to meet some customers' unmet needs.

During Operational Strategy, we test these hypotheses about unmet needs. Practically speaking, during the first set of questions in the interview process, we find out which specific improvements or additional features the interviewee deems important. For example, if a particular individual has said that mean time between failure is totally unimportant, we skip the elicitation of willingness-to-pay for improvements therein.

There is a good reason why we do not elicit willingness-to-pay for features that the interviewee initially considered unimportant. The interview process is very tiring, as the interviewee extracts from her brain things that she did not really know. The indifference process (which we will explain in more detail later) forces her to do so. The drawback is that this takes time, while the interview is limited to a time span of about an hour and definitely no more than 90 minutes: even if the interviewee would not mind continuing, she is brain dead by that time. Hence, the maximum number of features to include should never exceed ten, and five to seven is even more manageable.

Let us point out here that the importance of a feature to a customer is a necessary but not a sufficient condition for his willingness-to-pay. If a feature is considered important, it *may* command willingness-to-pay. There are plenty of examples to prove the point that it is not sufficient. Let us go back to you, dear reader, visiting a store to buy a new TV, and this time in a bricks-and-mortar store. Say you are not really a techie, but in no time a salesman comes up to you asking if you need some help. You sure do. He explains everything about 1080i versus 1080p, the importance of having 200 Hertz instead of 100 or 50 Hertz to get a smoother motion (but apparently, people either do not see it or do not find the appearance of such motion realistic), OLED versus LED (remember?), number of pixels, and the existence of features such as PiP, PVR and the like.

His explanations are obviously very important to you, as it allows you to make up your mind as to which model to buy, given your implicit willingness-to-pay and the prices of these models. But when the salesman asks you which model you want to purchase, you may well hem and haw before coming up with one of the salesman's most dreaded responses: "I will read up on it some more and be back tomorrow," or "I got to check that with my partner first," or the simpler version "I got to sleep on it." The reality is that, after the salesman's impeccable clarifications, you probably made up your mind, and may even have written down the model number inconspicuously. So before going to sleep, you may very well visit a web-shop, and simply order the chosen model at a lower price. Conclusion: you find the explanations very important but were not willing to pay for them.

There is a second criterion for deciding which features to include in the analysis of willingness-to-pay. We should only include features that the company can influence through R&D, product or service improvements and the like. If there is no chance to deliver on improved or additional features, it is managerially speaking irrelevant to know what the customer is willing to pay for these. To keep it simple, we are pretty sure that there is a huge willingness-to-pay for the feature that "you will live forever." However, if no company can generate this benefit, then there is no point in wasting time on measuring that willingness-to-pay and on finding out how it differs across "segments."

The same applies in the pump example. If the company knows for sure that it will never be able to improve the mean time between failure beyond, say, 12,000 hours, whatever R&D investments it may make, then there is no point in trying to figure out what the willingness-to-pay is for improvements beyond 12,000 hours. It does, however, want to know what the willingness-to-pay is for improvements from the currently feasible level (say 1500 hours) to whatever level can be estimated to be feasible, provided it makes sufficient investments. This is particularly important, as the decision to improve the feature level (and hence the benefits associated with it) precisely depends on trading off the customer's extra willingness-to-pay (and the translation thereof into extra company revenues) against the additional cost (R&D, capital expenditures (Capex) and operating expenses (Opex)) of generating this extra benefit.

Bearing this in mind, we now explain the process of understanding the potential customer's utility of improvements in feature levels (eventually translated into willingness-to-pay) *above her minimum requirements*. While we eventually want to understand the interviewee's willingness-to-pay, we never ask that question directly. We assume that the interviewee does not want to reveal her willingness-to-pay, but we want to extract it from her anyhow. For the trade-off method to retain its validity, it is also necessary to validate that assumption 3 (additivity of preferences) to a great extent holds. In general, we will have picked the features in such a way that it is the case. In the following discussion, we focus on the core of the method and assume that additivity is valid instead of overcomplicating matters because of some unlikely exceptions.[16] Here is how we proceed. Again, bear with us; it takes some time before getting to the willingness-to-pay question.

To start with, we define a gauge for the process of eliciting willingness-to-pay. For instance, the gauge could be an increase in warranty from, say, 0 to 6 months. We use the term "utility" as unit for this gauge, for the simple reason that it is in line with microeconomic preference terminology. So, an increase in warranty from 0 to 6 months increases total utility by 1 unit (if you are confused why we are doing this, we do understand; again, bear with us. . .). Such utility increase by 1 unit commands a willingness-to-pay, which we don't know at this point.

Why did we take an increase in warranty from 0 to 6 months as our gauge? For no good reason. It is totally arbitrary, and we could surely have taken another gauge, say, a decrease in delivery time from 6 to 4 weeks. The analogy with temperature is perhaps telling. Here too, it is totally arbitrary whether we use the centigrade (Celsius) or Fahrenheit scale, and a temperature increase of 1 degree Celsius is not the same as an increase of 1 degree Fahrenheit. What matters is that we take the same decisions about clothing, vacation planning or drinks for a given outside temperature, whether expressed in centigrade or Fahrenheit.

The same applies to utilities. It is totally arbitrary whether we define one utility as the increase in willingness-to-pay for an increase in warranty from 0 to 6 months, or as the increase in willingness-to-pay for an increase in warranty from 2 to 5 months, or as the increase in willingness-to-pay for a decrease in delivery time from 6 to 4 weeks. The important thing is that no matter how we define the utility, our forecast of willingness-to-pay and willingness-to-buy for any pump launched will be totally unaffected by the initial choice of the gauge. Our methodology guarantees that this is the case.

The next step is to elicit utilities for improvements of every other feature than the one we used as gauge. We do this sequentially per feature. That is, we first extract the utility of improving, say, efficiency. When we are done, we do so for improvements in mean time between failure and so on.

How do we do this? By asking pairwise trade-off questions that force interviewees to *indifference*, or, equivalently, to situations where they can no longer choose between two alternatives.[17] Table 3.3 shows the question we would ask to elicit the utility (later translated into willingness-to-pay) of efficiency improvements above the customer's minimum requirements.

Unlike other methods, we are forcing the interviewee to indifference, to the point where she can no longer choose between the two pumps. It is clear that

TABLE 3.3 Trade-off question between warranty and efficiency

	Question: Fill out the missing value for which you are indifferent between pump 1 and pump 2	
	Pump 1	Pump 2
Efficiency	50%	__ %
Warranty	6 months	0 months

pump 1 is better than pump 2 as far as warranty is concerned, so one would expect the interviewee to fill out a higher value than 50% for pump 2. As interviewees typically have a hard time with the first question of the interview, it is critical to take more time here and not rush through the questionnaire.

If the interviewee does not understand, a good way to proceed is to present no-brainer questions. For instance, ask her the question: of the following two pumps, which ones do you prefer (see Table 3.4)? This is obviously an easy question as it is clear that pump 1 is superior to pump 2a: they have the same efficiency but pump 1 has a higher warranty. Unless the interviewee really does not value warranty at all, she will prefer pump 1. The question is stupid, so to speak, but it is important to ask such questions to make the interviewee feel at ease (and to make her think that the interviewer is stupid inasmuch as that that makes her feel better).

The next step is to ask the interviewee for a value of efficiency for which she would definitely choose pump 2 (see Table 3.5). It is important that the interviewer does *not* plug in that value himself because it will, in behavioral economic terms, anchor the interviewee's subsequent answers. If the

TABLE 3.4 Facilitation question #1

	Question: Which pump do you prefer?	
	Pump 1	Pump 2a
Efficiency	50%	50 %
Warranty	6 months	0 months

TABLE 3.5 Facilitation question #2

	Question: Fill out the missing value for which you definitely prefer pump 2b	
	Pump 1	Pump 2b
Efficiency	50%	__ %
Warranty	6 months	0 months

interviewer plugs in the value 80% as opposed to 90%, that will influence the interviewee's answer to the subsequent indifference question.

Suppose therefore that the interviewee answers that if pump 2 had an efficiency level of 99%, she would definitely prefer pump 2b. If she can't find a value for efficiency at which she would prefer pump 2b, then we can already infer that she values efficiency less than an increase in warranty from 0 to 6 months.

Now, if the interviewee answers that at 99% efficiency she prefers pump 2b over pump 1, we can explain easily what we are after when we are looking for indifference. Here is the storyline: "Madam, in the first exercise (with an efficiency of 50% for the pump 2a) you preferred pump 1 over pump 2a. When we compared the same pump 1 with another pump with an efficiency of 99% (pump 2b), you preferred pump 2b. Thus, it must be the case that there is a value between 50% and 99% in which you switched from pump 1 to pump 2. We want to know that switching value." That value is indeed the value for efficiency that generates indifference.

At this point interviewees understand what we are after. For the first question, it typically takes a while to answer the question, and interviewees can get angry simply because indifference is so difficult to find. For instance, suppose the interviewee answers that an efficiency of 60% is the point at which she is indifferent (see Table 3.6).

The interviewer now suggests that he will select the pump for the interviewee and selects pump 1. This is a way of testing whether the interviewee is really indifferent: if she resists and wants the interviewer to select pump 2 instead, then obviously the interviewee's statements reveal that she is not

TABLE 3.6 Facilitation question #3

	Question: Are you indifferent between these two pumps then?	
	Pump 1	Pump 2
Efficiency	50%	60%
Warranty	6 months	0 months

really indifferent: she prefers pump 2 over pump 1. The implication is that the value of 60% is not the switching value. It is too high. Now the interviewee gets another chance to find her indifference point, and eventually she may converge to a value of, say, 55% (see Table 3.7). If the interviewer now takes a shot at challenging the interviewee again and asks: "Can I pick for you?", this may trigger her to snap back: "Pick whichever you want! I don't care." "Are you sure?" "Totally, I really don't know or couldn't care less." Heavenly! We finally found the indifference point: not being able to choose is a sign of indifference. Clearly, forcing people to indifference is a difficult but very important exercise, as it is here that we are really extracting their preferences.

What do we know at this stage for this interviewee? That the utility of increasing the warranty from 0 to 6 months is exactly the same as the utility of increasing efficiency from 50% to 55%. By the same token, the willingness-to-pay of this interviewee for increasing warranty from 0 to 6 months is exactly the same as the willingness-to-pay for increasing efficiency from 50% to 55%. At this stage, we just do not know yet what that willingness-to-pay is, but we do know it is the same. It is at a later stage that we will infer the value (willingness-to-pay) of a utility. But we won't tell the interviewee, as her only task is to reveal her preferences (or "needs" in the business jargon).

Process-wise, the most difficult part is done: the interviewee fully understands the questions. Now we can speed up the process. How do we do this? For those who studied microeconomics: we want to construct the interviewee's utility curve. For those who did not: ignore what we just said. Intuitively we want to understand which additional increments in efficiency give her the same extra utility (hence, willingness-to-pay) corresponding to the utility of increasing warranty from 0 to 6 months.

TABLE 3.7 Facilitation question #4

	Conclusion: Indifferent	
	Pump 1	**Pump 2**
Efficiency	50%	55%
Warranty	6 months	0 months

Here is how we proceed. We just take the switching value obtained in the previous question and substitute it in pump 1 (instead of the original minimum requirement of 50%), then ask the next indifference question again between the two pumps (see Table 3.8).

Now there is no need to explain at length what the question is about. She understands! What is critical is to tell the interviewee that how she feels is all that matters, that there is no right or wrong answer here. We do this, because some people may think that they are silly if they do not fill out the value of 60% for pump 2. But that is not necessary. For all you know, the increase in perceived value from 50% to 55% is very important for her, but increases beyond that are less critical. This could be for many reasons, but they do not really matter for the exercise, because we just want to know her preferences.

In that case, an interviewee faced with the choice shown in Table 3.9 may still prefer pump 1. That is, the increase from 55% to 60% in efficiency does not compensate for the decrease in warranty from 6 to 0 months. In economic jargon: if that is the case, there is decreasing marginal utility to efficiency. The

TABLE 3.8 Constructing the utility curve #1

	Question: For what missing value are you indifferent between pump 1 and pump 2?	
	Pump 1	Pump 2
Efficiency	55%	__ %
Warranty	6 months	0 months

TABLE 3.9 Constructing the utility curve #2

	Question: Which of these two pumps do you prefer?	
	Pump 1	Pump 2
Efficiency	55%	60%
Warranty	6 months	0 months

indifference outcome in the first trade-off question revealed that an increase in efficiency from 50% to 55% was worth exactly the same thing as an increase in warranty from 0 to 6 months. The second trade-off question reveals that an increase in efficiency from 55% to 60% is worth less than the increase in warranty (if it were the same, she would be indifferent again). Obviously, if we were to increase efficiency of pump 2 from 60% to 99%, it is likely that this considerable extra efficiency may make her switch again to pump 2. Her indifference point or switching value is surely higher than 60% but below 99%.

Suppose the switching value is actually 65% for this individual, i.e., she is indifferent between the two pumps shown in Table 3.10. And she will get there quickly after the intense agony suffered in the first trade-off question.

What do we know at this stage? We will illustrate this by a number of statements to familiarize the reader with how we deduce things from these indifference points. We know that an increase in efficiency from 50% to 55% gives the interviewee the same utility as the increase in warranty from 0 to 6 months. We also know that that same increase in warranty from 0 to 6 months gives her the same increase in utility (1 utility) as an increase in efficiency from 55% to 65%, or consequently, that increasing efficiency from 50% to 65% gives her 2 extra utilities. Hence, the increase in utility stemming from an increase in efficiency from 50% to 55% is the same as the increase in utility stemming from an increase in efficiency from 55% to 65% (by transitivity of preferences). By extrapolation, her willingness-to-pay from increasing efficiency from 55% to 60% is only about half the willingness-to-pay for a warranty increase from 0 to 6 months.

We will ask yet another question, using the new switching value as the starting point (see Table 3.11). If the interviewee truly has decreasing marginal utility, it could be that her indifference point is now 85%.

TABLE 3.10 Constructing the utility curve #3

	Conclusion: Indifferent!	
	Pump 1	Pump 2
Efficiency	55%	65%
Warranty	6 months	0 months

TABLE 3.11 Constructing the utility curve #4

	Question: For what missing value are you indifferent between pump 1 and pump 2?		
		Pump 1	Pump 2
Efficiency		65%	__ %
Warranty		6 months	0 months

TABLE 3.12 Constructing the utility curve for efficiency

Efficiency (%)	Utility
50	0
55	1
65	2
85	3

How many more questions do we ask? Until the point where our technical capabilities will never allow us to realize the feature level improvement. If indeed, we can never, with whatever R&D effort, expect to reach levels exceeding 85%, then there is no point in asking yet another question. Let us say that it is the case, which means that we have obtained for this interviewee a utility table for improvements in efficiency over the minimum requirement (see Table 3.12).

We will now elicit utilities for all other features that the interviewee finds important, in the same manner. In the interview process, things accelerate as the interviewee by now has become quite familiar with the process. Let us go through the process of eliciting utilities of improvements in the second feature, mean time between failure (MTBF), over the minimum requirement of this interviewee (see Table 3.13).

We will not need to fill out "1000 hours" in pump 2 for the interviewee to understand the question. She will relatively quickly come up with a value for which she is indifferent. Let us assume that the value is 1500 hours (see Table 3.14), which means that she cannot choose between pumps 1 and 2. Thus, the improvement in MTBF from 1000 to 1500 hours commands

TABLE 3.13 Trade-off question between warranty and MTBF #1

		Question: Fill out the missing value for which you are indifferent between pump 1 and pump 2	
		Pump 1	Pump 2
MTBF		1000 hours	__ hours
Warranty		6 months	0 months

TABLE 3.14 Trade-off question between warranty and MTBF #2

		Conclusion: Indifferent	
		Pump 1	Pump 2
MTBF		1000 hours	1500 hours
Warranty		6 months	0 months

TABLE 3.15 Trade-off question between warranty and MTBF #3

		Conclusion: Indifferent	
		Pump 1	Pump 2
MTBF		1500 hours	2000 hours
Warranty		6 months	0 months

the same utility increase (1 utility) as the increase in warranty from 0 to 6 months.

What is also true is that the interviewee has the same increase in utility from increasing MTBF from 1000 to 1500 hours as she has from increasing efficiency from 55% to 65%. Why? Because they both have the same value as the increase in warranty from 0 to 6 months. And so on. Without going into detail, imagine now that the following are the answers to the next preference elicitation questions related to MTBF (see Tables 3.15, 3.16 and 3.17).

TABLE 3.16 Trade-off question between warranty and MTBF #4

	Conclusion: Indifferent	
	Pump 1	**Pump 2**
MTBF	2000 hours	2500 hours
Warranty	6 months	0 months

TABLE 3.17 Trade-off question between warranty and MTBF #5

	Conclusion: Indifferent	
	Pump 1	**Pump 2**
MTBF	2500 hours	3000 hours
Warranty	6 months	0 months

It appears that this interviewee's preference for MBTF is totally linear: an increase in MTBF by 500 hours commands the same utility whatever the initial level of utility. As we said earlier, preferences do not necessarily reveal decreasing marginal utility. If this is how this interviewee feels, then that is what we record. Again, we stop asking questions if technically we can never improve MTBF above a particular level. In this case, that happens to be 3000 hours.

We can now summarize the preferences of this interviewee, that is the extra utilities associated with improvements in MTBF above the base minimum requirement (see Table 3.18).

Now we know that an increase in MTBF from, say, 2000 to 3000 hours commands the same willingness-to-pay as an increase in efficiency from 50% to 65%: both constitute 2 utilities. They are both equal to twice this interviewee's willingness-to-pay for increasing warranty from 0 to 6 months. Or to take another example, an efficiency improvement from 55% to 85% commands the same willingness-to-pay (2 utilities) as an increase in MTBF from 1500 to 2000 hours (1 utility) *combined with* an increase

TABLE 3.18 Constructing the utility curve for MTBF

MTBF (hours)	Utility
1000	0
1500	1
2000	2
2500	3
3000	4

TABLE 3.19 Constructing the utility curve for the feature used as original gauge #1

	Question: Fill out the missing value for which you are indifferent between pump 1 and pump 2	
	Pump 1	**Pump 2**
Warranty	0 months	__ months
Efficiency	55%	50%

in efficiency from 50% to 55% (1 utility), and so on. Again, all of this is only possible if, for this interviewee, the additivity assumption holds across the features, that is, if she does not have to answer with "I cannot answer this question unless I know the level of feature X (say, mean time between failure)." As we said, in practice and with sensibly selected features, this is more of a theoretical issue.

We can go on with all other features that, first, we can influence and that, second, the interviewee finds important. For simplicity of the exposition, let us assume that we can also elicit the utility curve for the delivery time of the pump, the delivery time of spare parts, and the level at which no external cooling is needed. Then there is only one other feature (other than price, of course) for which we do not have the utility curve yet, that of the gauge: warranty. You may wonder how we elicit the utility curve of warranty if it has been the gauge for all the other features. The way to proceed is to use one of these other features as the gauge for the elicitation of changes in the level of warranty. In fact, we have many options, and could for instance use efficiency changes from 50% to 55% as our reference point (see Table 3.19).

If the interviewee is rational and consistent, her answer to this question should in principle be 6 months. Why? Because we elicited the utility of improvements in efficiency from 50% to 55% from the comparison of an increase in the level of warranty from 0 to 6 months. However, as we said, we are helping individuals at identifying and crafting their preferences, which is a difficult task. We are scraping it out of their brain, so to speak. So, imagine that the interviewee comes up with the answer shown in Table 3.20.

That inconsistent value is obviously a bummer, but the appropriate response by the interviewer is surely not: "Are you stupid or what? In the first question, you got to an indifference at 6 months of warranty whereas now you are at 4 months?" Or "Hey, we are rewarding you to do this, so don't mess with us." To the contrary, it is normal that interviewees are not entirely consistent – we are not robots, after all. The best response is to show the interviewee the discrepancy, to tell her that this is normal as this is a difficult task, and to ask what level she really feels most comfortable with. In all likelihood, that will be 6 months, as she already spent so much time to force herself to indifference then. If that is not the case, one may need to revisit question 1 again, and start the process all over. This is, however, unlikely to happen.

The converse of this explanation is also true: if the interviewee is completely erratic, then we may have to conclude that we need to throw out this data point, as this interviewee is really messing with us. There may be some deviations from transitivity of preferences but not to such an extreme case. So, let us assume she feels most comfortable with her initial indifference level (see Table 3.21).

As before, we then go to the next question (see Table 3.22).

TABLE 3.20 Constructing the utility curve for the feature used as original gauge #2

	Answer: Indifferent	
	Pump 1	Pump 2
Warranty	0 months	4 months
Efficiency	55%	50%

TABLE 3.21 Constructing the utility curve for the feature used as original gauge #3

	Conclusion: Indifferent	
	Pump 1	Pump 2
Warranty	0 months	6 months
Efficiency	55%	50%

TABLE 3.22 Constructing the utility curve for the feature used as original gauge #4

	Question: Fill out the missing value for which you are indifferent between pump 1 and pump 2	
	Pump 1	Pump 2
Warranty	6 months	__ months
Efficiency	55%	50%

Here it is quite likely that preferences for warranty are not linear, though the type of non-linearity varies from individual to individual (with some individuals having linear preferences, of course). So, it should not be surprising that the interviewee values the first 6 months of warranty more than the increase in warranty from 6 to 12 months (i.e., at 12 months of warranty for pump 2, she prefers pump 1). Hence, she needs considerably more warranty above 12 months to make up for the given decrease in efficiency associated with pump 2. If she is comfortable with this answer, this implies again that her willingness-to-pay for an increase in warranty from 0 to 6 months is the same as her willingness-to-pay for an increase in warranty from 6 to 18 months (see Table 3.23). While we do not quite know the shape of the non-linearity between 6 and 18 months, we can roughly extrapolate that her willingness-to-pay for an increase in warranty from 6 to 12 months is about half her willingness-to-pay for an increase in warranty from 0 to 6 months.

Let us now say that the answers to the next indifference elicitation questions are as shown in Tables 3.24 and 3.25.

TABLE 3.23 Constructing the utility curve for the feature used as original gauge #5

	Conclusion: Indifferent	
	Pump 1	Pump 2
Warranty	6 months	18 months
Efficiency	55%	50%

TABLE 3.24 Constructing the utility curve for the feature used as original gauge #6

	Conclusion: Indifferent	
	Pump 1	Pump 2
Warranty	18 months	36 months
Efficiency	55%	50%

TABLE 3.25 Constructing the utility curve for the feature used as original gauge #7

	Conclusion: Indifferent	
	Pump 1	Pump 2
Warranty	36 months	72 months
Efficiency	55%	50%

Let us say we stop right there (given the typical lifetime of a pump and the fact that offering warranty beyond 72 months is excessively expensive). The corresponding utility table is shown in Table 3.26.

We can now also put all the utility values next to each other in one table (see Table 3.27), where we show how we can improve utility by 1 using various feature level improvements. We can also combine improvements across

TABLE 3.26 Constructing the utility curve for warranty

Warranty (months)	Utility
0	0
6	1
18	2
36	3
72	4

TABLE 3.27 The utility curves for the various features

Utility	Efficiency (%)	MTBF (hours)	Warranty (months)
0	50	1000	0
1	55	1500	6
2	65	2000	18
3	85	2500	36
4	NA	3000	72

features to obtain a given utility improvement (of, say, 4 utilities above minimum requirements).

So far, we have discussed the elicitation of utility for improvements of a continuous existing feature. The trade-off method can also easily handle discrete features rather than continuous ones, whether they be totally new in the market or (modifications of) existing features. Examples of discrete features are zero-one features such as "with or without alarm when the pump is overheating," distinct colors, or the year of construction. In such cases, the pump is presented with and without the extra feature, and the interviewee is asked how much MTBF (or any other continuous feature) she is willing to give up to have this extra feature. Suppose the interviewee is indifferent between a pump with the alarm and an MTBF of 1500 hours on the one hand, and a pump without the alarm and an MTBF of 2300 hours, then we know that the alarm is worth 1.6 utilities.

Let us go back to the original table. We now know many things. For instance, for this interviewee, the willingness-to-pay for an increase in warranty from 0 to 6 months combined with an increase in efficiency from 50% to 55% is the same as the willingness-to-pay for an increase in MTBF from 2000 to 3000 hours (namely 2 extra utilities).

Or that an increase in warranty from 36 to 54 months combined with an increase in efficiency from 65% to 75% is about the same as the increase in willingness-to-pay for increasing MTBF from 1500 to 2000 hours. As a result of additivity of preferences, all these increases are equivalent to a 1 utility increase, which is the willingness-to-pay associated with an increase in warranty from 0 to 6 months.

Expressing willingness-to-pay in monetary terms

The key question of course is: what is, in monetary terms, the willingness-to-pay for an increase in 1 utility, as defined earlier? As we mentioned before, we better extract this willingness-to-pay indirectly than by asking what a particular improvement is worth to the interviewee. There are many indirect ways to infer willingness-to-pay, and many ways to cross-check our results for consistency. It is the combined outcome of these cross-checks that will give us plenty of confidence in the true willingness-to-pay associated with 1 utility increase.

We need to make one assumption: the utility of money is linear. In other words, the first dollar is worth as much as the second dollar. This assumption is generally accepted, reasonable and supported by scientific evidence (as long as we are not talking about huge amounts of money, because for most of us, $100 million is actually not equal to 10 times $10 million; most of us would describe both as a whole lot of money).[18] For most decision-making problems, the assumption that, say, $20 is worth twice $10, or $2000 is worth twice $1000 is surely reasonable. And in B2B settings, where the buyers are profit-maximizing companies, the linearity assumption makes sense, even for larger expenditures: money is money, so to speak.

How do we then infer the willingness-to-pay for such utility? We take an arbitrary hypothetical pump, and again force the interviewee to indifference. Here is an example. Imagine that we ask the interviewee to find the value for the warranty level for which she can no longer choose between the two arbitrary pumps shown in Table 3.28. She will then carefully review the pumps, and understand that pump 1 is considerably better than pump 2 as far as MTBF is concerned (in our terminology, it is 2 utilities better, since 2500 hours of MTBF provides this interviewee 2 utilities more than 1500 hours of MTBF). On the other hand, the price of pump 2 is higher by $500 and the efficiency is slightly better (in our terminology, it provides 1 more utility) than that of pump 1.

TABLE 3.28 Willingness-to-pay for 1 utility #1

	Question: Fill out the missing value for which you are indifferent between pump 1 and pump 2	
	Pump 1	Pump 2
Warranty	36 months	__ months
MTBF	2500 hours	1500 hours
Price	$4000	$4500
Efficiency	55%	65%

TABLE 3.29 Willingness-to-pay for 1 utility #2

	Conclusion: Indifferent	
	Pump 1	Pump 2
Warranty	36 months	12 months
MTBF	2500 hours	1500 hours
Price	$4000	$4500
Efficiency	55%	65%

Since we do not know what a utility is worth, as that is what we are trying to find out, it is impossible to predict whether the missing value for warranty in pump 2 will be higher or lower than 36 months. It depends on how much the interviewee values a utility monetarily. Imagine she is most comfortable with 12 months (see Table 3.29).

Let us sum the utility difference between the two pumps associated with the pump features other than price. We reproduce it in a table (see Table 3.30).[19]

Since the interviewee is indifferent between the two pumps, the utility associated with both pumps is the same for her. Thus, it must mean that the

TABLE 3.30 Willingness-to-pay for 1 utility #3

Feature	Pump 1	Pump 2	Utility of pump 1 – Utility of pump 2
Warranty	36	12	+1.5 (by extrapolation)
MTBF	2500	1500	+2
Efficiency	55	65	−1
TOTAL			+2.5

TABLE 3.31 Cross-check #1

Question: Fill out the missing value for which you are indifferent between pump 1 and pump 2

	Pump 1	Pump 2
Warranty	36 months	18 months
MTBF	1500 hours	1000 hours
Price	$4400	$4000
Efficiency	65%	__ %

difference in price of $500 is worth 2.5 utilities, so that 1 utility is worth $500/2.5 = $200.

We can validate this result through a number of cross-checks, which are some form of inconsistency and lie detector. If indeed the interviewee is rational and does not lie, then we can forecast what she should be answering to the indifference question shown in Table 3.31.

You can do the calculation. If $200 is indeed the value of 1 utility inferred from the earlier question, or, conversely, the willingness-to-pay for a 1 utility increase is $200, then we can construct a similar table, knowing the utility value of the price difference (see Table 3.32).

That is, without considering efficiency, the utility value of pump 1 is exactly the same as that of pump 2. The hyper-consistent truthful interviewee would

TABLE 3.32 Cross-check #2

Feature	Pump 1	Pump 2	Utility of pump 1 – Utility of pump 2
Warranty	36	18	+1
MTBF	1500	1000	+1
Price	4400	4000	−2
TOTAL			0

TABLE 3.33 Cross-check #3

	Predicted value of efficiency for pump 2 that generates indifference between pump 1 and pump 2	
	Pump 1	**Pump 2**
Warranty	36 months	18 months
MTBF	1500 hours	1000 hours
Price	$4400	$4000
Efficiency	65%	65%

then need to have the same efficiency level for the two pumps, namely 65%, to be indifferent (see Table 3.33).

In reality, people are of course not hyper-consistent robots. So, some averaging out will need to be done. Imagine for instance that the interviewee would have answered 70% instead of the predicted 65% efficiency (see Table 3.34). Since her answer implies indifference, it turns out that x should be equal to −1.75 utilities. This means that 1 utility is worth $400/1.75 = $228.

If we only had this one cross-check, then we would take the average of $200 and $228 and deduce that the value of a 1 utility increase is worth $214. With one more cross-check, we would get an even better picture. We would throw out the data points related to individuals who are totally inconsistent, as they may not understand the questionnaire or take it seriously.[20]

To simplify the exhibition, let us assume for now that we inferred from the previous questions that a utility improvement of 1 unit is worth $200. Then

TABLE 3.34 Cross-check #4

Feature	Pump 1	Pump 2	Utility of pump 1 – Utility of pump 2
Warranty	36	18	+1
MTBF	1500	1000	+1
Efficiency	65	70	–0.25
Price	4400	4000	x
TOTAL			0 (by indifference)

TABLE 3.35 Utility table including price

Utility	Efficiency (%)	MTBF (hours)	Warranty (months)	Price ($)
0	50	1000	0	5000
1	55	1500	6	4800
2	65	2000	18	4600
3	85	2500	36	4400
4	NA	3000	72	4200

we can construct a table representing different ways in which utility can be increased by improving one feature of the pump relative to the minimum requirement for that feature (which we again arbitrarily call utility = 0). Utility in price is linear, to the tune of $200 per utility increase, and obviously increases with a decrease in price (see Table 3.35). As you have understood from the preceding, we can also combine changes across the various feature levels to generate a specific utility change.

As preferences are additive, we can now construct hypothetical pumps with different combinations of features, and forecast which pump this interviewee prefers, provided she satisfies the completeness, transitivity and additivity assumptions (see Table 3.36). This interviewee prefers pump 4 over pump 3 despite a higher price, simply because the strong features of pump 4 command sufficient willingness-to-pay to cancel out the relatively negative price effect. She in turn prefers pump 3 over pumps 1 and 2, and is indifferent between pumps 1 and 2.

We have now done what we claimed we could do at the outset of this exhibition: to forecast *for any type of pump* (out of the thousands that we can

TABLE 3.36 Utility for various hypothetical pumps

Feature	Pump 1	Pump 2	Pump 3	Pump 4
Efficiency (%)	55	60	55	65
MTBF (hours)	1500	2500	2000	2500
Warranty (months)	12	0	6	18
Price ($)	4500	4700	4400	4800
Utility	6	6	7	8

construct) what the interviewee will prefer, without having to ask her the question directly. Realize that this has been done by asking just a limited number of questions, in fact about three to four indifference questions per feature, and one additional question plus a few cross-checks for the translation of utility into willingness-to-pay, leading to a total of about 15 questions. With continuous features, the number of pumps that can be constructed is obviously infinite. The method allows us to forecast accurately the preferences of this interviewee, that is, what she will choose, provided that the preferences satisfy the very reasonable assumptions on preferences.

Eliciting willingness-to-buy

The preceding analysis allowed us to elicit an individual's preferences and willingness-to-pay for improvements in feature levels or additional features. It did not (yet) allow us to predict her willingness-to-buy: whether she would actually buy a particular pump, or what it would take for her to do so.

Let us tell you up front what we will *not* do. We will not try to identify all the pumps available on the market from other manufacturers, and to somehow measure the utility of each of those pumps, including ours (and including thus other dimensions like the utility of brand, relationship, look-and-feel etc.), and then compare these utilities with each other, to conclude that the utility of our pump is higher or lower for this interviewee than that of all these other pumps. This is often being done in alternative methods, but we find it both terribly inefficient and terribly irrelevant.

It is terribly inefficient because to do so, one would need to compare all the features of the products one by one, not only the ones that we can influence (in the preceding example: efficiency, price, warranty and MTBF) but also everything else, such as ISO certificates, look-and-feel, proximity of the manufacturer, brand value, value of the relationship with the sales person of the manufacturer, value of the available pump colors, and a whole lot of things that are in fact unknowns (for instance, exceptionally good or bad experiences with the manufacturer). It would truly take forever to do so, and the interviewee would be exhausted and angry at the end of the exercise.

Besides, the analysis may very well be done to no avail because it is unlikely that the interviewee would be able to recall all the elements of value creation or destruction related to all other available pumps. Neither may she be willing to reveal all her experiences with her best alternative, nor the price that she typically pays.[21] Our method, by way of contrast, does not depend on her revealing this price, nor even what her best alternative pump is.

The exhaustive analysis is also terribly irrelevant because not all of these pumps matter. The only thing that matters, at the end of the day, is the interviewee's best alternative, which could be either the pump that she would be buying should we not launch our hypothetical pump, or simply "nothing" (if she is not sure that she will buy a pump at all). Let us assume, for simplicity, that she would buy a best alternative pump. The most important thing to know is that all other pumps do not matter.

What we will do, therefore, is to infer the difference in utility between the interviewee's best alternative pump and one of our pumps, typically but not necessarily our hypothetical launch pump. The hypothetical launch pump (called, say, LP) could be what management had in mind *before* digging deeply into the preferences of the ultimate decision-makers, the customers. LP has a particular look-and-feel and is specified by a number of feature levels, as described in Table 3.37.

The question to ask to the interviewee is now shown in Table 3.38.

To make things, well, complicated, so that you really understand the process, we assume that when asked whether she would choose her best alternative pump or our hypothetical launch pump, she reveals that she prefers the former.

If she prefers the best alternative, we would really want to know "by how much," that is, by how many utilities (this is only between you and us, the word

TABLE 3.37 Features of hypothetical launch pump LP

Feature	Level
Efficiency	55%
Warranty	12 months
Mean time between failure (MTBF)	2000 hours
Delivery time of pump	4 weeks
Delivery time of spare parts	48 hours
Price	$4600
No external cooling required below a temperature of	80°C
Pump standard	EVX
ISO Norm	2424
Speed	Variable
Noise reduction feature	Included

TABLE 3.38 Comparison with best alternative

Which pump do you prefer?

	Pump 1	Pump 2
Type	Your best alternative pump	Our hypothetical launch pump

utility is obviously never used during the interview). The difference in utility between the best alternative pump and this hypothetical launch pump will give us an indication of the minimum improvement in utility needed over this hypothetical launch pump for the interviewee to switch and buy our pump instead. Whether such improvement is worth it for us obviously depends on costs, imitability and the like, as well as on how other customers in the target market feel. We will come back to these issues in Chapters 4 and 5.

Imagine we were to ask the interviewee how much she is paying for her best alternative pump. She may well be lying through her teeth, or may simply not answer the question (despite being rewarded for participating in the interview). While we could probably prod her into telling us what her best alternative pump is (in which case we could verify the levels of the features), she may not do so. This highlights that it is important that our method does not depend on this information. At least in our experience, we can extract the switching value in another way, provided our questions are not threatening.

The question we can ask is: "What is the level of MTBF that our pump would need to have for you to be indifferent and thus no longer be able to choose between our (enhanced) pump and your best alternative (keeping all other features constant)?" If you need to explain it further, you can indicate to the interviewee that, at an MTBF of 2000 hours for pump LP, she prefers her best alternative. The question now is by how much our MTBF would have to be raised above 2000 hours for her to be indifferent between her best alternative and our pump. Imagine she says: "3000 hours." We can of course double-check this by presenting a new hypothetical pump and asking her whether she would choose this pump or her best alternative (see Table 3.39).

If the answer is that she now prefers this pump, then 3000 hours is obviously too large a value, and we will need to go through a similar process as in our first trade-off question to uncover the true value of MTBF for which she really can no longer choose. Suppose it is actually 3000 hours. In that case, we know that this specific interviewee needs 2 extra utilities over the hypothetical launch pump LP for her to be indifferent between that pump (described in Table 3.39) and her best alternative. That is the case because of the utility information we have about the increase in utility from the original 2000 hours for the LP and 3000 hours (see Table 3.35).

Let us cross-check this result. Imagine we go back to the original hypothetical launch pump LP which the interviewee did not want to buy. Now we can ask the question: "What is the improved level of efficiency that this pump

TABLE 3.39 Features of new hypothetical launch pump

Feature	Level
Efficiency	55%
Warranty	12 months
Mean time between failure (MTBF)	3000 hours
Delivery time of pump	4 weeks
Delivery time of spare parts	48 hours
Price	$4600
No external cooling required below a temperature of	80°C
Pump standard	EVX
ISO Norm	2424
Speed	Variable
Noise reduction feature	Included

would need to have for you to be indifferent between this pump and your best alternative (keeping all other features constant)?" Again, you can indicate to the interviewee that, at an efficiency level of 55%, she prefers her best alternative. The question now is by how much this efficiency would have to be raised above 55% for her to be indifferent. If she is consistent, her answer should really be an efficiency level of 85%, as the increase in utility from 2000 hours MTBF to 3000 hours MTBF equals the increase in utility from 55% efficiency to 85% efficiency, namely 2 extra utilities.

We could cross-check one more time and use the warranty variable (12 months in the original hypothetical launch pump). You guessed it, the predicted answer of the hyper-consistent interviewee should be 54 months. Obviously, we will not get that level of consistency all along, and may need to average out these utilities. If the switching values related to the three checked features (MTBF, efficiency and warranty) correspond, for example, to utility increases of 2, 1.6 and 1.8, then we can take the average switching value of 1.8, or we can play it safe and say that it is maximally 2.

Some of you may wonder why we do not cross-check with the price variable as well. That is, ask for what value of price ($4600 for the hypothetical pump) the interviewee would be indifferent between her best alternative and our pump, keeping all other variables constant. The forecasted answer is obviously $4200 as a decrease of $400 corresponds to 2 utilities. Such price questions may be worth trying, and surely so for inconspicuous buyers, but they remain tricky, especially for astute purchasers in B2B settings. The good news is that we do not need the price questions, as we understand how to translate utilities into price cuts. And who says that we want to offer price cuts to attract buyers anyhow?

So, let us say our safe estimate of the switching value is 2 utilities. This switching value represents the sum of the values of the following four components to this interviewee:

1. The differences in value she attaches to the measurable features (MTBF, delivery time, price, ISO certification, etc.) and the look-and-feel dimensions of the two pumps.

2. The switching costs she has to incur, if any, from switching from the one pump to the other, that is from her best alternative pump to our hypothetical pump.

3. The differences in brand value between the two pumps.

4. If the best alternative pump is made by her current supplier: the positive or negative value of working with this specific supplier (if positive, this includes the perceived risk of working with a new supplier).

If the two pumps are exactly the same in terms of features and in terms of look-and-feel, and if switching costs are zero, then it means that the switching value of 2 utilities relates to the last two of the preceding four components. It then captures the additional pure brand value (which stands for a number of softer characteristics, such as better and proven reliability) and, possibly, the better perceived experience of dealing with the company that manufactures the best alternative pump.

By showing that the switching value covers so many differences between alternative choices, we hope to reinforce our earlier claim that it is impossible to predict customer choices by disaggregating pumps into all their measurable and non-measurable components. There are just too many to consider, and interviewees do not necessarily remember what features mattered in their choice decisions. In addition, all we need to know is what would make her switch from her best alternative. The preceding method captures that well. It is not dependent on information about the best alternative or the current supplier (if any) that the interviewee may not want to reveal. The cross-checks increase the chances that the switching value inferred is maximally accurate.

The implication of the preceding is that, at least for this interviewee, we can predict whether she will or will not purchase any pump within our capabilities. All we need to know is whether the pump has at least 2 more utilities than the hypothetical launch pump. Two utilities are not sufficient, as this is where she is indifferent between the two pumps. Theoretically, 2.01 utilities are sufficient. But let us play it safe, and allow for some inconsistency of the utilities derived from the comparisons with the best alternative. As a consequence, let us assume the interviewee will buy a pump from the manufacturer instead of her best alternative if the former has at least 2.1 utilities more than the latter.

Table 3.40 shows some examples of pumps that she would or would not buy. We obviously only change the values for the features whose values can be changed by the manufacturer – these are in the first four rows.

TABLE 3.40 Examples of pumps to offer

Feature	Pump 1	Pump 2	Pump 3	Pump 4	Pump 5	Pump 6
Efficiency (%)	60	55	75	85	65	55
Warranty (months)	18	12	24	36	24	0
Mean time between failure: MTBF (hours)	2500	2000	2400	1000	3000	3000
Price ($)	4550	4150	4800	4300	4550	4400
Delivery time of pump (weeks)	4	4	4	4	4	4
Delivery time of spare parts (hours)	48	48	48	48	48	48
No external cooling required below a temperature of (°C)	80	80	80	80	80	80
Pump standard	EVX	EVX	EVX	EVX	EVX	EVX
ISO Norm	2424	2424	2424	2424	2424	2424
Speed	Variable	Variable	Variable	Variable	Variable	Variable
Noise reduction feature	Included	Included	Included	Included	Included	Included
Utility over hypothetical launch pump	$0.5 + 0.5 + 1 + 0.25 = 2.25$	$0 + 0 + 0 + 2.25 = 2.25$	$1.5 + 0.83 + 0.8{-}1 = 2.13$	Below min. requirement on MTBF	$1 + 0.83 + 2 + 0.25 = 4.08$	$0{-}1.5 + 2 + 1 = 1.5$
Will interviewee buy (YES/NO)	YES	YES	YES	NO	YES	NO
Revenue generated from interviewee ($)	4550	4150	4800	0	4550	0

Let us discuss each of these pumps briefly. Pump 1 induces switching toward the new pump with minimal effect on price, since sufficient value is brought through the other three features. Pump 2 induces switching, but it is based on a price cut, a notoriously easily imitable action. Pump 3 is a more creative option: it raises price and yet induces switching, as the perceived value increase from the improvement in efficiency, warranty and MBTF is more than 3.1 utilities larger than the decrease in value from the price increase, ending up with a total utility increase of 2.1. Pump 4 is quite attractive as it improves value on three dimensions, namely efficiency, warranty and price. However, the dip in MTBF is too large and does not satisfy the interviewee's minimum requirements.

Pump 5 definitely induces switching, as it generates much more utility to the interviewee than needed for her to switch. In fact, it generates 4.1 utilities whereas 2.1 is sufficient to switch. We should wonder, however, whether we have delivered too much value to the customer relative to the cost of offering the super-performance on the features. It surely is nice if we like to hold a bubble bath discussion on how important it is to super-please the customer, or to pamper the customer, or what have you. Yet from a margin perspective (and our shareholders may ultimately care more about that), pump 1 may be vastly superior to pump 5. It makes the customer switch, but presumably at a lower cost, and hence with higher margins for the manufacturer.

Generally, to know what is best from a profit maximization perspective, we need cost information, competitor information and information about preferences of other interviewees in the representative sample, not just one potential customer. In Chapter 4 we will explain how we obtain such aggregate revenue and margin forecasts. Note that we illustrated our method with six potential pumps only. We can in fact forecast the choices of the interviewee for any type of the thousands of possible pumps at various price levels.

Some closing methodological remarks

The conclusion of the foregoing is that the method not only allows us to know what to offer to make a customer switch, but also what not to offer and still make a customer switch. We find that quite powerful. Nevertheless, some of the more skeptical readers may still have questions such as:

1. Do customers in real life go through the process of figuring out where they are indifferent?

2. Is the analysis not fundamentally determined by the gauge we used up front (in our case, the difference between 0 and 6 months of warranty)?

3. Do customers really behave the same way in real life as in the experimental setting?

4. Can the method predict what individuals will do if we are planning to bring more than one pump to market?

5. How should the method be adapted to predict and influence customer's willingness-to-buy for experience goods or hybrid goods (both in B2C and B2B settings)?

6. This appears complicated and costly. What if we don't have the time or money? Are there any shortcuts?

Let us address each of these questions separately.

Question 1. Do customers in real life go through the process of figuring out where they are indifferent? The answer is no, but the observation misses the point. What we are trying to do with the indifference questions is to find an as clean as possible way to extract preferences, based upon a minimum number of assumptions (completeness, transitivity and additivity) that do make sense and are generally accepted. At the end of the day, when a customer makes a choice, his preferences dictate that choice. The customer may not pay attention to all the features of a specific product, but then this also means that the customer would have found these features unimportant. Our method would have picked that up, and we would not have gone through the elicitation of utilities for improvements in unimportant features anyhow. To predict a given customer's choices, the best way forward is to understand his preferences as accurately as possible, and to do so in a rigorous, scientifically founded way.

Question 2. Is the analysis not fundamentally determined by the gauge we used up front (in our case, the difference between 0 and 6 months of warranty)? Here the answer is negative. Whatever gauge we had used, the predicted choices of the interviewee would remain the same. Imagine that we had taken a difference in MTBF from 2500 to 1500 as our gauge in the utility elicitation questions (i.e., we would have defined 1 utility as the increase in MTBF from 1500 to 2500), as opposed to defining it as the increase in warranty from 0 to 6 months. Ex post, we know that an increase in MTBF from 1500 to 2500 for this interviewee is worth 2 times an increase in warranty from 0 to 6 months or, conversely, equivalent to an increase in warranty from 0 to 18 months, which has the same value as an increase in efficiency from 50% to 65%. In the translation of utility into willingness-to-pay, it would also turn out that 1 utility, defined as the delta between 1500 hours and 2500 hours in MTBF, would then come out to be $400.

One needs to pre-test somewhat the appropriate gauge internally before starting the interviews. For instance, an increase in MTBF from 1500 to 2500 is relatively large to elicit the utility associated with increases in efficiency. In fact, with such a large gap, the interviewee may not be able to answer certain questions. For instance, she would still be able to answer the first set of questions: she needs an efficiency of 65% combined with an MTBF of 1500 to be indifferent with a pump with an efficiency of 50% and an MTBF of 2500 (from Table 3.35). But she may not be able to answer the second set of questions (see Table 3.41). It could be the case that even with an efficiency of 100% for pump 2, the interviewee still prefers pump 1. In that case, we do not know much about the incremental value of increases in efficiency beyond 65%, other than that an increase from 65% to 100% is worth less than an increase from 50% to 65%. In addition, the answer is not that useful if we can in any event not generate 100% efficiency. We want to know the value of improvements within our (extended) capabilities, not beyond these capabilities.

Question 3. Do customers really behave the same way in real life as in the experimental setting? Here the answer is also negative, which is unfortunate. We will have a margin of error as a result of the experimental nature of the setting. This is common to any method of preference elicitation. However, we try to minimize the bias by putting people in choice and comparison situations, which is what people actually do in real life. We also clearly explain to the interviewee that we are helping her at crafting her preferences, which is a necessary condition for us to forecast actual behavior. That other factors

TABLE 3.41 Example of pre-test

Feature	Pump 1	Pump 2
Efficiency	65%	x% =?
MTBF	2500 hours	1500 hours

may intervene at the time of the actual purchasing decision is beyond our control, and there is not much we can do about it. What we do is to control all the controllable factors, and get to understand the interviewee's true preferences, keeping all other factors constant, while accepting that they may eventually not be (or that preferences may have changed by the time of purchase).

Question 4. Can the method predict what individuals will do if we are planning to bring more than one pump to market? Absolutely. Going back to what we explained before, individuals want to maximize the deal value. They want to maximize the difference between the value of the pump and the actual price paid, provided again that the pump meets the minimum requirements.

Let us see how this works by going back to the six pumps presented in Table 3.40. We inferred, first, that pump 1, priced at $4550, was worth an extra 2.25 utility over the original hypothetical pump; and second, that the interviewee needed at least 2 utilities over her best alternative to buy the original hypothetical pump. Hence, pump 1 is worth 0.25 utilities more than her best alternative. Thus, the extra monetary value of pump 1 before reaching the point of indifference is $0.25 \times \$200 = \$50$ (remember, we figured out that one utility is worth $200), and its total value is $4550 + \$50 = \$4600$. The deal value of pump 1 is thus simply equal to the monetary value over the best alternative ($50). That is, we do not really need to calculate the value of the pump: calculating the monetary value over the best alternative suffices.

We can fill out the value of the five other pumps, as well as their deal value (see Table 3.42). The interviewee would never buy pumps 4 or 6, for reasons that we explained before. If pumps 1, 2, 3 and 5 are launched simultaneously, she would buy pump 5.

Question 5. How should the method be adapted to predict and influence customers' willingness-to-buy for experience goods or hybrid goods (both in B2C and B2B settings)? Experience goods are goods that can be accurately evaluated only after the product has been purchased and experienced. Many B2C products (such as chocolate bars and drinks) and services fall into this category. Other B2C products and services only partially fall into the category of experience goods (e.g., all kinds of telecommunications packages, financial services, hotel services and the like). Many services that are traditionally categorized as an experience good have moved more into the search good

TABLE 3.42 Deal value of alternative pumps

Feature	Pump 1	Pump 2	Pump 3	Pump 4	Pump 5	Pump 6
Efficiency (%)	60	55	75	85	65	55
Warranty (months)	18	12	24	36	24	0
Mean time between failure: MTBF (hours)	2500	2000	2400	1000	3000	3000
Price ($)	4550	4150	4800	4300	4550	4400
Utility over hypothetical launch pump	0.5 + 0.5 + 1 + 0.25 = 2.25	0 + 0 + 0 + 2.25 = 2.25	1.5 + 0.83 + 0.8 −1 = 2.13	Below min. requirement on MTBF	1 + 0.83 + 2 + 0.25 = 4.08	0 − 1.5 + 2 + 1 = 1.5
Will subject buy (YES/NO)	YES	YES	YES	NO	YES	NO
Value of the pump ($)	4600 (4550 + 50)	4200 (4150 + 50)	4826 (4800 + 26)	None	4966 (4550 + 416)	None
Deal value of the pump ($)	50	50	26	<0	416	<0
Preferred pump (YES/NO)	NO	NO	NO	NO	YES	NO

category over time and are therefore a hybrid of the two categories. Hotel services is one of them, as they can be selected through objective criteria provided by hotel booking platforms. Even the subjective dimension (i.e., the "experience" of staying at the hotel) is increasingly evaluated through measurable criteria; witness the massive use of the average review score of the hotel and the distribution thereof.

While our method can be tailored to practically *all* goods and services, it is easier to apply to (1) search goods and (2) all experience goods that have a search component to it, that is, for which at least one objective and, ideally, a continuous feature (such as review scores) other than price is used in the purchasing decision. In the case of an experience good, such as medical gloves, the potential customer does indeed have to experience the good: in this specific case, the interviewee has to try on the glove, as she cannot understand the value of, for instance, a decrease in the thickness by x microns unless she tries them on.

The same applies even more to the case of food and beverages. Imagine the question: how much increase or decrease in potassium would you need to be indifferent with a given decrease in the phosphoric acid content? The interviewer would surely be asked to take a hike. In cases like these, we would have to put the interviewee in choice situations between two food products (the proposed one and her best alternative), have her try both products, and ask the question which of these two she prefers. As long as one can work with one objectively understandable variable that is continuous (e.g., calories per serving), it is feasible to find points of indifference between the two offerings and switching values and predict customer behavior.

When a good is a pure experience good (that is where no objective continuous criterion other than price is evaluated prior to purchase), the method needs a further adaptation. That being said, such adjustment is only required for very few goods, as even chocolate bars do have objective features that are relevant in the purchasing decision (calories, fat content and the like) and are traded off extensively. In fact, these objective features are probably the reason why we don't eat more of them, and they thus clearly influence our purchasing decision.

Question 6: This appears complicated and costly. What if we don't have the time or money? Are there any shortcuts? For one thing, for explanatory purposes, we made the example a bit more complicated than it usually is:

preferences for all but one feature (i.e., MTBF) appeared to be non-linear whereas in reality *quite a few* may be linear. If that is the case, the interview will be less complicated.

For another, it does make sense to spend time and money here. Doing this exercise is the basis of the most important information that a company can have about a strategy: designing the right products and services with the highest revenue and margin potential, where revenues are generated bottom-up, based on understanding customer preferences and on forecasting choices. Hence, before thinking about shortcuts, think about the important information that you may be tossing away.

That being said, the exercise may be too costly on a cash basis for a small company or a start-up. In that case, it makes sense to talk to at least a number of customers (10 or so) rather than doing nothing. You should ask them at least the question "which one do you prefer" (your hypothetical launch product or their best alternative), and then ask them what you would need to do to your product, service or solution to make them switch, if at all possible. You will at least obtain some important, yet incomplete information about key enhancements and minimum requirements for some customers, without being able to infer willingness-to-pay and make revenue forecasts. That is surely a lot better than making decisions solely based on gut feel.

▶ CONCLUSIONS

The behavioral assumptions and the willingness-to-pay elicitation method explained in this chapter suggest that we should reconsider the way of thinking about strategy. Suppose, for example, that a Grand Strategy exercise culminates in the intent to enter a particular market by launching a new offering. A typical strategist would then go about answering three questions sequentially:

> *Question 1. Should we or should we not enter the market?* If the answer to this question is positive, he moves on to the second question.

> *Question 2. What products or services should we develop for that market?* Here, he defines the specifications of the products or services (which features are included, which ones are not, what is optional, etc.), within the limitations of the company's capabilities, and the number and types of products to develop. When this is done, he

moves on to the third question (as part of a set of marketing questions, which also include questions related to the level of promotion, advertising, channels, USP and the like).

Question 3. What price should we charge for the products and services? In good value pricing mode, the answer, of course, will be to charge the price that is slightly below the average customer value to which we referred before.

Our approach is different from your typical strategist's. We combine and answer questions 2 and 3 first, and answer question 1 at the end. More specifically, we proceed as follows:

Question 1. For any given product specification within the limitations of our capabilities, what is the distribution of willingness-to-pay (i.e., the real demand curve), estimated over the next 3 to 5 years? The outcome hereof is a set of distributions of willingness-to-pay (the number being equal to the number of possible specifications, as the willingness-to-pay varies with the features included or excluded in the product).

Question 2. For each of these product specifications, what is the price that maximizes operational profits (profits minus variable costs) over the same period, assuming that profit maximization is the objective? The outcome hereof is a set of profit figures, one per specification or, more generally, per launch option.

Question 3. Which of these options are likely to trigger competitor imitation, and how would that affect the profit figures? Obviously, the ease or willingness to imitate will fundamentally affect the figures. In general, the company will select options that are harder to imitate or for which incumbents have little imitation capabilities.

Question 4. For each of these operational profit figures, what are the needed capital investment levels over the agreed-upon horizon, and what are the ensuing NPVs of each launch option? If the company has another objective than NPV maximization or considers other factors (payback time, etc.), these will need to be calculated for each of the options. Now the commercial return for each of the launch options can be ranked in descending order, and the optimal launch strategy (product, price, channel, USP) is the one associated with the option on top of the list.

Question 5. Is the highest possible return obtained in Step 4 actually acceptable for management, and can the decision to enter the market thus be confirmed? Theoretically, if the NPV calculation took the correct discount rate, this should be. However, as other factors may play a role and other measures may matter, this is not unambiguously the case.

Our approach is likely to lead to vastly superior results, in that our business plan figures will turn out to be much closer to the actually realized revenues and margins than your typical strategist's business plan ever can be. The fundamental reason is that we do not start from top-down averages but from an in-depth understanding of differences in individual customer preferences.

▶ NOTES

1 Experience from many projects reveals that managers then tend to embellish that disappointing finding by considering "superior customer relationships," "a trusted partner" or something along those lines as their superior assets.

2 For an interesting debate on this topic, see Gerd Gigerener, *Risk Savvy: How to Make Good Decisions* (London: Penguin Books, 2015); see also Daniel Kahneman, *Thinking, Fast and Slow* (London: Penguin Books, 2011).

3 For the sake of brevity, we leave out a chapter or two on whether one can really ever confirm a hypothesis.

4 Note that the type of reasoning and analysis would be exactly the same when the question for the Grand Strategy exercise is not about geographic expansion but product diversification or differentiation, for instance.

5 Forgive our little excursion here, but we can state the rule of thumb, without generalizing too much, that whatever is good for government is bad for business. That is surely the case for "perfect competition" as described by microeconomic textbooks (i.e., companies making zero economic profits in the long run). Incidentally, we cannot resist to interject a small warning sign: don't be overly scared off by the atrocities of perfect competition (for the companies, that is – governments love it). The microeconomic textbook assertion that no one makes money in perfect competition is totally driven by the assumptions that all companies have the same cost structure (and a weird cost structure for that matter, unobserved in reality, with marginal cost curves that take on very, very peculiar shapes) and that in the long run companies enter until they cannot make any economic profits. The reality is of course that even in perfect competition (or

whatever approaches perfect competition), some companies have much lower marginal costs than others. For instance, Chilean copper producers have a lower cost than Zambian or US copper producers, and can make healthy profits even in the long run. Secondly, the long run can take a very, very long time to kick in and, in the meantime, plenty of supernormal profits can be made, making this perfectly competitive market not such a bad place to be. Some people (think of Ari Onassis) even get to become the wealthiest individual in the world from operating in a perfectly competitive market, which oil tanker shipping is. This is because the long run takes a lot of time to happen: it takes years to build new oil tankers (that was at least the case during his lifetime) that meet the needs of the customers. And when capacities cannot adjust, prices will shoot up well above cost (whichever one: marginal cost, average cost, etc. – make your pick). Sorry about this side-note. Chances are that our analyst may not have picked that up during classes, but that may be okay for the case of the payroll services company. It turns out not to be as lucky as Onassis was.

6 In addition, most economists only look at this from a theoretical angle to make policy implications. They love markets with high levels of consumer surplus. Anyhow, bury the thought, as a business has different objectives: it is one thing to be customer-oriented, it is another to give all the value to the customer and not let him pay for it.

7 The following is a true story: one of the authors, though having been engaged in high-end strategy consulting for decades, in fact had no TV for a very long time. Is he irrational? Not quite. Or does he simply have different preferences than the other author (who just "must" watch college basketball or international soccer games)? Or, worse, do we need to conclude that basketball or soccer game fanatics are a different "segment" than those who do not care about it? As you can sense, we can go on for a long, long time to agree upon the appropriate customer "segments."

8 For simplicity of the argument, we ignore here that the customer may stay with Lohn Inc., in the expectation that Lohn Inc. would lower its price to €99,000. In any event, under the current assumptions, there is no need to do so, as the current supplier Lohn Inc. is not better than Payroll Inc.: their respective services are both worth €140,000.

9 See for instance Peter Wakker and Daniel Deneffe, "Eliciting von Neumann-Morgenstern Utilities When Probabilities Are Distorted or Unknown," *Management Science* 42 (1996): 1131–1150 and references therein. For the more techie reader only, as we will point out, our method is in fact an improvement over (adaptive) choice-based conjoint analysis, which is the most commonly used method for preference elicitation in the marketing area. There are many variations of conjoint analysis, but they all face similar problems. For example, empirical studies reveal that conjoint analysis does not accurately predict real purchasing behavior, that is, there is little correlation between intended purchase and actual purchase. This is due to various methodological flaws and the weak behavioral foundations. See,

for example, Linda F. Jamieson and Frank M. Bass, "Adjusting Stated Intention Measures to Predict Trial Purchase of New Products: A Comparison of Models and Methods," *Journal of Marketing Research* 26 (August 1989): 336–345; see also Brian Roe, Kevin J. Boyle and Mario F. Teisl, "Using Conjoint Analysis to Derive Estimates of Compensating Variation," *Journal of Environmental Economics and Management* 31 (September 1996): 145–159.

10 We take the example of industrial pumps rather than continuing to build on the payroll services example, as the former is more tangible and requires less country-specific legal information.

11 See for example Sawtooth Software, "The CBC/HB System for Hierarchical Bayes Estimation," Version 5.0, www.sawtoothsoftware.com/download/techpap/hbtech.pdf

12 See, for instance, Elie Ofek and Olivier Toubia, "Conjoint Analysis: A Do It Yourself Guide," HBS: Case Collection 9-515-024 (August 2014): 11. See also the University of Virginia's www.coursera.org/lecture/uva-darden-bcg-pricing-strategy-customer-value/conjoint-analysis-step-4-and-product-preferences-IOTKy and https://www.coursera.org/lecture/uva-darden-bcg-pricing-strategy-customer-value/attribute-trade-offs-vgkRt that both explain the conjoint results for the *average* customer (golfer in this case).

13 See Thomas T. Nagle, John Hogan and Joseph Zale, *The Strategy and Tactics of Pricing* (Oxon, UK: Routledge, 2016).

14 See, for example, the following quotes from Wikipedia (http://en.wikipedia.org/wiki/Preference_(economics)):

> For instance, if asked to choose which one of one's children will be killed, as in Sophie's Choice, there is no rational way out of it. In that case, preferences would be incomplete, since 'not being able to choose' is not the same as 'being indifferent'. We do not face such ethical or philosophical issues when trying to understand whether a customer prefers pump A over pump B, or vice versa, or is indifferent between the two.

15 Michel Regenwetter, Jason Dana and Clintin P. Davis-Stober, "Transitivity of Preferences," *Psychological Review* 118 (January 2011): 42–56.

16 We can validate this by asking whether the interviewee's satisfaction level with improvements in any feature (say, efficiency) depends on the level of the other features. In the unlikely event that the answer is positive, the interview becomes more complicated as more questions will need to be asked.

17 This is fundamentally different from "choice-based conjoint analysis" and guarantees accuracy. In addition, it is valid under the assumption of additivity and forces the interviewee to think about clear trade-offs.

18 Matthew Rabin, "Risk Aversion and Expected-Utility Theory: A Calibration Theorem," *Econometrica* 68 (2000): 1281–1292.

19 A word of explanation about the extrapolation. The utility difference between a warranty of 6 months and that of 18 months equals 1. Hence, an increase of 12 to 18 months corresponds to $(18 - 12)/(18 - 6) = 6/12$ or 0.5 of a utility. Add to that the 1 utility associated with the increase from 18 to 36 months. The total utility difference between 12 months of warranty and 36 months of warranty thus equals 1.5.

20 An alternative, more sophisticated approach is to assume a (typically uniform) distribution across the various extreme values for the utility, though this is typically an unnecessary step that adds more complications than needed, particularly since we will aggregate the results at the end.

21 In this context, realize that list prices are quite irrelevant, given the discounts granted to most, if not all, customers.

Part 2
Applications of Operational Strategy

4

Operationalizing a new market entry strategy

Enough talk about foundations. Let us get to the heart of the matter: how do we go about defining our Operational Strategy in practice, and how do we obtain reasonable revenue and margin forecasts? Let us recall that the starting point for our Operational Strategy is the one or the other Grand Strategy decision (or, more accurately, a hypothesis, as we explained in Chapter 3). In this chapter, we will explain how to define the Operational Strategy if the Grand Strategy decision was to go and find profitable growth in some broadly defined new market.

Of course, the Grand Strategy decision could also have been to stick to one's knitting, that is, not to expand into new markets but to gain strength in the company's core markets. That situation is the focus of Chapters 5 and 6. In Chapter 5, we will walk you through ways of thinking about defending one's turf in one's core markets against other players and particularly aggressive new entrants. In Chapter 6, we will deal with the situation where the customers in the company's core markets care about price only, and, as a consequence, it is very difficult for the company to gain a competitive advantage.

In this chapter, we focus on the company's entry into a new market. A new market may be a new geographical region to the entrant, a new product market to the entrant or to the world as a whole (a newly created Blue

Ocean®, if you wish), or a new application to the entrant or to the world as a whole (e.g., a new vehicle market segment, the German payroll market, the medical labels market or the industrial pumps market, to take just a few of the examples mentioned earlier), either through an acquisition or a greenfield initiative. The strategy can involve a totally different market area, or may simply relate to an extension to the company's current geographical scope or product line. However, the way to operationalize a new market entry strategy and put numbers on it remains fundamentally the same, whatever the type of new market entry envisaged. The approach consists of eight steps (see Figure 4.1).

The idea is as follows. Whatever our growth ambition may be, the first and critical step is to agree on what we are trying to achieve, what our degrees of freedom and constraints are, and how we will measure success. Then, in Steps 2 through 7, we want to understand the extent to which customers in the target market are likely to be responsive to our strategy and our possible offerings. The Grand Strategy implicitly assumed, on the basis of a high-level analysis of unmet needs and our capabilities, that a sufficiently large chunk of customers would switch. In the Operational Strategy, we

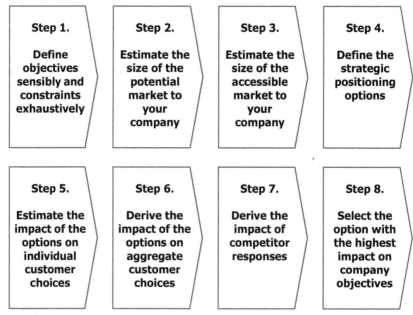

FIGURE 4.1 Steps in the operationalization of a new market entry strategy

put numbers on this, based upon real customer choices, as opposed to our beliefs about what customers should choose.

More specifically, we answer the following questions in Steps 2 through 7:

▶ Step 2: What fraction of the customers in the target market are potentially receptive to having their known or unknown needs met by a new supplier rather than by their best alternative (their current one or by none at all)?

▶ Step 3: Of those customers that are potentially receptive, how many of these are receptive to our company's specific offering?

▶ Step 4: What range of options (that are within our current capabilities or within our extended capability set) do we have that can make the receptive customers actually switch?

▶ Steps 5, 6 and 7: Given the distribution of customers' preferences and their switching costs, and given competitors' likely responses to each option, what is the proportion of customers that is expected to actually switch to our company for each option?

In Step 8, finally, we calculate the financial implications (revenues, margins, cash flows) of the forecasted customer choices for the company, and then select the option with the best financial return.

We detail each of these steps next. The examples used to illustrate each step are drawn from different real cases (passenger cars, payroll services, medical gloves, medical labels, industrial pumps, etc.), simply because some are more suitable to illustrate a given point than another. In any case, the approach explained herein will always have to be tailored to the specific product or service market (B2B, B2C, etc.) of the company concerned.

▶ STEP 1. DEFINE OBJECTIVES SENSIBLY AND CONSTRAINTS EXHAUSTIVELY

Sensible objectives

The first step is to understand the objectives of the Operational Strategy. This is critical, as different resolutions of conflicting objectives lead to different strategic positioning outcomes. Or, even worse, if the objectives do not involve trade-offs, the outcome of the Operational Strategy will be straightforward, but absurd. Let us illustrate this with three examples.

The first example concerns an aggressive automaker, where there was not much doubt about its objective: "market share." The second example concerns a consumer durables company, whose objective consisted of multiple components that were expressed additively as "revenues and profits." The third example concerns a perimeter protection company, whose objective was again expressed additively as "volume and price." None of these objectives actually make any sense. To avoid problems in the optimization of the Operational Strategy later on, it is important to agree on sensible objectives up front, and not halfway down the Operational Strategy project.

Let us take each of the preceding objectives one by one. Our automaker wanted market share. It was not clear what he meant, so we wondered: "What market share? Volume or value?" Management's response: "Volume." Before even starting, we are already done with the Operational Strategy, as that objective implies the following: "Make the best possible vehicle given the company's technological and marketing constraints. And then give the vehicle away for free. Or even better, pay customers for purchasing this best and fully loaded model instead of them paying you."

The problem is that the defined objective does not involve trade-offs between a benefit and a cost, as any economic activity should (yep, the good old concept of marginal benefit versus marginal cost from microeconomics is rearing its ugly head again). In this case, the objective is volume (that is the benefit), and volume can always be increased through lower prices and better quality. Since the cost of generating extra volume appears nowhere in the market share objective, one ends up with the absurd outcome of giving the vehicles away for free.

The management at the automaker (which remained very volume-driven) readily understood the absurdity of this outcome, and it was forced to adjust its objective into something meaningful. It adjusted it to "we want to sell at least 40,000 vehicles in a number of predefined geographic markets at maximum possible profits in the first year of the launch, net of launch costs." This constrained objective is well-defined. In fact, it is tantamount to saying that the objective is to maximize profits (as opposed to volume) and that the constraint is to sell at least 40,000 vehicles. It also points to the implications for further analysis (see Figure 4.2).

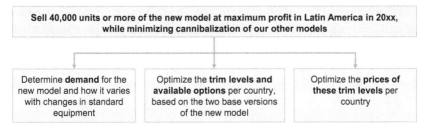

FIGURE 4.2 Example of a well-defined objective with implications

How about our consumer durables company? It wanted to maximize both revenues and profits. This is like asking to draw a circular triangle, which is just impossible. The problem is that the strategic choice that maximizes profits is different from the one that maximizes revenues, and often significantly so. Suppose variable contribution margin is 20% of sales, and forecasted sales without a particular investment equal $100 million. Suppose also that improving a particular feature of a product requires a $10 million investment and is expected to generate an extra $30 million in sales. If variable production costs are not affected, then such investment will generate an extra $6 million (20% of $30 million) in contribution margin. So, from a sales perspective, the investment is sensible, but it is not from a profit perspective. If we fail to pin down a sensible objective clearly up front, endless discussions inevitably will emerge down the road.

Finally, let us take the case of a company manufacturing perimeter protection products. Its CEO told us that his objective was economic profits, or EBITDA minus the cost of capital. This objective translated into cost minimization for the production department, and "volume and price" for the sales force. In this case too there is a problem of contradictory objectives. To begin with, raising prices in the market invariably leads to a drop in volume due to the marginal customer walking off (remember the demand curve). In addition, salespeople who are incentivized based on sales being generated have all the incentives in the world to more than please their customers by offering them all kinds of services, often for free. And contrary to popular belief, this is not what salespeople ought to do: a salesperson of a profit-maximizing company should offer services up to the point where the incremental revenue generated from the services offered exceeds the incremental cost of these services. If the objective is price or volume, then, obviously, the incremental costs of these services will not enter the equation, and the salesperson does not maximize company profits.

The "volume and price" objective is common in companies selling commoditizing products. Its very costly implication is that salespeople will tend to offer their customers whatever they want free of charge, particularly in B2B settings: offering free rush orders, accepting order cancellations with a smile, offering costly weekend shipments, allowing the customer to have multiple requests for having the product tested to make totally sure that it meets the specs, and the like. In one case (of a smart card company), such testing of the product exceeded $1000 per test, and customers were free to ask for such tests whenever they wanted to. The sales department happily had the products tested over and over again, while that practice alone hurt the bottom line by close to 0.3% of sales.

This "volume and price" objective has a second-order effect: not only do salespeople offer things for free, but customers also start to change their behavior and increase the cost-to-serve even more. If rush orders are free of charge, why should a customer place regular orders? There is no gain whatsoever in doing so. At a rush order cost of an easy $700 per order (not per customer) in some industries, this again often adds up to 0.3% to 0.5% of sales. Or if orders can be cancelled at no cost, why not order enough to be on the safe side, and cancel later on? Such behavior is very costly, and remedies are not straightforward when such "abuse" has become the standard.[1]

Exhaustive constraints

For now, we do hope that the message is clear: objectives must be defined clearly and sensibly. What about constraints? It is of paramount importance to define these exhaustively. Not doing so will backfire at a later stage, with plenty of time wasted when time is running out. Constraints can be related to various activities, such as sourcing, development, production or marketing.

For example, at the automaker that was trying to achieve the objective of selling 40,000 vehicles, the key constraint was linked to the degrees of freedom at each stage of the new product development cycle. The automaker was in the final stage of the development of the new model: the prototype was already finished, and potential customers were ready to be walked through the so-called pricing clinic. As a consequence, most model features were no longer subject to change. The only degrees of freedom were the trim levels and the prices thereof, based upon the two available base versions of the new model. That is, the horsepower levels of both base versions were a constraint: 180HP for the one and 225HP for the other. The horse-power could not be changed at this stage of development, even if the pricing research would reveal that, say, a small increase in horsepower would command a significant increase in willingness-to-pay and potential revenue. Conversely, it was also too late to suggest a small decrease in horsepower, should customer choice analysis reveal that such decrease would have a minimal direct negative effect on willingness-to-pay of the vast majority of potential buyers, while generating a proportionally larger decrease in incremental costs (apart from the ex post regret that it would also have saved the company a substantial development expenditure).

It turned out that not only horsepower but most of the production and look-and-feel aspects of the model were not subject to change, with the exception of some features that were not impacted by the design of the base versions, such as the types of wheels or tires, the car communication system, the navigation system and the like. Knowing what could be removed from the various versions was equally important, as this helped us understand whether some trim levels really could be created as basic versus loaded. It also turned out that removing controls or gauges from the dashboard often costs more than leaving them in, and that degrees of freedom are often limited here as well, especially when wanting to avoid the particularly odd look of omitted gauges (not to mention the discomfort thereof, as with the 1960 VW Beetles or some 1970 Fiat 500s that came without fuel gauges, for instance).

We observed the same issue, though with severe ethical questions, at a producer of upgradeable pacemakers who had to decide which patient health-monitoring features had to be excluded from the base model and included in the upgrades. In sharp contrast to the context at the automaker, though, most features were still variable at the time of the pricing research.

The preceding highlights an issue in strategy formulation to which we have alluded before: one should not leave the pricing dimension to the last phase of the new product development and launch cycle, when all other features have pretty much been fixed. To the contrary, knowing the willingness-to-pay and the distribution thereof, in relation to expected development costs and production costs, should maximally influence which features to include in the models in the first place, and what levels they should have. Knowing this willingness-to-pay, or lack thereof, is in fact the most important piece of information from a revenue perspective, and should maximally be gathered up front in the development cycle.

Other constraints are related to marketing. The automaker simply decided to offer a limited number of vehicle packages, such as the business package, rather than to leave all options open and have the customer select from the myriad of features. It is true that such a choice may turn some customers away from buying in the first place: for car fanatics, creating the optimal bundle of features is one of the best things about buying a new car; but many other customers prefer to select only from a limited number of packages, as they simply do not want to dig into the best communication package for a vehicle that is used for business travel purposes (what speakers to select, what navigation system is about right, etc.).

Finally, constraints can also be driven by the business focus and boundaries imposed by the company's owners or its other stakeholders. In the case of a particular patient safety device company, the company's vision and the owners' determination to stick to that vision were in fact pretty detrimental to the company's very survival. The company faced competition from low-priced Chinese players and was losing significant market share as a result. Meanwhile, the company had built up unique capabilities in designing top-end devices that enabled the company to meet the needs of the most demanding buyers of devices and their influencers. Those buyers are looking for devices that are smooth and don't irritate the often fragile or brittle skin of babies and elderly patients. At the same time, they prefer devices that are quite difficult to remove, as patients need to be identifiable at all times (many patients, especially those in psychiatric hospitals, would not hesitate to try to tear them apart, and should not be able to do so). They should also be lasting (at least for the duration of the hospital stay), and the patient nametag should be water-resistant, just to name a few benefits that some of the most demanding hospital buyers may expect from safety devices.

In view of the Chinese competitors and the reluctance of many hospitals to continue to want to pay for the superior performance of some of these features, the company had no other choice than to diversify into new non-medical areas where its core capabilities could be highly valued and leveraged. The new areas envisaged included horticultural plant protection (water resistance is key, and the product should be robust, should some rodents roam around the plant), youth penitentiary systems, or cheaper substitutes for collars for all types of animals. These were just a few ideas that needed to be further looked into through ideation sessions (the structured brainstorming sessions in which participants creatively look for new marketspace opportunities). It at least seemed more than worth exploring these diversification opportunities, given the limited available alternatives for the company, including doing nothing and losing market share, revenues and profits.

But these ideation sessions never took place. The company's vision did us in. While the company's management was quite receptive to the idea of building a strategy that was based on the company's core capabilities and that was unconstrained by its current market, its owners (a private-equity company) refused. They only wanted to diversify into healthcare-related markets, in line with the company vision that they had defined. The foregone profits associated with willfully sticking to this constraint when markets dictated otherwise are likely to have been substantial.

Whatever the constraints may be, it is critical to know them all early in the Operational Strategy process. When the strategic choice is to diversify into new areas, you need to know what is fixed and what you can play with up front. This is so for two reasons.

First, it makes the process more efficient, as there is no point in wasting time and money to propose options that are in any event not feasible for whatever reason. Brainstorming about the diversification options for the patient safety device company turned out to be a waste of our and management's time. It does not make any sense either to know how a change in a particular feature would increase or decrease willingness-to-pay and affect production or development costs if this feature cannot be changed anyhow. And if we find out too late what all the constraints are, then research about customer preferences and willingness-to-pay will have to be done over again, at least partially, which in turn may push back the planned launch date of the company's new products or services.

The second reason for knowing the constraints up front is the flipside of the first one. Knowing them allows you to get a better view of the real degrees of freedom. All possible opportunities for investigation will have been agreed upon clearly. Making sure that you know what is feasible (or in-scope, to use consulting terms) guarantees that the maximum potential from the Operational Strategy is being investigated. In markets where competitive advantage is so difficult to attain, this is the least one should do.

▶ STEP 2. ESTIMATE THE SIZE OF THE POTENTIAL MARKET

For each strategic option in the Operational Strategy, we will eventually have to come up with a revenue and margin forecast. To take the example of entry by the payroll services company from the Netherlands into Germany, the revenue forecast will be based upon an estimation of how many buyers (companies in this case) in Germany would buy a number of particular payroll service packages at what price.

To construct this forecast, we use a cascade approach that is totally based upon customer choices (see Figure 4.3), which is surely much more accurate than revenue forecasts based upon some internal hockey-stick projections that ignore any consideration of customer decision-making.

We start with estimating the potential market. This potential market consists of the number of buyers who may *consider* buying a new product or service from any new supplier in this (potentially totally new or existing) market. They may consider switching from their best alternative, which could be their current supplier or their current way of satisfying their needs (which could be by buying nothing), to an alternative supplier. To put it differently, customers that are not in the potential market are not interested in buying a new product or service. It is not part of their agenda. Anything outside of the potential market is therefore simply unattainable for *any* new entrant, i.e., not just for the company designing the Operational Strategy of entering into this market. If the potential market is small relative to the actual market (measured, for example, by last year's market volume), it means, first, that a large chunk of the market is captive to the incumbent players, for whatever

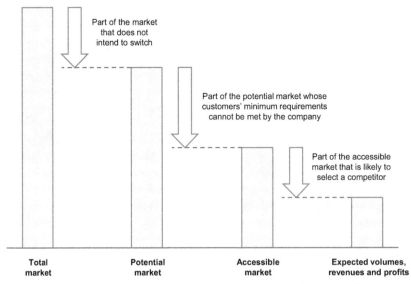

FIGURE 4.3 The cascade used to make revenue and margin forecasts

reason (long-term contracts or otherwise), and, second, that the growth of the market (from new buyers, who by definition are not captive to any company) is relatively limited.

Understanding the size of the potential market is just the first stage in the construction of our revenue forecasts. At a later stage (Step 3 in this chapter), we will need to figure out what share of the potential market (and not of the total market, as the share of the captive part is by definition zero) the company can reasonably obtain with its various entry options.

Let us work with an example to make the case as practical as possible. Specifically, we return to the Grand Strategy decision of Payroll Inc. to diversify geographically by offering payroll services in Germany (see Chapter 2). To construct the size of the potential market, we looked at two subsets of customers (or segments, if you prefer): first, companies that currently do outsource and, second, companies that currently do not outsource but process their payroll in-house (also referred to as the insourced market). These two subsets accounted for 34% and 66% of all companies in Germany, respectively.

Of the companies that outsourced, 70% did not consider switching suppliers within the next three years, i.e., they were captive to their current suppliers, whereas 30% did consider switching if a better alternative emerged. These 30% constituted 10% of all companies, as only 34% of all companies in this market made use of outsourced payroll services (see Figure 4.4).

One may wonder why just about any company that already outsources payroll services is not interested in switching if a better alternative is being offered.

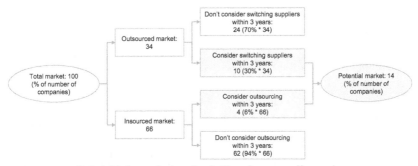

FIGURE 4.4 Potential market calculation in payroll services

Theoretically the answer is that they all should be, but in practice this is not the case. The possible reasons for not considering switching are varied, and one typically hears things like: "It is not one of our priorities in the coming years," "We are happy with the current provider," "We are contractually committed to our current provider for another three years," "Payroll servicing is too small an expense and it is not worth spending efforts at searching for cheaper alternatives," "The cost of switching is too high," "We believe that suppliers are ultimately all the same, and the market mechanism will guarantee that we are not overpaying for our current supplier," and the like.

Of the companies that insourced payroll processing, only 6% considered switching from doing it in-house to outsourcing it to an external provider. These 6% constituted 4% of all companies, as 66% of all companies in this market insourced payroll services.

The key takeaway from the preceding example is to devote energy to sizing the potential market, and not to take the total current market as a reference point. Many managers who consider entry into a new market painstakingly try to accurately measure the size of the current market, and then assume a supposedly reasonable market share. The preceding shows that this may not be the best measure to look at, as the potential market and the total market overlap only partially, whereas it is the potential market that matters. On the one hand, only a relatively small fraction of the total current market (that is, the companies that already do outsource) is part of the potential market (in the preceding case: 30%). On the other hand, there are companies in the potential market that do not belong to the current market (in the preceding case: a whopping 4 of the 14 in total, or more than 30% of the potential market). To put it simple: it really does not make a lot of sense to spend time at finding out in detail whether the size of the total current market is $4 billion or $4.2 billion, since the revenue potential in this market is a lot more influenced by whether roughly 30% versus 70% of the roughly $4 billion current market is part of the potential market.

Obtaining information on the potential market can be quite an eye-opener up front, and puts a lot of realism on what can be expected from entering the market, especially when compared to the standard hockey-stick projections that we referred to a number of times before. For instance, suppose that management was expecting to obtain a 10% share of the total market by the end of the third year after entry. This implicitly assumes that, as a new entrant, it would capture around 70% (that is, 10 of 14) of customers who consider switching (from insourcing to outsourcing, or from their current supplier to a new supplier). In a market with more than five incumbents, this is a phenomenally high figure that can only be achieved through some difficult to emulate superior service that is yet to be invented in payroll services.

The information on the potential market immediately raises a number of strategic positioning questions, such as: which customers to target? On the one hand, the companies that insource appear to be better targets, as their switching costs are lower than those that are currently outsourcing. On the other hand, companies that outsource appear to be five times (30% versus 6%) more likely to consider switching (to an alternative supplier) than companies that insource (and would switch to outsourcing).

How do we obtain that crucial information? In this case, it was simply based upon short telephone calls to a random sample of some 450 HR-directors of potential buyers (companies). The percentage of respondents who said that they considered switching was then applied to the entire population of buyers (all companies are inherently potential buyers of payroll services, and their number is known) to get a sense of the size of this potential market.

Sometimes the potential market coincides with the total market, which makes it simpler to size it. For instance, to understand the size of the potential market in, say, the compact vehicle segment, it suffices to know the size of the total market (how many people bought such vehicle in the last 12 months), and add a market growth rate to it. In the case of automobiles, it is a tad easier simply because there is no captive market of automobile buyers, i.e., buyers who cannot switch to a new supplier due to, say, contractual obligations to buy the same brand when replacing their current vehicle. Of course, an automobile buyer may choose not to switch to another type of vehicle for other reasons. It is hard to imagine, for instance, a passionate BMW 5 series driver switching to, say, a newly launched Nissan model. That is something we will pick up in the analysis of the accessible market (see Step 3 as follows).

The implication is also that, even when the size of the potential market can sometimes be estimated without any customer interviews, such customer interviews will always be required to estimate the part of the potential market that is accessible to your company. It is only through customer interviews that one can understand the deep customer preferences that will determine whether a customer considers your company's offerings as a viable alternative to his otherwise preferred option.

▶ STEP 3. ESTIMATE THE SIZE OF THE ACCESSIBLE MARKET

To understand the revenue and, ultimately, margin potential of a particular entry option, it is not sufficient to know the size of the potential market in general. One should also know which part of that potential market is *accessible* to *your* company, because customer-specific entry barriers may make it impossible for your company to access these customers. In short, these customers are considering switching (that is why they are in the *potential* market), but unfortunately your company is not a candidate to switch to for them.

We will therefore need to construct the size of the accessible market. This consists of the number of customers in the potential market for whom your company satisfies all minimum requirements. These must-haves obviously differ across customers. We talked about minimum requirements already in Chapter 3, but let us elaborate some more at this stage.

By definition, if the new supplier fails on any of the minimum requirements of a particular customer, he will not be considered, even if the supplier scores well on all other features. In the case of the automaker, it could be that for some potential customers, a minimum requirement is at least 250 HP. Since the automaker's base versions had a horsepower of 180 HP and 225 HP, those customers are not part of the accessible market to this automaker. Some other customers may have as minimum requirements that their vehicle is not a foreign brand, simply because they just buy American no matter what.

How do we find out? This depends on the type of products and services. If at least a number of these minimum requirements can be expressed verbally and maximally objectively (which is the case for search goods), these requirements will be obtained through customer interviews from a sample of customers from the potential market, i.e., from the sample of customers who have been identified as being potential buyers in, say, the next 12 months. If these minimum requirements cannot be expressed verbally and maximally objectively (which is the case for experience goods), the identification of the potential market will be different and involve actual consumer trials, as consumers cannot express their minimum requirements without actually experiencing the good.

Let us assume we are dealing with search goods. Customers are then asked a number of qualitative questions about the importance of a number of features (such as horsepower level), about their minimum requirements on each feature, and on the performance of their current best alternative on each feature. In practice, it turns out that interviewees have a tendency to indicate their desired level of horsepower, but that is actually not the question. The question is about the minimum required level, which is below the desired level. In fact, the minimum required level is the horsepower below which the customer would never buy the car, even if all other features were all perfect. With this clarification, interviewees typically lower the bar for what constitutes their minimum requirement.

Table 4.1 has a very simplified illustration of how we identify which customers in the potential market are in the accessible market, and which ones are not. It appears that in this example only two of the five interviewees (2 and 4) are in the accessible market. If we have a larger representative sample of customers in the potential market, it is possible to apply the same ratio to the estimated population of the potential market to infer the accessible market size.

Not all minimum requirements can be measured or be expressed verbally. For example, a particular car may pass all the measurable minimum requirements but not satisfy the minimum look-and-feel requirements. The more the look-and-feel features can be simulated up front in the interview process, the more accurate the Operational Strategy will be. But no matter what, it will not be complete until, at some stage, one puts customers face-to-face with prototype vehicles.

TABLE 4.1 Identifying customers in the accessible market

Car feature	Sample of customers in potential market				
	Interviewee 1	Interviewee 2	Interviewee 3	Interviewee 4	Interviewee 5
Horsepower	N	Y	N	Y	N
Engine size	Y	Y	Y	Y	Y
Number of seats	Y	Y	Y	Y	Y
Brand	Y	Y	N	Y	Y
Other feature	N	Y	Y	Y	N

Notes:
Y = Planned model does meet interviewee's minimum requirements
N = Planned model does not meet interviewee's minimum requirements

To take another example, let us go back to the entry strategy of the company that could design a new type of non-latex medical glove. While working on the minimum requirements for a number of the company's potential customers, we identified protection against HIV as an important feature. This feature could be measured as the likelihood of not getting infected by the HIV virus in the event that the scalpel was to perforate the glove. But for another feature, namely glove flexibility, it was not possible for the interviewees to express a minimum requirement numerically. Glove flexibility is directly related to the thickness of the glove, measured in microns. Needless to say, no single physician would be able to express the thickness that would make this particular glove unacceptable, whatever the level of the other features. In this very case, we had to have some specific samples of prototype gloves of different thickness manufactured, and simply had the interviewed physician wear them. At that stage, it became much easier to express the minimum requirements on thickness.

The key takeaway from the preceding example is that entry barriers at the customer level are often the most important ones to overcome. In many of our Operational Strategy projects, we find that these barriers can be daunting – and much more important than the long list of possible barriers to entry, such as economies of scale and the like, that are presented in any entry-level strategy textbook.

Identifying minimum requirements from the sample of customers is often a major eye-opener. Let us go back to the entry strategy case of Payroll Inc., the payroll services market leader in the Netherlands. The company believed that its home market recognition and reputation would give it plenty of credibility for entry into Germany, thus facilitating its acceptance as a viable alternative to potential customers' current local payroll suppliers. The voice of the customer told a different story, though, which yet again underscores the extreme importance of Operational Strategy. It turned out that in our sample of customers in the potential German market, no single customer was willing to switch to the Dutch player.

The reason was the Dutch company's lack of experience in the German market, as measured by the number of reference clients that it could refer to (see Figure 4.5). Of all customers in the sample of the potential market, no single one of them was even considering the Dutch market leader as a possible supplier as long as it had zero reference clients in the German market; only

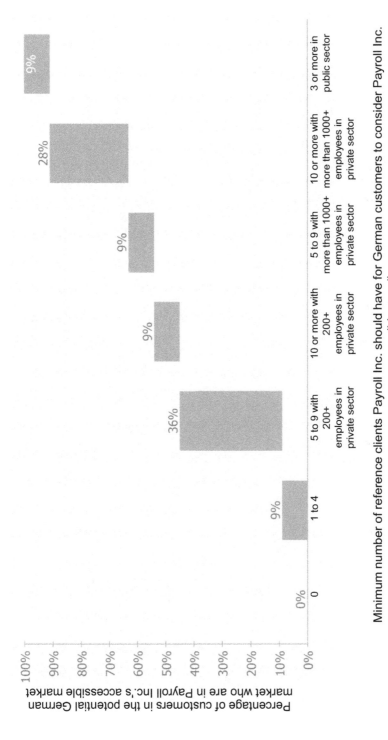

FIGURE 4.5 Example of entry barriers at the customer level

9% was considering doing business with the new entrant if it had one reference client in Germany; and so on.

While we explain the approach here, we would like to interject a comment on the content as well. The existence of reference clients as a barrier is actually a recurrent (and for management often discouraging) observation: to do business in the new market, one needs to have references in that market; but these are very difficult to obtain, as references are needed to do business in the first place. If that is the case, the company often has only one option, that is, to offer the service for free to some customers, and let them find out for themselves how reliable it really is. This can be an acceptable proposition to many customers, as they continue to work with their original supplier and in parallel experience, at no charge to them, the quality of the company's service.

There are two benefits of doing so for the company. First, the potential customer may get convinced of the quality of the company's service and may consider switching for good at standard rates. Second, the company is building up its base of reference clients, which establishes the needed credibility for other customers. Obviously, the more it offers free services to more customers up front, the higher its initial costs and cash outflows, but the faster it builds up a critical level of reference clients. With the preceding figures for Payroll Inc., it would not make sense to invest in just one reference client, as still only 9% of the customers in the potential market would become accessible by the end of the first year. In the preceding case, after doing the numbers, it turned out that an investment in minimally five reference clients was needed.

▶ STEP 4. DEFINE THE STRATEGIC POSITIONING OPTIONS

Once we have identified customers in the accessible market, we still just know one thing: these customers are in fact just willing to talk to us. They have not switched yet. In fact, these customers have no reason to switch to a new entrant unless two conditions are met, as discussed in Chapter 3. First, the new entrant should be willing and able to offer them more deal value than their best alternative option (which could be their current supplier, if any). Second, that value should exceed their switching costs, which we defined earlier as the monetary and non-monetary costs associated with moving from their current supplier (or from "no supplier" if that is the case) to another.

Defining strategic positioning options (i.e., what are the various types of products that we would like to launch at what price) requires that we clarify internally what we can feasibly offer to the customer, possibly through partnerships. The set of strategic options consists of all possible combinations of the product or service feature levels, and at different price levels (e.g., for the industrial pumps, product option 1 = delivery time of 4 weeks, plus efficiency of 80%, plus warranty of 12 months, plus price of $4000, etc.; product option 2 = delivery time of 6 weeks, plus efficiency of 90%, plus warranty of 24 months, plus price of $4500, etc.). Since some of these features are continuous in nature (e.g., delivery time, efficiency, warranty period, to name a few), theoretically an infinite number of possible strategic positioning options exists.

But there is actually no gain in defining the various combinations of feature levels at this stage. Instead we define for each product or service feature the feasible range that we could possibly offer to our customers: the minimum level and the maximally achievable level. The latter level may very well not be feasible today, and may require an investment. Whether this investment is justified depends on the cumulative incremental operational margin that offering such a superior level will bring relative to its development or acquisition cost, which in turn depends on the willingness-to-pay for this hypothetically achievable level by a sufficient number of customers.

For example, in the Payroll Inc. entry case, the key question is which base service package we bring to the market at what price. A secondary question is which optional features we offer at what price. The more features we bring, the costlier our service offering will be both in terms of Capex and Opex, but the higher the likelihood that, at any given price, customers will switch from their preferred alternative to ourselves. For each feature, we will need to assess whether an improvement in the service level commands sufficient willingness-to-pay that it is worth spending money on its development. Obviously, we will not dig into willingness-to-pay for features that we in no way can feasibly deliver.

Table 4.2 shows some of the approximately 15 features that had to be optimized at Payroll Inc. Some of these, such as response time, are continuous. Others, such as payroll-related tax & legal advice, are discrete, i.e., they

TABLE 4.2 Example of feasible ranges per feature

Feature	Minimum level	Best level (after investment)
Indemnification for errors in processing of pay-slips (too late, inaccurate, etc.)	Redo pay-slips	Redo pay-slips, plus up to 6 months of free service
Payroll calculation time	One business day	By 8:30 am if requested between 4 pm and 8 pm, or within 4 hours otherwise
Response time of single point of contact	On the phone within a business day	On the phone within 4 hours
Payroll-related tax and legal advice	Not included	Proactive advice on the latest legal developments affecting payroll
Response time for requests to relaunch pay-slip calculations	Completed within 48 hours	Completed less than 2 hours after request

take on a limited number of values (1 = no advice; 2 = on-demand advice; 3 = proactive advice on the latest legal developments affecting payroll).

Once we have identified these ranges for the continuous features and the possible levels for the discrete features, we can identify per customer in the sample of the accessible market what value she attaches to improvements in each of these features, using the methodology explained in Chapter 3. Eventually, as we will explain in more detail later on in this chapter, we can also forecast what we really want to know: for each feasible strategic positioning option, the number of customers who would switch from their best alternative at what price, and hence how much revenue we can expect.

In some cases, the company's current capabilities may be too limited to be able to offer differentiating features that make a sufficient number of customers switch. It could also be that the company is not even able to satisfy the minimum requirements for many customers, so that the ability to offer differentiating features does not quite cut the mustard. In both cases, it may be worth it to consider offering an expanded set of features through a partnership with a company that offers complementary assets and capabilities. The analysis of customers' willingness-to-pay is then extended from the features that the company can offer on its own (i.e., through a greenfield investment strategy) to the features that it could potentially offer through partnerships. Should the forecasted revenue stream from the partnership scenario ("all options open") be significantly superior to the forecasted revenue stream from the greenfield scenario ("limited offering"), then such partnership may be envisaged. Obviously, if all the features are offered by the partner, the biggest chunk of the commercial returns from the partnership is likely to flow to the partner rather than the company, and the partnership may not be viable.

To illustrate this point, let us take the example of a manufacturer of medical accessories. The company was considering entry into the market of medical labels that are used in various hospital applications (admissions, nursing, pharmacy, laboratory, etc.). Since the company could not offer all potentially differentiating features on its own, it considered both a partnership and a greenfield scenario (see Table 4.3). To simplify matters, we represent the features as discrete, binary variables, indicating whether the feature is present or not. For example, the company could not offer on its own an on-label temperature indicator that reveals the log of the temperature variations of the stored product to which the label was attached. This feature may be critical for laboratory or pharmaceutical products that need to be stored at constant temperatures. As the inability to offer this feature might put a new entrant at a disadvantage, the company considered how the picture would change should it be able to offer this and other features under a partnership scenario.

TABLE 4.3 Ability to offer features under the partnership and greenfield scenarios

Feature	Partnership scenario	Greenfield scenario
Hospital process improvement services	Y	N
Durability of label	Y	Y
Portfolio includes medical accessories X, Y and Z	Y	Y
Resistance against water, alcohol and UV	Y	Y
Temperature indication	Y	N
Portfolio includes printers	Y	N
System integration	Y	N
Compatibility with existing printers	Y	Y
Service flexibility	Y	Y

Notes:
Y = Feature can be offered
N = Feature cannot be offered

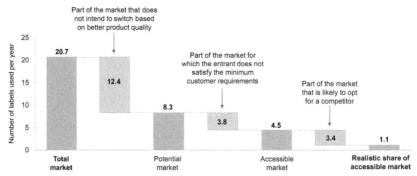

FIGURE 4.6 Cascade leading to realistic share of accessible market in greenfield scenario

To make a long story short, it turned out that the greenfield scenario provided a much more limited revenue potential than the partnership scenario. We leave out the methodological details on how to obtain the revenue potential from either option, as we will cover this in Steps 5 through 8. What we do want to show at this stage is that making the distinction between what can be offered internally versus through partnerships is often an eye-opener and an important input for decision-making.

Specifically, in this case, the greenfield entry option was abandoned altogether, as the maximum volume that the entrant could achieve in this specific market under this scenario was 1.1 billion labels a year, which corresponded to about 5% share of the total market (see Figure 4.6). It was not even worth digging into cost figures for this scenario, since the achievable revenues could never cover even the most conservative launch and operational cost estimates. By way of contrast, the realistic market share under the partnership scenario was three times higher.

▶ STEP 5. ESTIMATE THE IMPACT OF THE OPTIONS ON INDIVIDUAL CUSTOMER CHOICES

Once we have defined the strategic positioning options, we have to estimate the impact of these on individual customer choices, while keeping competitor responses constant. The objective of this step is to forecast most accurately how any individual customer in the accessible market would respond to improvements (or deteriorations) in product or service features (including price) relative to some hypothetical launch offering. This hypothetical launch offering is what the company has in mind a priori when thinking of entering a specific market. As explained in Chapter 2, it is the outcome of Grand Strategy thinking and managers' gut feel, which in turn is driven by experience or some cursory market research, possibly a limited number of internal and external interviews, and the like. We will continue building here on the example of the hypothetical launch pump that we gave in the preceding chapter.

As we have explained our individual customer forecasting method in detail in Chapter 3 using the example of the industrial pumps case, we will be brief here. It led, amongst other results, to the hypothetical launch pump shown in Table 4.4. In addition, the pump has a number of look-and-feel options that cannot be described but that can be drawn or shown via real or simulated 3D prototypes.

Obviously, a company may launch different products at the same time at different prices, or have a base launch offering with various additional options. Our method can easily address the issue of multiple launches, as we explained in the closing remarks of Chapter 3. In this chapter, we keep the example simple to get the core logic across. Hence, we assume that the company has just one base launch offering in mind.

We should note that the selection of such a hypothetical launch offering is primarily a pure methodological choice: we need such a specific hypothetical

TABLE 4.4 Example of feature levels of hypothetical launch pump

Feature	Level
Efficiency	55%
Warranty	12 months
Mean time between failure (MTBF)	2000 hours
Delivery time of pump	4 weeks
Delivery time of spare parts	48 hours
Price	$4600
No external cooling required below a temperature of	80°C
Pump standard	EVX
ISO Norm	2424
Speed	Variable
Noise reduction feature	Included

pump only to understand an individual customer's switching value between a pump and her best alternative, as illustrated in Chapter 3. In the example of the pumps, the choice of the hypothetical launch pump is totally arbitrary in the sense that the subsequent forecasts of customer choices for any other pump are in no way affected by its specifics. Whether we take this specific hypothetical launch pump or any other one (a much better or worse version), the outcome of the customer choice analysis will be exactly the same, and the forecasted customer's choices will be unaffected as well. The base pump is a natural anchor that makes sense, is easy to explain to management, and is in all likelihood different from the pump that the company will eventually launch. Of course, going through the process explained in this chapter, we will also be able to forecast the revenue and margins of launching this hypothetical launch pump (just like for *any* other pump for that matter).

What we really want to understand, for each interviewee in the sample, is whether for each possible pump with features within the capabilities of the company, the interviewee will or will not buy the pump at a particular price. At this point, for each interviewee in the sample, we know that she will not buy the pump if the pump does not satisfy all minimum requirements. And even if it did, what we do not know is whether she would buy the hypothetical launch pump instead of her best alternative.

We can conceptually categorize the customers in the accessible market into two categories, which for the sake of convenience we call Believers and Non-believers. Believers are customers who prefer the hypothetical launch pump over their best alternative option. Non-believers are customers who prefer their own best alternative option over the hypothetical launch pump. In the preceding chapter, the customer whose preferences we elicited was assumed to be a non-believer: when faced with the option of buying her best alternative versus the company's hypothetical launch pump, she chose the best alternative option. Obviously, whether one is a Believer or Non-believer totally depends on how this hypothetical base pump is defined in relation to a customer's preferences.

A Believer sees more perceived value in the hypothetical launch pump than in her best alternative option. That is, the deal value of this hypothetical base pump is larger than the value of the best alternative by some switching value. If the entrant offered a pump with a lower value than the hypothetical launch pump (through a deterioration of feature levels, a removal of some binary features, an increase in price, or a combination hereof), it is still possible that the Believer would choose this "adapted" pump of the entrant. At some point, however, when this perceived value *to her* decreases too much, she would become indifferent between the pump of the entrant and her best alternative. That is, she can no longer choose between the two. And if the value reduces even further, she would prefer her best alternative to the pump of the entrant. In short, it is possible to reduce the feature levels (thereby typically decreasing costs) or increase the price (thereby increasing revenues) of the pump without affecting the choices of a Believer. By how much this can be done depends on the magnitude of the switching value, as measured in the way explained in Chapter 3, and by the changes in the willingness-to-pay due to changes in the features or a decrease in the value of the deal due to an increase in price.

For a Non-believer, the opposite is true. She sees more perceived value in her best alternative option than in the hypothetical launch pump. That is, the value of the deal of the hypothetical pump is lower than the value of the deal of her best alternative. Hence, to make her switch to the entrant launching the pump, she would need more deal value from the launch pump. The entrant can increase the value through an improvement of the feature levels for which the Non-believer is willing to pay, through a reduction in price or a combination of both. At some point, with sufficient increased value, with a lower price, or a combination of both, the Non-believer becomes indifferent between her best alternative and the pump of the entrant. And with just a tiny bit more value or an even lower price, the Non-believer prefers the pump of the entrant over her best alternative option.

Whether all of this is worth it *for the company* depends, of course, on the cost of generating this extra value and on the number of *other* customers whose switching behavior would be affected, and hence on their specific preferences. This is an aggregation issues that we will address in Step 6, but let us lift the veil of the underlying logic already somewhat here.

Imagine two extreme cases 1 and 2. In case 1, most interviewees are Believers. This implies that the hypothetical launch pump carries too much value to them. That is, the optimal pump will have worse features and/or a higher price than the hypothetical launch pump. Which feature levels will need to be reduced depends on the distribution of preferences of customers, as elicited using the trade-off interviews, and on the cost savings from reducing the feature levels. In the extreme case, if no interviewee sees any value destruction from a reduction of the MTBF from 2000 hours to, say, 1500 hours, and the cost savings to the company from offering this reduction are substantial, then it is likely that the optimal pump will turn out to have a lower MTBF than 2000 hours. It may even go hand in hand with a higher price if it turns out that most interviewees still prefer this new pump (with lower MTBF and higher price) over their best alternative option.

In case 2, most interviewees are Non-believers. This implies that the hypothetical launch pump carries too little value to them or at least less deal value than their best alternative. As a consequence, it is critical to either add value to most interviewees or to lower price. Which value will be added depends again on the distribution of customer preferences, the imitability of adding such value (an issue we address in Step 7), and on the cost of adding this value. Imagine, for instance, that it is not very costly to increase the warranty from 12 months to 24 months (simply because the company knows it has very reliable pumps). Imagine, in addition, that doing so would turn most Non-believers into Believers. In that case, such increase is likely to be commercially beneficial. A price cut is also likely to do the job but has two drawbacks: it cuts right into the bottom line, and it is also easily imitable, thereby destroying the advantage.

The question gets increasingly complex, of course, when there is a mix of Believers and Non-believers, and when customers differ in what their minimum requirements are and in what they value above the minimum requirements. That is often the case in real-world situations. As a consequence, to be able to forecast aggregate customer choices, it is critical to understand individual customer choices first, recognizing that each individual is different, whatever "segment" he may be in, as discussed in earlier chapters. We should understand whether an individual customer is a Believer or Non-Believer, and by how much. We should also understand what improvements or deteriorations in value are generated through improvements or deteriorations of the feature levels relative to the hypothetical launch offering. In fact, we should look at improvements relative to a customer's minimum requirements. Going below the minimum requirements is a guarantee that the customer will select his best alternative option, whatever the level of the other features.

We have explained in Chapter 3 how to do so at the individual level, for one potential customer. What we want to do now, is to understand how many pumps of a particular type we would be selling at alternative prices to all customers in the target market. To know how much the market would buy, we need of course not just interview one individual but a representative sample, and then make inferences based on this sample.

At this point, you will probably ask: "What should the sample size be?" Our short answer is: "Be real!" Our foremost priority is accuracy, which is an absolute must when dealing with willingness-to-pay. Hence, we prefer a small sample of long interactive interviews over a large sample of short phone interviews or non-interactive questionnaires. An interactive interview takes between 60 and 90 minutes. It is performed face-to-face, ideally in person, though in many cases and particularly for search goods, a virtual face-to-face interview is feasible. The important thing is that the interviewer can interact with the interviewee and make sure that the interviewee understands the questions and is minimally affected by external stimuli. For some products where the look and, especially, the feel are critical, the interview obviously has to be in person.

What do we mean by a small sample? And how large does the sample minimally need to be? In many B2B situations, this is really a non-issue, simply because the answer is more driven by two constraints than by what we ideally would like to have. The first constraint is the number of potential customers in the accessible market who are willing to participate in a face-to-face interview. The second constraint is the time and money needed to hold these interviews.

Let us take the example of the industrial pumps. The number of companies in a particular market buying this product may be less than 1000. Of those, perhaps only half consider buying new pumps over the next three years. Of those, our company perhaps can satisfy the minimum requirements of only 20%, which brings us down to less than 100 customers. Knowing that a response rate of 30% is very high, we would be happy to interview all these approximately 30 customers in the sample.

Add to this that an interview takes 60 to 90 minutes of time, and that usually some financial or other incentive needs to be provided to persuade a customer to participate. Non-financial incentives (for instance, receiving a summary of the non-confidential results of a broader survey) are obviously the cheapest, and they do work in certain sectors like hospitals. But things tend to be different when interviewing decision-makers at, say, telecom companies, where the financial incentive for participating in an interview may exceed $300. This is not because these managers want to make extra money, but because they want to create a barrier to being interviewed by every Tom, Dick and Harry. Usually these managers do not use the money for private purposes but give it away to charity, or use it to have lunch with some of their staff members. In other cases, we have used (high-end) restaurant vouchers for two people as a token of our appreciation, which at the same time may be less offensive than offering sheer money. Whatever reward being used, the total cost of an in-depth interview can easily reach $500. So, even if there were 1000 potential customers in the accessible market, would we want to interview them all at that cost?

We talked about B2B markets. In B2C markets the total population size is obviously larger, and it is easier to obtain a larger sample of customers as well. In addition, the reward for participation in a survey is typically considerably smaller. In this case, we typically use a two-phased approach: we first do an in-depth elicitation with a limited number of customers (50 to 100 or so) and then validate the results through a web-survey.

▶ STEP 6. DERIVE THE IMPACT OF THE OPTIONS ON AGGREGATE CUSTOMER CHOICES

After having understood the preferences of a representative sample of individual potential buyers (Believers and Non-believers), we want to derive the impact of the strategic positioning options on aggregate customer choices, volumes, market shares, revenues and margins. This sounds like a complex task requiring plenty of statistical analyses. The reality is that such statistical analyses only induce extra error, as explained in Chapter 3 and are in fact not needed. To the contrary, to aggregate the results, we need to have recourse to a simple mathematical program that we are all familiar with: the summation! Here is how.

We already showed previously that we could make a best possible prediction about whether a particular interviewee would or would not buy a specific pump at a specific price. As explained in Chapter 3, specifically the discussion about the pumps to offer (see Table 3.40 and Table 3.42), we could infer which of six different pumps the interviewee would buy at whatever price, and we could also do so if we were to launch different pumps at the same time.

Other interviewees obviously have different preference structures. But by making use of the same trade-off method as earlier, we can infer, for all other interviewees, their minimum requirements, their willingness-to-pay for improvements above these minimum requirements, and their positive or negative switching values with their best alternatives. We can then ultimately do exactly the same thing as we did with the interviewee in Chapter 3: predict for each interviewee in the sample whether he will or will not buy a particular pump. If the sample is representative of the population, we can forecast market demand in terms of volume for any type of pump, that is, the number of pumps that people would buy at any given price. The predicted revenue is then also easy to forecast: it is simply the volume times the price.

Let us show how. We start by reproducing the table showing which pumps our first interviewee would buy (see Table 4.5, row "Will interviewee 1 buy (YES/NO)"). Suppose we now have ten interviewees in the sample (this surely is too small a sample, but we simply want to spare you the trouble of looking at a table with an excessive number of rows). For each of these interviewees, we can predict whether or not they will buy a particular pump, by applying the same method as we did for our first interviewee. For instance, if we were to bring only one pump model on the market, interviewee 2 would, say, buy pump 2 and 4, but not the others. Obviously, if we were to bring both pump 2 and pump 4 on the market, then interviewee 2 would buy the pump that gives him the highest deal value (as in the discussion about Table 3.42). So, whether we launch one, two or six pumps, we can always forecast what interviewee 2 would do.

Aggregating across interviewees, and, assuming for the time being that every customer buys just one pump, it turns out, for this sample of potential customers, that pumps 2 and 4 generate the highest volumes (five pumps sold) whereas pump 4 generates the highest revenues (5 × $4300 = $21500). So, purely from a revenue perspective, it is the one pump to launch, assuming the simplest case where we only launch one pump.

From a profit perspective, one would need to add the expected Capex and Opex needed to develop and produce each of the pumps. In fact, pump 4 may then not come out as the better pump. Compared to pump 2, for instance, it has a much higher efficiency (85% versus 55%), a higher warranty (36 months versus 12 months) and the same MTBF (3000 hours). Hence, the expenditures required to develop, launch and produce are very likely to be higher for pump 4 then for pump 2. It is the relative magnitude of these expenditures relative to the increased revenue that would determine the commercially most successful launch pump.

TABLE 4.5 Forecasted behavior of all interviewees in the sample

Feature	Pump 1	Pump 2	Pump 3	Pump 4	Pump 5	Pump 6
Efficiency (%)	60	55	75	85	65	55
Warranty (months)	18	12	24	36	24	0
MTBF (hours)	2500	2000	2400	1000	3000	3000
Price ($)	4550	4150	4800	4300	4550	4400
Will interviewee 1 buy (YES/NO)	YES	YES	YES	NO	YES	NO
Will interviewee 2 buy (YES/NO)	NO	YES	NO	YES	NO	NO
Will interviewee 3 buy (YES/NO)	YES	NO	NO	NO	YES	NO
Will interviewee 4 buy (YES/NO)	NO	YES	NO	YES	NO	NO
Will interviewee 5 buy (YES/NO)	YES	NO	NO	NO	NO	YES
Will interviewee 6 buy (YES/NO)	NO	NO	NO	NO	YES	NO
Will interviewee 7 buy (YES/NO)	NO	YES	NO	YES	NO	YES
Will interviewee 8 buy (YES/NO)	NO	NO	YES	YES	YES	YES
Will interviewee 9 buy (YES/NO)	NO	YES	NO	YES	NO	NO
Will interviewee 10 buy (YES/NO)	YES	NO	NO	NO	NO	NO
Total forecasted number of pumps bought	4	5	2	5	4	3
Total revenue ($) generated	18200	20750	9600	21500	18200	13200
Average revenue ($) per interviewee	1820	2075	960	2150	1820	1320

How do we now forecast the revenues for the market as a whole? To keep it simple for the sake of the exposition, suppose our interviewees constitute a representative sample of the customers in the potential market, and that we launch pump 4. Then our maximum revenue forecast for the market is simply the average revenue per interviewee per launched pump times the size of the potential market. For instance, suppose that there are 10,000 buyers in the potential market and, for simplicity, they all are expected to buy one pump, then the maximum revenue forecast in the first year is $2150 × 10,000 = $21.5 million. Another way to calculate this is to understand that the potential market volume constitutes, say, 10% of the total market volume. Pump 4 induces 50% of the customers in the sample to switch, whereas pump 6 for instance induces 30% to switch. Hence with pump 4 we expect to gain a realistic 5% market share (0.5 × 10%), whereas with pump 6 that is 3%. Value market share for pump 4 would be 5% × (price of pump 4)/total market sales, and so on.

It is also possible to forecast the real-world demand curve and hence the revenues for *any* of the hundreds of possibly newly launched pumps. Such top line information is one of the most important pieces of information that a company wants to have with maximum accuracy. As we explained in Chapter 3, a demand curve specifies the volume (denoted Q) that would be bought of a specific product at different price levels (denoted P). If we have the demand curve for the product that we will launch, we can forecast how volumes, revenues and margins are affected by changes in the price of the product. This is useful precisely because this demand curve is not linear: above certain price thresholds, volumes can drop significantly.

To show how such a demand curve is created, let us take, for example, pump 3. At a price of $4800, it turns out that two interviewees would buy the pump. This is the case because the price of $4800 is below the value of the pump, i.e., the price below which the interviewee prefers this specific pump over his best alternative. What happens when we lower the price of pump 3, keeping all other features constant? Then, obviously, the two interviewees who would have bought at a price of $4800 would still buy at a lower price. Others may still not buy this pump, either because it does not satisfy their minimum requirements (they are hopeless for pump 3, as they will not buy even when prices are very low), or because that price is still above the value of the pump to them: they still prefer their best alternative to pump 3.

Lowering the price below $4800 does, however, increase the attractiveness of pump 3 for the interviewees for which pump 3 satisfies the minimum requirements, that is, for interviewees in the accessible market. In fact, for these interviewees, we can precisely forecast at what price each of them is indifferent between his best alternative pump and pump 3: if the price is lower than that switching price, they will buy pump 3; if it is higher, they will buy their best alternative. Hence, as we lower the price of pump 3, more and more interviewees start switching to pump 3; conversely, as we increase it, interviewees start switching back to their best alternatives at specific price points. For interviewee 1, we traced out the entire set of preferences in Chapter 3, and determined the value of pump 3 to be $4826. Hence, we know that she will not buy when the price is higher than $4826, and will buy when it is lower. Through this process, we can trace out the demand curve for pump 3, for the other five pumps previously described, or for any of the hundreds of other pumps that we could consider launching.

For the sake of clarity, we included a number of simplifications in the preceding exposition. This may raise the following questions:

1. Can we extrapolate reliably from the sample to the total market?

2. Even if the sample is representative, can we assume that customers in the market are as informed as the interviewees in the face-to-face interviews?

3. How do we handle customers buying more than one pump?

Without going too much into methodological detail, let us briefly point out that these issues can be addressed by tailoring the approach to the specific situation at hand.

Question 1. Extrapolation from the sample to the total market

The extrapolation from the sample to the market is indeed an important real-world issue. It assumes that the sample is representative. If that turns out to be incorrect, then revenue and margin forecasts will be biased. We acknowledge this issue. It is, however, not specific to our approach, but rather an age-old problem common to all sampling-based methods. The so-called solutions that are typically brought forward are to select the sample carefully, and to increase sample size.

In our view, these solutions are a tad academic. Often, all one can do in the real world is to hope that the potential customers who want to be interviewed are representative. As far as increasing the sample size is concerned, we simply need to trade off the benefits from an increased sample size with the incremental costs of doing so, as we have shown that these can be significant. This is more a matter of business judgment than a statistical issue.

While the sample size issue is common to all sampling-based methods, do recall that, for good reasons explained in Chapter 3, we are after estimating the important *differences* in preferences across individuals, not some population mean, population median or whatever other so-called higher order moments of the population (for readers unfamiliar with this statistical jargon, please rest assured that you do not miss anything if this sounds like gibberish to you). We want the differences per se.

More importantly, we do not use any type of statistical or econometric technique to infer, from the interviewees' answers, the preferences of "the representative customer." By now, you understand that information about this so-called representative customer or about that average customer value is useless. We do what we need to do: adding the choices of individual interviewees to infer, first, total volumes at given price levels and, second, total revenues, which are simply these price levels times these volumes. This is the only way to take into consideration differences in customer preferences. At the same time, econometric or statistical errors are eliminated simply by not recurring to these methods in the first place. And these errors can be significant for a number of reasons that we mentioned in Chapter 3 but that we reiterate here briefly. Without going into detail, one reason is that econometric methods in some way or another impose some functional form (e.g., linear or a specific form of non-linear estimation), whereas preferences may be of a different non-linear nature. We hit two birds with one stone!

Question 2. Dealing with uninformed customers

The preceding extrapolation from the sample to the total market assumes that customers in the potential market are as well informed of the benefits of the newly launched pump as the interviewees in the sample. This is not the always the case. To address this problem, we need to adjust our forecasted market revenue by taking into account the assumed advertising and promotional reach. If it turns out, for instance, that the salespeople will cover only 80% of the geographical area and are expected to reach only 60% of the potential market, then the forecasted revenue figures would have to be adjusted downwards to reflect that 60%. Again, common sense is in order.

Question 3. Customers buying multiple pumps

As we mentioned, the pump launch case is a disguised description of a real-world entry project. In that project, customers typically bought more than one pump. If the pumps are for the same application (say, pumping water), the approach can simply be tailored to reflect the fact that different customers in the sample buy different volumes. If these differences in volumes across interviewees in the sample can be assumed to be representative of the population, one simply adds the volumes across individuals in the sample to get forecasted market volumes. In doing so, one naturally attaches a weight that is proportional to the volume that each of those individuals intended to buy.

If these differences in volumes are not representative, and one has a good reason to believe so, then one needs to subjectively weigh the responses, and assign less or more weight to some interviewees. This is not the preferred route, as it is ideal to let the data speak for themselves and minimize the subjectivity in the analysis. But in practice, it may be a needed adjustment if these are simply the customers that agreed to be interviewed.

▶ STEP 7. DERIVE THE IMPACT OF COMPETITOR RESPONSES

So far in the discussion, we assumed everything constant when forecasting customer behavior and the impact thereof on volumes, market shares, revenues and margins. In reality, though, this assumption does not hold. Not all of the proposed options that generate sufficient switching behavior by customers in the potential market are equally sustainable: some improvements in the product features can be imitated by some or all competitors, while others cannot. The sustainability of the advantage that induces customers to switch depends fundamentally on competitors' willingness and ability to respond.

A lot has been written about the sustainability of a competitive advantage, and even more has been written on the theoretical foundation thereof, namely game theory, which deals with anticipating competitor responses. What is remarkable, though, is that few practical game-theoretic approaches exist.[2] The art, and clearly not the science, is to make a best estimate of competitors' likely responses, based upon a thorough understanding of their objectives, capabilities and past behavior. Making such estimates is a totally necessary step, since the forecasts we made so far optimistically assumed that competitors cannot or do not want to respond. For some improvements that increase the deal value of the entrant's offering and make some customers switch, this is unlikely. For instance, price cuts are much easier to imitate than improvements in MTBF or efficiency.

How do we go about assessing this, and how does that affect our revenue and margin forecasts? First, we specify a time horizon, say one year after launch. Then we ask ourselves the question whether within that year, specific competitors will be able and willing to match our offering, or at least take action that minimizes the impact of the thing that hurts them the most, namely customers switching to our company. If the answer is no, we keep our original forecasts as they are. If the answer is yes, we adjust our original forecasts to reflect the number of competitors that can match our offering or that act to minimize its impact on customers switching to us. We do so by dividing the forecasted revenues by the number of competitors that can match plus one, to reflect that customers will have various options to choose from. If, say, two competitors are able and willing to imitate our offering within said horizon, we assume that we will obtain a third of the original revenue forecasts, since the customer has three options to choose from. The corresponding contribution margin and EBIT are calculated accordingly.

You may wonder whether it is reasonable to assume that, should n competitors be able to imitate rapidly, we will be able to get $1/(n+1)$ of the potential market. This is indeed a simplifying assumption that is open for discussion, but for lack of a better alternative, we use the preceding best possible assumption. In reality, it all depends on how many customers we can convince to switch to our offering before competitors manage to imitate. Once customers have switched, they are unlikely to switch back to the other players afterwards, since these customers' switching costs are now in our favor, given customer inertia and the like. So, we are aware that it is a simplifying assumption that we are happy to discuss with the management and sales team, and adjust if the real-world situation calls for it (for instance, if it is difficult to switch back when customers somehow get locked in).

With the assumption that we obtain $1/(n+1)$ of the potential market, and again assuming 10,000 customers in the potential market, we would adjust our initial revenues (as was shown in Table 4.5) to those shown in Table 4.6.[3]

TABLE 4.6 Forecasted revenue taking competitor responses into account

Feature	Pump 1	Pump 2	Pump 3	Pump 4	Pump 5	Pump 6
Efficiency (%)	60	55	75	85	65	55
Warranty (months)	18	12	24	36	24	0
MTBF (hours)	2500	2000	2400	1000	3000	3000
Price ($)	4550	4150	4800	4300	4550	4400
Average revenue per interviewee from launching this pump, **assuming no competitor response** ($)	1820	2075	960	2150	1820	1320
Forecasted revenue, **assuming no competitor responses** ($ million)	18.2	20.8	9.6	21.5	18.2	13.2
Number of competitors that are willing and able to imitate the pump within time horizon	3	1	1	1	0	0
Forecasted revenue **incorporating competitor response** ($ million)	4.55	10.38	4.8	10.75	18.2	13.2

You may wonder where these figures about competitors come from, and how accurate they are likely to be. They are based 20% upon game-theoretic considerations, and 80% upon management judgment. Game-theoretic considerations do matter somewhat. While they have a limited predictive power, we incorporate some of the key takeaways. One of the takeaways is that large rational established players have little incentive to respond with price to small low-priced entrants. We will elaborate on this issue in Chapter 5 when discussing defense strategies.

Some large established players deviate from this response, and put volume before value. Whatever the reason may be (irrationality, or simply the rational creation of a reputation for being irrational), such zero-tolerance behavior also exists and we have seen it with many of our clients or their competitors. We even observed both types of behavior within the same (medical devices) company, with one geographic area having the zero-tolerance policy and the other area "preserving the value in the market," as it was called.

The point is that theoretical game-theoretic considerations are one input to the discussion. Much more critical are competitive intelligence (reports, press and website announcements) and management's assessment of their competitors' ability and incentives to imitate. Is that judgment always correct? No. Is it reasonably accurate? Surely a lot more accurate than assuming that competitors do not respond. One simply needs to do the best one can. And the best one can is in our experience reasonably good, because many managers pursue careers within the industry and have held positions at many competitors. As a consequence, they have a good judgment about how their former employers are likely to respond. One of our friends (a former client) started his career at a medical devices company; at this point, in his mid-50s, he has had seven positions, you guessed it, all at medical device companies. While such managers are obviously not allowed to share confidential information about the competitors where they worked before, they do have a good sense of these competitors' competitive cultures.

The combination of experienced management judgment, competitive intelligence and a tidbit of useful game-theoretic considerations is not perfect. If you are not happy with it, dear reader, then our question to you is: what is a better alternative? If you do have input on this, be sure to let us know, and we will incorporate it in our next edition, with full acknowledgments.

▶ STEP 8. SELECT THE OPTION WITH THE HIGHEST IMPACT ON COMPANY OBJECTIVES

The final step in the decision-making process is to select the launch option with the highest impact on company objectives. Suppose, for simplicity, that the objective is to maximize the NPV of future cash flows. Since there are hundreds of possible pumps to launch (the combination of the various levels of all features within the capabilities of the company), one could theoretically find the NPV-maximizing pump using a sophisticated optimization algorithm. While we occasionally use mathematical algorithms, we prefer to go about it more pragmatically, in two phases.

First, we select a number of possible launch pumps (say, three to five) based upon a combination of feature levels that are valued most by a large set of customers in the potential market. We then forecast the revenue streams based on the customer interviews and estimate the required Capex and Opex for each of these pumps. In this option evaluation phase, we can thus derive the forecasted NPV.

Second, we vary the prices and feature levels of the preferred pump slightly to infer its effect on the commercial returns. Eventually we work out the business plan for the best performing pump or set of pumps.

▶ CONCLUSIONS

In this chapter, we have shown why it is crucial to start with a proper base, and, more importantly, how to establish a rigorous, accurate real-world estimate thereof. We have shown that the assessments of the market shares that a company can successively secure with its new offerings must not be based on some a priori estimates of seemingly reasonable percentages. To the contrary, these estimates must be derived from an understanding of individual customers' preferences, their switching behavior and the choices these customers make, as well as competitors' likely responses. The trade-off method described in Chapter 3 does exactly that. It is only by using a behavioral logic that projections in business plans can claim to be reasonably valid and surely a lot better than the way these plans are typically created.

The examples we have given are from companies entering already established and primarily B2B markets (like medical supplies, payroll services, industrial pumps and the like) rather than totally newly created markets (so-called Blue Oceans®). We did so because for 99% of companies (and hence our readers) diversification means diversification into existing markets with enhanced products, not the creation of Blue Oceans®. The companies that create totally new markets make the news but are the exception rather than the rule. For instance, Apple revolutionized the smartphone market in June 2007 when releasing the first iPhone. But from then onwards, entry into this market with differentiated products for latecomers such as Samsung, Huawei or even Nokia *is* similar to the problem we went through earlier. They need to attract customers away from their best alternative. The same applies to car manufacturers entering new segments. Only one company created the segment while the majority are latecomers.

That being said, our method *is* totally applicable to the creation of totally new Blue Ocean® markets. In that case, the best alternative to the potential customer is by definition "nothing." It is precisely one of the strengths of the approach that it does not require that we even know what that best alternative really is, or that that offering is an offering by another company rather than "nothing." In fact, in the case of payroll services, the best alternative was "nothing" for companies in the potential market that did not outsource payroll but considered doing so.

We deep-dived into two B2B examples because of the continuity of the argumentation: it is better to work with one or two examples and work them out completely so that the reader really understands (we hope so) than to scratch the surface of various cases. But we are happy to summarize how B2C markets differ. For B2C markets it is actually easier to interview customers, as they are (1) easier to find and (2) less second-guessing the interviewer's intentions (for example, what he will do with their answers or, in the worst case, whether he will hold their answers against them at a later stage). Finally, many B2C goods are partially an experience good, which requires an adaptation to the method as we discussed at the end of Chapter 3.

▶ NOTES

1 There are, however, some interesting remedies to these problems of "customer abuse." We will return to this point in Chapter 6.

2 While it is obviously difficult to judge without a thorough understanding of all the disciplines in the world, game theory appears to be one of the disciplines where the ratio of the number of theoretical developments over the number of applied approaches gets close to infinity. This is because the numerator is countless and the denominator is close to zero. In fact, when Daniel Deneffe was doing his PhD in Economics in the mid-80s, it was totally uncool not to focus on game theory. Students who were doing applied work tended to be considered second-class citizens. The difficulty for the PhD students was actually to find examples for their game-theoretic constructs, as these papers actually assumed hyperrationality from all market participants. Many business professionals would surely have a hard time agreeing with that assumption.

3 The figures for forecasted revenues are calculated in the same way as we did before: we multiply the average revenue per interviewee in the sample (assuming no competitor response) by the number of customers in the potential market. For simplicity, we assume a potential market of 10,000 buyers and we assume 100% coverage and promotional support.

5

Operationalizing a defense strategy against a new entrant

In the previous chapter, we explained how to operationalize a strategy when the outcome of the Grand Strategy exercise was a company's decision (or better: a hypothesis) to enter a new product or service market. That could be entry either into a newly created market (with no incumbent players) or into a market that is new to the company that enters with a differentiated offering. In the current chapter, we will explain how to act when the Grand Strategy outcome is not to enter a new market but, quite to the contrary, to defend the company's position as an incumbent.

There is ample business literature about the question whether increased competition from new entrants poses a problem for incumbents. As is often the case with the business literature, the answer depends on which article you read, and on the anecdotal evidence that the author of such article selects to prove her point. In an article whose title says it all ("When Companies Underestimate Low-Cost Rivals"), the author Adrian Ryans, professor at IMD, makes the claim that established companies "often underestimate [the challenge]. Sometimes executives are so focused on their traditional competitors, they don't even recognize the threat developing from low-cost rivals."[1]

Our own experience from working with executives across numerous industries facing entry, typically by low-priced players (such as in domestic appliances, chemicals, cement, telecommunications equipment and medical supplies) is that the word "sometimes" in Adrian Ryans's sentence ought to be replaced by "it can happen that." Incumbents in most cases do not underestimate the threat by low-cost rivals: they are close to being totally paranoid about them, and often justifiably so.

Our experience that incumbents take new entrants very seriously is probably biased, as companies often call us for support precisely when those low-cost or, more generally, low-priced entrants are wreaking havoc on their core business. So, let us take a more general source, such as PWC's 18th Annual CEO Survey (2015).[2] For the 1322 CEOs surveyed in 77 countries, the second most disruptive force of their industry in the next five years was indeed increased competition. More precisely, 61% of the interviewed CEOs felt that the increase in the number of significant direct and indirect competitors would be a disruptive (or more precisely, anything ranging from "somewhat disruptive" to "very disruptive") trend. Only changes in industry regulation were seen as more disruptive.

The threat of new entrants, particularly of low-cost competitors, is thus foremost on the minds of CEOs. It is also perceived to be more dangerous now than it was 10 to 15 years back. We do recall a business unit manager claiming that low-priced Indian and Chinese players were not that reliable, and that none of his customers wanted to have them as primary suppliers. He felt that the quality of their products was inadequate, and that these suppliers often failed to meet minimum requirements for supply guarantee and supply reliability.

We do not need to tell you that the situation is totally different now. Established players are under attack. Even more importantly, their customers do realize that formerly marginal entrants often have a satisfactory product and service quality, but at a much lower price. In fact, established players are often relegated to the secondary-supplier role, thereby providing their customers some insurance value should the new entrants fail to deliver properly.

Incumbents should be concerned about new entrants. In this chapter, we will first describe the traditional logic that is often applied when establishing a defense strategy against new entrants. We will point to some limitations of such a traditional defense logic, as it is often based on unfounded managerial beliefs or generic decision rules. A response to new entrants must not be a matter of beliefs or simple decision rules, but should be the result of a clear consideration of objectives and risks, customer choices and competitor reactions. The response should take into account the particular conditions of the threat, and hence personal beliefs or generic decision rules are in fact non-generalizable and very risky.

In the second section of this chapter, we will explain an alternative defense strategy framework that is based on behavioral logic. In the subsequent two sections we will show how this framework is applied in practice by referring to two real cases. The first case describes the differentiation strategy applied by a telecommunications company. The second case describes the fighting brand strategy applied by a cement manufacturer.

▶ THE LIMITS OF THE TRADITIONAL DEFENSE STRATEGY LOGIC

In this section, we will describe three ways of thinking about defense strategies against new entrants: trusting managerial beliefs, following generic decision rules, and applying behavioral logic.

Defining a defense strategy by trusting managerial beliefs

Executives are often adamant about the best response to the threat posed by new entrants. It is as though the response is a matter of "beliefs" (such as "always match prices," or "never destroy the value of the market"), more so than of a thoughtful analysis of customer choices. To put it bluntly, many of these beliefs are plain unfounded.

What makes us make such a bold statement? It is the simple observation that often, in one and the same situation, the one manager is convinced about response A being the best to cope with a new entrant, while the other manager is equally convinced about the effectiveness of the opposite response B. Unless we want to open up a medieval discussion about the existence of one versus multiple truths – which is not exactly the subject of this book – one of the two must be plain wrong.

For example, one of our clients in the cement industry was under attack by low-priced (in this case, not even low-cost) competitors. Interviews revealed that the managers concerned agreed to disagree, and adamantly so. In this case the proposed responses could be categorized into four categories (one of them being "do nothing"), with no manager wanting to budge a bit initially, convinced as they were about the effectiveness of their suggested responses. We will extensively revisit this case in the last section of this chapter, and explain the approach needed to come to a founded decision rather than a decision driven by subjective convictions and in-company power struggles.

Another example concerns a leading medical devices company with product categories such as medical stents, defibrillators, pacemakers and the like. The company was one of two incumbents that dominated a particular type of medical stent market in EMEA (Europe, Middle East & Africa). Their EMEA Director wanted support in what he called a pricing project. The objective was to achieve agreement among the regional Vice Presidents who reported to him (VP Nordic, VP Iberia, VP Central Europe, etc.) about the best response to a low-priced threat to their so-called core business.[3]

That threat was the following: the medical stent business, which was high priced and high margin, was under attack by a number of low-priced players that had entered the various geographic markets at the low end. The price response to this entry, which was very much in the hands of the regional VPs, differed across countries. Some VPs had dropped prices significantly in their region, while others had not (see Figure 5.1, with year 0 being the year preceding the start of the project). Overall, though, and partly as a result of the commoditization of the product, the average price trend of the company's stents was downward everywhere.[4]

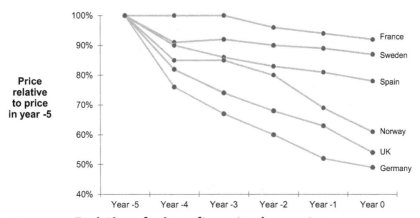

FIGURE 5.1 Evolution of prices after entry, by country

One could of course put the blame for the price de-escalation on the one other large incumbent, but the EMEA director rebuffed this argument straight away, and rightly so: "I refuse to believe that these price drops are primarily triggered by our main competitor." That is, his view was that differences in the beliefs of his VPs about the optimal response to a given competitive threat were responsible for the differences in price de-escalation across countries. That view appeared to be consistent with the available evidence. For example, taking just two neighboring countries, prices dropped by about 12% in Sweden over five years, whereas in Norway they dropped by close to 40%. This difference cannot be explained by a different competitive environment, since the prediction would go the other way: prices dropping faster in the more competitive market, which typically would be the largest market, in this case, Sweden.

The differences in price response were indeed the result of differences in beliefs as to what was best. Some VPs believed that a "zero-tolerance policy," as they called it, was best. That is, they felt that it was necessary to keep prices low to keep the entrants out. VPs in other countries believed that it was better, again in their terms, to "preserve the value of the market," and hence not to respond with price cuts to the low-priced entrants.

The outcome of acting differently because of different beliefs could actually have been quite alarming. If one country decides to go for a price-matching strategy, while the other does not respond and keeps prices high, parallel trade is likely to emerge, given the relatively low transportation costs for lightweight and compact products such as medical stents: traders will buy the products cheap in a low-priced country and sell it at a higher price in the high-priced country, thereby significantly hurting the high-priced country's margins and the overall EMEA margins as well. Fortunately for this company, the damage from parallel trade was relatively minor because each product had to be approved by the local health authority and hospitals did not want to take the risk of buying a non-approved stent sourced from another country.

We observed the same discussions in similar competitive situations at many other companies. All managers agree on the ultimate business objective, that is, to maximize long-term profits. Yet they disagree on how to achieve it, because defining the best response to the threat seems to be a matter of trusting the automatic pilot of one's own beliefs, even though everyone struggles to explain the foundations of these beliefs.

Defining a defense strategy by following generic decision rules

Rather than going by personal managerial beliefs, some business scholars propose so-called generic strategies such as "sell solutions," "differentiate, differentiate, differentiate, but don't cut price" or "don't offer good services, but offer ever better services than your competitors." By using well-picked examples, these scholars can claim that their generic strategies, unlike managerial beliefs, are at least somehow consistent with some anecdotal evidence.

But just like managerial beliefs, these generic strategies suggest an unconditional way forward. And when digging somewhat deeper into their underlying logic, one often finds two things. The first finding is that the generic strategy only holds under a specific set of assumptions. This in fact means that other recommendations would actually follow under a different set of assumptions. The second – and more disconcerting – finding is that these assumptions are not made explicit, either by ignorance or neglect. This in fact means that many managers are unknowingly misled when they apply the recommendations.

The lack of generalizability applies to any type of generic strategy, including the well-known generic strategies "differentiation" versus "cost leadership" versus "focus," advocated in numerous general management textbooks following the publication of Michael Porter's book on competitive strategy.[5] Another example thereof are the three generic competitive strategies, or "value disciplines," advanced by Michael Treacy and Fred Wiersema: "operational excellence" versus "customer intimacy" versus "product leadership."[6]

The reason why the preceding generic strategies cannot be said to be valid in general is that they only hold under a number of specific assumptions on two critical things, namely (1) the distribution of customer preferences, and (2) the competitive positions of other players. For example, a cost leadership strategy, in the sense of offering a no-frills product, can be successful only if two conditions are fulfilled: (1) there are a lot of customers out there who value the low-frills products but do not value the extra product or service features, and (2) there are few competitors offering such products. If few customers want such products (for instance, wine in one-liter cartons at $1.99) and/or if other competitors offer such products at low cost as well, a cost leadership strategy is unlikely to be successful. Conversely, a differentiation strategy is unlikely to be successful if very few customers, if any, want to pay for the differentiating elements, which is the case for commoditizing products, as we will explain in Chapter 6.

The same argument holds for the generic strategies that specifically address defense situations. For example, in "Strategies to Fight Low-Cost Rivals," Nirmalya Kumar sets up some sort of decision tree to determine how to respond to a low-cost entrant, based upon research of 50 incumbents and 25 low-cost businesses.[7] As an example, the first question of the tree is: "Will the low-cost entrant take away any of my present or future customers?" If the answer to that question is "no" (node 1 of the tree), the decision tree recommends not to take on the new entrant. If the answer is "yes" (node 2 of the tree), the decision tree recommends not to launch a price war, but to increase product differentiation by using a combination of tactics. Later, further questions are asked to refine these recommendations. Let us have a look at these first two nodes of the decision tree, and try to understand whether they are really generalizable, that is, whether they hold as often as is claimed implicitly.

The situation at node 1 is pretty straightforward. The recommendation not to take on the new entrant does make sense if it is indeed the case that the low-cost entrant will not take away any of the incumbent's present or future customers. One may question, however, the added value of this node in the decision tree. If the entrant's product is launched in the product segment of the incumbent, it is inevitable that the answer to this question is "yes." Let us go back to very, very basic microeconomics. If a low-priced substitute enters the market, the demand for the incumbent's product will decrease. This does not mean that customers will massively abandon the incumbent; it simply means that some of the most price-sensitive customers will be lost to the new entrant.

This is pretty much always the case, unless the entrant enters a totally unrelated business. For instance, it is obvious that the entry of low-priced Kia Motors in Europe inevitably took away customers from Ford, Opel, Renault and Citroën, and that it has not or at best only minimally affected Rolls-Royce's sales. But that is simply because Kia Motors and Rolls-Royce do not serve overlapping market segments. Should Kia Motors enter this top-end luxury sedan market, Rolls-Royce would almost inevitably lose *some* customers to Kia Motors, that is, the ones who hesitate buying a Rolls-Royce but cannot find an alternative that gives them a higher deal value than Kia Motors does.

Let us turn to the recommendation at node 2 of the decision tree: do not launch a price war but increase product differentiation by using a combination of tactics. Where does this recommendation come from? Is this statement really true under all reasonable behavioral assumptions? And what is meant exactly by "do not launch a price war": that the incumbent cannot go down on price, or that the incumbent cannot match the price cut of the new entrant? Without specifically focusing on the previously mentioned article per se, what we would like to demonstrate is that, under some reasonable assumptions, this is simply not an appropriate recommendation. It is therefore not generalizable.

To demonstrate our point (that is, the lack of generalizability of a generic defense strategy such as "do not start a price war, but increase product differentiation"), we need to show that under at least one reasonable condition (that is, a set of real-world assumptions that can reasonably be applicable), it does make sense to respond with price; we can equally think of many situations where it makes sense not to differentiate either. We will describe this as case 1. Likewise, we can show that, under certain conditions, even a third defense strategy, namely "do nothing" makes sense. We will describe this as case 2.

Before detailing case 1 and case 2, let us point to something that readers with some background in game theory will understand easily: that the best response to low-priced entry fundamentally depends on numerous factors such as the cross-price elasticity of the incumbent's product relative to the entrant's product (more on that later); the extent to which the incumbent's product can be differentiated, in a way that the customer is willing to pay more for the differentiation than it costs; the objectives of the entrant (profits, volume, revenues); the size and capacity of the entrant; and the time horizon of both players, to name the most important ones. Let us now detail the two specific cases.

Case 1: "tit-for-tat" is better than "do not start a price war, but increase product differentiation"

Suppose, for instance, that the incumbent's product is a commodity or commoditizing product (e.g., a medical label, an intermediate chemical, a cobalt-chromium stent), that the entrant is rational, that the entrant has loads of excess capacity, and that his objectives are profits both in the short and long term. Suppose further that the products of the incumbent and the entrant are perceived to be close to perfect substitutes to each other, that is, the cross-price elasticity of the incumbent's product relative to that of the entrant's is positive and sizeable: the incumbent would lose a lot of volume (say, more than 50%) in response to even a small price cut by the entrant. Suppose further that customers may appreciate or be satisfied with a number of features that differentiate the incumbent's product from the entrant's but are not willing to pay for it.

Under these assumptions (which can be reasonable, but do not always hold) it is in the incumbent's best interest to respond with price, and not to differentiate. Responding with price is the right thing to do because the volume effect is bigger than the price effect: the margins lost from losing so much volume as a result of the high price gap with the entrant are simply higher than the margins lost from lowering prices and limiting volume losses. *Not* differentiating is the right thing to do because there is no differentiating feature that customers want to pay for. What we just described is the classical prisoner's dilemma used so often in business school economics or strategy courses. In the circumstances described, a tit-for-tat strategy is most advisable in the long run.[8]

Incidentally, and we are sure you guessed it, there are exceptions to the preceding tit-for-tat rule as well. For instance, the rule may be inappropriate if the entrant will cut prices further in response to the incumbent's price cut. Here again, we must ask ourselves in which situations this assumption (further price cuts by the entrant) can be expected to hold. One situation is when the entrant uses competitive-based pricing and has a very simple pricing rule such as "our price is the incumbent's price minus 10%." In that situation, a tit-for-tat strategy by the incumbent sends prices and margins plunging. Another situation is when the entrant is simply irrational and does not think through the implications of its actions on the anticipated response of the incumbent.[9]

Case 2: "Do nothing" is better than "do not start a price war, but increase product differentiation."

Suppose that that infamous cross-price elasticity is still positive but much lower, that is, a decrease in price by the entrant only has a small negative effect on the volume sold by the incumbent. In that case, the incumbent's best response to a low-priced entrant may be to keep prices high. For example, assume that the incumbent is the Coca-Cola Corporation and that it gets attacked by a low-priced unbranded product in one of its product categories. Assume, in addition, that Coca-Cola has 99% market share, that the new entrant entered at a somewhat lower price than Coca-Cola, and that Coca-Cola's superior brand name and Coca-Cola customers' loyalty prevented the entrant from obtaining more than 1% market share. If the entrant now decides to get aggressive and cuts prices further by 20%, its market share may increase from 1% to 2%. If Coca-Cola does not respond with price, and if the entrant's unit variable costs are not too high, such price cut is a meaningful proposition for the entrant, since after all it doubles its volume. For Coca-Cola, however, responding with an equivalent 20% price cut to keep 99% instead of 98% market share is way too costly relative to accommodating the entrant and accepting a minor erosion of its market share. This is so because the profits lost from lowering prices over all of its volumes is larger than the profits regained from keeping its prices high. In game-theoretic jargon, not responding is called a dominant strategy. Under these circumstances, neither differentiation nor price cutting is the right defense strategy for the incumbent.

Our more general point from this section is that it is too simplistic to come up with so-called natural recommendations that invariably hold. Instead, it is necessary to dig deeper and capture the most reasonable assumptions in the real world, and then derive the correct recommendation per combination of assumptions. Admittedly, this is not so much fun as having simple recommendations for a particular business situation such as the entry of low-priced players. And perhaps there is an abundance of literature that suggests simple recommendations without making these assumptions explicit for that very reason: it is much easier to read, much easier to do, and much less time-consuming. But it is simply non-generalizable and hence only correct when lucky.

Defining a defense strategy by applying behavioral logic

From the preceding sections, we can draw two conclusions about the best response to new entrants. First, the best response to a new low-priced entrant is not a question of the "preserve the value of the market" belief versus the "zero-tolerance" belief. The only belief that is relevant here is the belief to want to maximize the value of the firm.

Once that is established, the best response to such a new entrant depends on a number of reasonable evidence-based assumptions about parameters that we illustrated earlier (elasticities, available capacities, and the like). Making these assumptions explicit and deriving conclusions from them, possibly after some modeling, is a lot better than having long and often empty discussions that often kick in because the assumptions are not made explicit. Making assumptions explicit makes it much easier to enable management to eventually come to an agreement, in this case, about the best or most reasonable response to the new entrant.

The second conclusion is that the number of parameters that come into play is large. Hence, a simple decision tree that comes up with unconditional recommendations like "do not cut price, but differentiate" cannot but implicitly assume particular values for most of these parameters, and thus is bound to be misleading. As discussed, when differentiation is not feasible or is too costly, a price response may be justified, particularly when the entrant can take away a significant chunk of the business from the incumbent as a result of price cuts. Under other conditions, neither differentiation nor price cutting may the best response. For example, not doing anything may be the best response; or a combination of some differentiation and price changes, including price hikes, may be the best.

What we are saying, then, is that the best response to a new entrant in a specific case is conditional, that is, it depends on the specific conditions of that case. Of particular importance is to know the distribution of the preferences of the customers in the markets targeted by the incumbent and the new entrant. Also of high importance is the position and behavior of the various competitors in the market. Therefore, it is better to state these conditions and come up with recommendations per set of conditions, than to ignore the conditions and come up with just one simple recommendation.

In the next section of this chapter, we will explain the conceptual foundation for a sound way of thinking about how to respond to low-priced entrants. As you will see, it builds on the behavioral logic explained in Chapter 3.

▶ A DEFENSE STRATEGY FRAMEWORK BASED ON BEHAVIORAL LOGIC

We will first walk you through the logic of the approach for the simple case where the incumbent has to defend a business that has one customer. Once that logic is clear, we will demonstrate how it can be applied to more complex real-world settings with many customers, all having different preferences. At the end, we will explain how to get the required data.

Case 1: the simple case with just one customer at risk

In this simple case 1, we assume that the incumbent company has just one recurring customer. The notion of recurring is important, as the search for a strategy to cope with an attack and the resulting customer loss implicitly assumes that the company has recurring business with its customers. In case 2, we will be able to generalize the approach to a situation where the incumbent company has multiple recurring customers with different preferences.

The incumbent's product or service could be anything: an airplane ticket, electricity or, to take a B2B example, a particular medical device (how about a stent?). Let us call it the base package. Assume that the incumbent's customer is willing to pay for the base package, and that the incumbent knows the magnitude of the customer's willingness-to-pay, namely $120. Furthermore, the incumbent currently charges a price of $100, and the unit variable cost of the base package equals $70. To keep things simple, we assume throughout this case that the marginal cost of each unit is the same, which means that marginal cost and unit variable cost are interchangeable concepts.

From the mere observation of customer choice (economists would call it "revealed preference," as we explained in Chapter 3), it must be the case that the deal value to this customer of buying from this incumbent ($120 – $100 = $20) is larger than the perceived deal value he could obtain at any other incumbent supplier, minus the switching costs to that supplier. That is, even if another supplier charges $95, and if the customer's willingness-to-pay for the other supplier is the same ($120), the fact that the customer does not switch must mean that his switching costs are higher than $5. Put differently, his net willingness-to-pay (willingness-to-pay minus switching costs) must be lower than $115, unless he is either mental or ignorant.

Suppose now that a new entrant comes in at a price of $85. Suppose also that the customer's net willingness-to-pay for the entrant's base package equals $110 (see Table 5.1). Under these circumstances, if the incumbent does nothing, this customer will eventually switch over to the entrant, as the net deal value of buying from the entrant is now higher than the net deal value of staying with the incumbent.[10]

Let us have a look at the three defense options available to the incumbent.

TABLE 5.1 Comparison of deal value of incumbent's and entrant's base package

	Incumbent's base package	Entrant's base package
Customer's willingness-to-pay (net of switching costs, if any)	$120	$110
Price	$100	$85
Unit variable cost	$70	< $70 (guesstimated)
Deal value to customer (net of switching costs, if any)	$20	$25
Contribution margin	$30	> $15

TABLE 5.2 Comparison of deal value when adding a differentiating value destroying feature

	Incumbent's base package + differentiating feature A	Entrant's base package
Customer's willingness-to-pay (net of switching costs, if any)	$130	$110
Price	$100	$85
Unit variable cost	$90	< $70 (guesstimated)
Deal value to customer (net of switching costs, if any)	$30	$25
Contribution margin	$10	> $15

Option 1: differentiate (value destroying)

Suppose that the incumbent can add a differentiating feature, say, a particular technical service, to the base package. This differentiating feature A costs an extra $20, the customer's willingness-to-pay for feature A is $10, and the incumbent keeps the price of the package unchanged (see Table 5.2).

Now the incumbent's package becomes the preferred package. Compared to the "do nothing" scenario, the incumbent is no longer at risk of losing the customer, and makes a contribution margin of $10.[11] While the margin is lower than in the initial situation, and hence value is destroyed, it is still better than the $0 that eventually would materialize if the incumbent did nothing. The conclusion is that it makes sense to differentiate in such a way as to make the incumbent's product the preferred package, as long as the total margin of doing so is positive.

Option 2: cut price

If adding a differentiating feature costs more than it is valued monetarily by the customer, it is better to remove the feature, and return that same value to the customer in the form of a lower price for the base package.[12] Suppose the price cut is $10 (see Table 5.3). The customer's deal value of staying with the incumbent is larger than the deal value of switching to the entrant. Compared to the differentiation option, the incumbent saves $20, while the customer's willingness-to-pay decreases by $10. As a result, the wedge between willingness-to-pay and cost increases by $10. Lowering the price by $10 (from $100 to $90) thus gives the same deal value as the differentiation option ($130 – $100 = $120 – $90), which exceeds the deal value of switching to the entrant. The only difference is that the incumbent's margin is higher in this "cut price" option ($20) than in the "differentiate" option ($10).

A potential counterargument to option 2 would be that the entrant is more likely to cut his price when the incumbent pursues option 2 than when the incumbent pursues option 1. In reality, though, option 1 puts the incumbent in the more vulnerable position because his margin is lower.

The same logic applies of course to the base package itself. Without adding a numerical example, it is easy to see that, if the base package contains a number of features that are valued less than they cost, it is better to remove them in return for a lower price. Doing so creates value between

TABLE 5.3 Comparison of deal value when cutting price

	Incumbent's base package at lower price	Entrant's base package
Customer's willingness-to-pay (net of switching costs, if any)	$120	$110
Price	$90	$85
Unit variable cost	$70	< $70 (guesstimated)
Deal value to customer (net of switching costs, if any)	$30	$25
Contribution margin	$20	> $15

the incumbent and the customer. This is similar to the logic of the responses of legacy air carriers to low-cost carriers offering rock-bottom fares. Even in the absence of a fighting brand, these incumbents remove (for the price-sensitive customer) a number of features that cost more than many customers are willing to pay for, such as meals, extra bagging or other features that all become optional at a charge. As a result, while the incumbents are still more expensive than the low-cost carriers, more customers stay with them than should the incumbents have done nothing. Customer retention is increased, not because the price gap has been lowered, but because the deal value of the low-cost carriers has decreased relative to the incumbents.'

Option 3: differentiate (value creating)

Assuming no further price retaliation by the entrant, and assuming just one customer, it may be better to remove features and lower prices than to add those that add less value than what they cost. That was the logic of option 2. However, if features can be identified that generate more value (willingness-to-pay) than they cost, differentiation is the best option. Adding these features increases the deal value of staying with the incumbent relative to switching to the entrant. This in turn allows the incumbent not to have to lower prices (or by less than in the case of a pure price response). As a result, further price cutting by the entrant is less likely than in a pure price response.

Suppose that a new differentiating feature B is added to the incumbent's base package. Feature B increases the customer's willingness-to-pay by $20, whereas the unit variable cost of the feature equals $10 (see Table 5.4). In

TABLE 5.4 Comparison of deal value when adding a differentiating value creating feature

	Incumbent's base package + differentiating feature B	Entrant's base package
Customer's willingness-to-pay (net of switching costs, if any)	$140	$110
Price	$100	$85
Unit variable cost	$80	< $70 (guesstimated)
Deal value to customer (net of switching costs, if any)	$40	$25
Contribution margin	$20	> $15

other words, the feature increases the customer's willingness-to-pay by more than it costs, and value is created. Compare this to option 1, where value was destroyed, because the increase in willingness-to-pay for feature A ($10) was less than the unit variable cost of feature A ($20).

So, option 3 is quite attractive: the customer does not switch, as the deal value of staying with the incumbent is larger than the deal value of switching to the entrant; furthermore, the risk of retaliation is minimized. The fact that the incumbent's margin in this option 3 is the same as in option 2 ($20) is an artifact of the example: the unit variable cost of the feature equals $10, but if that cost had been lower (or higher), the margin in option 3 would have been higher (or lower) than the margin in option 2.

If we think simply in terms of "price cutting" (option 2) versus "value creating differentiation" (option 3), one can say that value creating differentiation can be superior provided:

▶ It increases the willingness-to-pay sufficiently so that the deal value of staying with the incumbent is larger than the deal value of switching to the entrant.

▶ The increase in cost from differentiation is less than the increase in willingness-to-pay.

▶ The increase in cost from differentiation is less than the minimum price cut needed to make the customer stay with the incumbent under no differentiation.

In the preceding example, the last condition is actually not satisfied. The increase in cost from differentiation is $10, whereas the minimum price cut needed to make the customer stay equals $6: at a price cut of $5, the customer is indifferent between switching and staying (see from Table 5.1). This simple example thus leads to the important point that "value creating differentiation," even when it can be achieved, is not necessarily superior to "price cutting."

The most important point of the example, however, is that binary thinking (that is, should we either differentiate or cut price) is not constructive. The best response can be a combination of differentiation and price cutting, but also of differentiation and a price increase. In this specific example, if we are

TABLE 5.5 Comparison of deal value when differentiation is combined
with price change

	Incumbent's base package + differentiating feature B	Entrant's base package
Customer's willingness-to-pay (net of switching costs, if any)	$140	$110
Price	$114	$85
Unit variable cost	$80	< $70 (guesstimated)
Deal value to customer (net of switching costs, if any)	$26	$25
Contribution margin	$34	> $15

faced with the options to do nothing, or to differentiate with feature A, or to differentiate with feature B, or to cut price, or to combine some form of differentiation with a price change, the actual best response to entry would be to go for the combination of differentiating with feature B and increasing price by $14 (see Table 5.5). The customer stays with the incumbent ($26 > $25) and the incumbent's margin ($34) is higher than under any of the other options (do nothing: $0; respond with optimal price: $26; respond with value destroying differentiation: $10; respond with value creating differentiation: $20).

Obviously the preceding does not work if the customer can buy the original base package and the differentiating feature separately, and if the differentiating feature can be added to the base package of the entrant. That is, the differentiating feature must either truly be part of the incumbent's base package or it has no value without the incumbent's original base package. Take the real-world example of camera-assisted parking as a feature that is added to an incumbent's vehicle: it is either part of the incumbent's base package or it cannot be added to an entrant's vehicle.

If the customer could buy feature B separately (even at $14) and add it to the entrant's base package, the incumbent's differentiation strategy would not lead the customer to stay. If the incumbent were to charge $100 for the original base package and $14 for the separate feature B, the customer would buy the base package from the entrant and feature B from the incumbent. The incumbent would then end up with a margin of just $4 ($14 – $10), and will have lost the biggest chunk of the customer's business.

Case 2: the generalized, more complex case with different customers

Let us now think through the case of two customers, instead of just one, to show how the incumbent's best response is determined. Once you understand this logic, you will also understand the logic of determining the best response when an even larger sample of customers is at risk.

Let us expand the example used in case 1, and consider the base package first (see Table 5.6). Suppose that customer 2 values the incumbent's base package more than its price ($110 > $100) but values it less than customer 1 does ($110 versus $120). Suppose also that customer 2 values the incumbent's base package more so than the entrant's package, at least after subtracting the switching costs ($110 > $105). Customer 2 would still switch because of the entrant's significantly lower price ($85 versus $100) and the higher deal value ($105 – $85 > $110 – $100). We also assume that the two customers have different costs for switching from the incumbent's base package to the entrant's.[13]

Let us now consider also the two features A and B. We assume that the features are truly differentiating for the incumbent's base package and cannot be added to the entrant's base package. Suppose that the two customers' willingness-to-pay (WTP) for the features is known, and that it is different across the two (see Table 5.7).[14]

TABLE 5.6 Comparison of deal value in case of different customers

	Incumbent's base package	Entrant's base package
Customer 1's willingness-to-pay (net of switching costs, if any)	$120	$110
Customer 2's willingness-to-pay (net of switching costs, if any)	$110	$105
Price	$100	$85
Unit variable cost	$70	< $70 (guesstimated)
Deal value to customer 1 (net of switching costs, if any)	$20	$25
Deal value to customer 2 (net of switching costs, if any)	$10	$20

TABLE 5.7 Comparison of willingness-to-pay and unit variable cost by feature

	Feature A	*Feature B*
Customer 1's willingness-to-pay	$10	$20
Customer 2's willingness-to-pay	$25	$22
Unit variable cost	$20	$10

The optimization logic stays the same. First, the customer is assumed to maximize his deal value. Second, all the incumbent can do, is to optimize his profits. And third, competitor responses and, in particular, imitation capabilities should be taken into consideration. Based on that logic, we can look at a variety of options.

Option 1: differentiation and high price increase for feature B

The option that was best in the case of just one customer (that is, add differentiation feature B to the base package, and increase price by $14) will not work. While customer 1 stays with the incumbent, customer 2 will not, since the deal value of switching to the new entrant is still higher ($20) than of staying with the incumbent ($10 for initial deal value, plus $22 WTP for feature B, minus $14 for the extra price of feature B = $18). The incumbent's total margin in this option is thus $34, as it was in the case of one customer.

Option 2: differentiation and moderate price increase for feature B

A better option would be to add differentiating feature B to the base package and increase the price by $11 instead of $14. That way, both customers would stay, and margins would increase to the tune of 2 × ($111 – $70 – $10) = $62.

Option 3: differentiation and high price increase for both features

An even better option would be for the incumbent to keep the price of the base package at $100, and charge $22 for feature A and $14 for feature B. Under these circumstances, customer 2 would buy feature A, making an extra $25 – $22 = $3 in deal value. She would also buy feature B, as she has a better deal from buying ($22 – $14 = $8) than from not buying ($0). Hence the extra deal value she obtains from these two features is $11. The total deal value of staying with the incumbent is now $10 (from the base package) plus

$11 (from features A and B), which exceeds the deal value of switching to the entrant ($20).

What about customer 1 in option 3? Customer 1 would buy feature B, as his willingness-to-pay ($20) exceeds the price ($14). He would not buy feature A. Hence, if we keep the price of the base package at $100, customer 1 would stay with the incumbent, as his total deal value would now be $20 (from the base package) plus $6 (from feature B), which exceeds the deal value of switching to the entrant ($25).

What margin does option 3 generate for the incumbent? Since both customers will buy the base package at a price of $100, the incumbent makes 2 × ($100 − $70) = $60 on the base package, plus 2 × ($14 − $10) = $8 from feature B, plus 1 × ($22 − $20) = $2 from feature A. The incumbent's total margin is now $70, which he obtains from adding options to the base package without cutting the price.

Obviously, should the entrant be willing and able to imitate feature A or B rapidly, all the benefits that the incumbent got from differentiating through that feature would be wiped out. But it is precisely these kinds of discussions that should be held to make the right decision. For example, if the entrant had the incentive and ability to imitate feature A easily but not feature B, the defense strategy would change: the incumbent should now offer feature B at a price of $11. Both customers would stay and the incumbent would make a margin of $62. It would not matter whether the price of the base package stayed at $100 and feature B is offered optionally at a price of $11 or, conversely, whether it would be included in the base package which would then cost $111. The latter choice makes sense when all customers value feature B more than it costs.

If the entrant imitated both features A and B, a price cut becomes more reasonable. Not doing so, that is, "preserving the value of the market," would simply mean that the incumbent loses the only two customers in the market, and has zero contribution margin as a result. How deep he would need to cut prices depends on his understanding of the entrant's incentives. It also depends on whether cutting prices even further would do him more harm than good. To keep customer 1, and assuming no further response by the entrant, a price cut to $94 is required. To keep customer 2, a price cut to $89 is required. If we know that the entrant would not respond by cutting prices even further (given that the incumbent's price of $89 still exceeds the entrant's price of $85), this would be the best defense option. However, if we know that the entrant may respond (when he does not make any money), a price cut to $94 may be more advisable, as it would leave half of the market to the entrant (customer 2) and half of the market to the incumbent (customer 1), The incumbent would then still make $24 ($94 − $70), which may be better than letting prices and profits plummet until the entrant gives up.

For example, suppose that we guesstimated the entrant's unit variable cost to be $65 per package. In that case, we do know that the entrant will never lower his price below $66, assuming that this unit cost reflects all of his opportunity costs. If the entrant sets the price at $66, the incumbent would need to charge $75 to keep customer 1: this customer values the incumbent's base package by $10 more than the entrant's, and he would have a better deal (by $1) from staying with the incumbent.

By analogy, if the entrant ended up rock-bottom at $66, the incumbent would need to charge $70 to keep customer 2. As the incumbent makes zero profits at that price (his unit variable cost being $70), he would never let this happen. He would prefer charging $75 and keeping customer 1, while letting go of customer 2. In this scenario, the incumbent would only make $5. Anticipating this downward spiral, the incumbent had better accommodate the entrant and charge $94, and thus make $24, hoping that the entrant would not cut prices further. This hope is justified, as the entrant would end up with a margin of $2 if he cuts price to $66. If the entrant is somewhat rational, it is unlikely that he would be cutting prices below $85: at a price of $85, he gets customer 2 and makes a margin of $20, in turn anticipating that the incumbent can reasonably be expected not to cut prices below $94.

The point of the preceding examples is that an incumbent who is faced with an aggressive entrant should address the problem not by following dogmatic beliefs or some unconditional generic decision rules, but by understanding, as well as possible, customer preferences, the choices customers make to maximize their deal value, and the entrant's incentives and likely behavior. Hopefully we made it clear that the optimal defense strategy totally depends on how customers prefer the entrant's offerings versus the incumbent's, on the differences in these preferences between customers, and on their switching costs.

Some will argue that it is too difficult to get that sort of customer information, and that therefore it is better to go by "simple rules" (such as "differentiate, do not cut prices"). We hope to have shown by means of simple examples that there is really no behavioral foundation for such rules. One might as well not say anything and flip a coin. The fundamental premise in this book is that it is better to do the right thing with imperfect information than take a shortcut that is easy to work with but has no behavioral foundation. We do not claim that we will have the information on customer preferences with accuracy. But we do claim that we know what to look for, and that we can do a lot better with our estimates or guesstimates than by flipping a coin.

Getting the data to define the optimal defense strategy

As we have made clear, defining an effective defense strategy requires a sound, data-based understanding of customer preferences and switching costs. There are two methods for getting these data. The first uses the company's salespeople as a source about customers, while the second involves talking to customers directly. Let us have a look at both.

Method 1: use the company's salespeople as a source

If you do not know your customers' costs of switching from your company to the new entrant, the least costly solution is to have a number of informed salespeople guesstimate these costs a priori. The results will be inaccurate, but again, one needs to compare it to simplistic shortcuts and coin-flipping. Furthermore, there are ways to improve your chances of getting reliable estimates from the salespeople.

First, make sure that the salespeople involved in this process are minimally biased by their current sales objectives. Salespeople have a tendency to say that switching costs are zero, thereby using the argument that their company's and the entrant's products are exactly the same. The fact that salespeople disproportionately accentuate the perceived entry threat is often rooted in their fear that their sales volume inevitably will fall more when the company takes on a rather accommodating stance (e.g., by keeping prices unchanged, without any differentiation) than when the company responds actively (e.g., by cutting prices, through differentiation, or a combination of both). As we have shown previously, however, such an active response may not be the best defense.

It is therefore essential to have a leading salesperson drive the process of gathering insights about customer preferences and establishing the defense strategy. Such a person should have a number of characteristics. First, she should have been in the organization for a sufficiently long time (say, at least 3 years) but not too long either, as people with over 20 years' experience may be defensive about what they have been doing during that period, or may even obstruct some innovative measures. Second, she must have the trust and respect of top management, and also be able to motivate other salespeople in the lower echelons. Third, she must have reasonably strong conceptual skills and be willing to go through an innovative thinking process to do what is best for the organization rather than what advances her own best interest.

With such a person in the driver seat, it will be much easier to motivate the salespeople to contribute to the defense strategy project, while minimizing their thinking about what is in it for them. Obviously, management must also reward salespeople for their objective participation, so that they do not think they are digging their own grave.

The second thing to ensure is that the guesstimates of customer preferences and switching costs are minimally influenced by cognitive biases or, specifically, by anchoring. Anchoring takes place when an individual uses an initial piece of information to make subsequent judgments. Admittedly, it is very difficult to avoid the anchoring problem, but it is important to do whatever it takes to minimize it.[15] In this case, it is important not to obtain the guesstimates by asking salespeople around in a workshop, as the guesstimate related to a particular product or service feature will be influenced by whatever the first person says. While at some point it will be necessary to collect the views of all participants, it will be even more important that these views are collected in a maximally unbiased fashion, that is, through individual interviews first. Once the views of all participants are collected independently of one another, the workshop will aim to get to a consensus.

The drawback of this minimal-effort approach is of course that it is subjective. Second, it is very unlikely that the salespeople will be able to find differences in customers' willingness-to-pay and switching costs. They will get a rather general view, and translate that in an average across customers, while inevitably ignoring the differences.

Method 2: talk to customers directly

Obviously, the best sources for understanding customers are . . . customers. And we know the question you will ask: how many customers do we need to talk to? We have addressed the issue of sample size already in Chapter 3 and Chapter 4. Our answer essentially remains the same: it depends on the time and money that you can and want to spend. That being said, one piece of advice is to talk to a number of customers (at least ten) rather than none. Is ten enough to understand differences between customers? Not quite, but it surely is enough to possibly adjust internal views on what matters to them.

If one wants to be more methodic and gather more information to understand differences in customer preferences and switching costs, gathering a larger, representative sample of customers is obviously advisable. This will allow one to do an in-depth assessment of (1) the differentiating product or service features (these are the things that will increase a customer's costs of switching to the new entrant), and (2) their current switching value (this is the difference in deal values net of switching costs to the new entrant).

The approach to obtain this information is exactly the same as the one worked out in detail in Chapters 3 and 4. Again, there is no magic number for the right number of customers to interview. The big difference with Chapter 4 is that the customers interviewed in that case were new customers (as Chapter 4 was about new market entry), whereas here they are your own (as the goal is to understand what to do to prevent your existing customers from switching to a new entrant).

▶ **THE TELECOMMUNICATIONS CASE AS AN EXAMPLE OF A "DIFFERENTIATION" DEFENSE STRATEGY**

In this section, we present a case example of the development of a defense strategy, in an evidence-based manner, in the telecommunications market. The incumbent company, which we call IncCom, was the market leader in a particular country. A well-known new entrant, which we call EntCom, was attacking IncCom by aggressively entering the market for EVPN services (private networks) through lower prices. IncCom was wondering what it should do to protect its current and future EVPN margins.

The approach followed by IncCom is explained in Figure 5.2. The logic should be rather straightforward, given the description earlier in this chapter. In Step 1 we simply agreed on the levers (that is, the product and service features) that IncCom could work with to possibly differentiate and increase the deal value of its offering to its customers. We

Step 1.

Diagnosis of IncCom's current offering and potential features

Activities

- Interview IncCom's key product managers and sales managers
- Assess existing price and usage of additional features
- Define and prioritize focus segments and product and service features
- Identify unit variable costs

Deliverables

- Clear understanding of hypothesized drivers of value and revenue at IncCom
- Hypotheses about segments
- Unit variable costs for base package and features

Step 2.

Estimation of switching values, willingness-to-pay, and sales and margin potential

- Develop questionnaire and templates, and test in 3 to 5 pilot interviews
- Conduct interactive face-to-face interviews with current customers (~50)
- Process interview results and identify segments
- Optimize offering, assuming no competitor reactions

- Accurate estimates of customers' willingness-to-pay and switching values
- Estimates of sales and margin potential of any combination of product features and price (total and per segment)

Step 3.

Analysis of competitive reactions, and finalization of product and price strategy

- Conduct workshop to discuss results with Marketing & Sales
- Evaluate various scenarios of competitor reactions
- Re-optimize to define the base package, add-on services and pricing
- Define pragmatic guidelines for future tactics

- Aligned understanding of optimal prices and product strategy, sales, margin potential and risks
- Pragmatic optimization tool for the EVPN offering

FIGURE 5.2 Approach for developing a defense strategy

also formulated hypotheses about the customer segments that we could distinguish. And we sought to understand the unit variable cost of Inc-Com's base package and of the extra features that it could add to the base package.

In Step 2 we interviewed a sample of customers to identify their switching values and their willingness-to-pay for improvements in the product and service features. The sample was relatively small (50 customers), for the two "be real!" reasons that we already mentioned in Chapter 4. The first reason relates to the cost of increasing the sample size. It is a sure thing that we could have increased the sample size to 500. But few managers at customers want to be interviewed for free during a full hour. And we need that hour to get accurate reliable information from the interview process. With a $300 reward per manager, our costs of adding 450 interviewees would increase to a mere $135,000, excluding the costs of holding the interviews. The second reason relates to the very possibility of recruiting that many interviewees. Recall that we are in a B2B setting, which means that there are far fewer customers than in a B2C setting. And we cannot force someone to participate. So, even with our $300 reward, it is dubious that we would have been able to recruit more interviewees.

In Step 2 we deep-dived into customer preferences and switching behavior using the trade-off method, and identified whether the hypothesized segments from Step 1 were actually true segments. Finally, we optimized our offering, using the logic that we explained for the preceding two-customers case, but now applied to the sample of interviewees. If at all possible and economically feasible to create separate offerings for the true identified segments, we would do so.

In Step 3 we re-optimized the offering, taking competitor responses into consideration. Whenever faced with uncertainties about competitors' ability and willingness to imitate, we worked with scenarios. The ultimate outcome was a new base package for EVPN, a new set of features and a new price for both the base package and the feature improvements.

Next we show some outcomes of the process. These are of course disguised illustrations, but they give you an idea of the wealth of information that can be obtained this way. They also point to the exceptionally solid margin improvement that digging deep into customers' minds can generate.

Switching behavior

IncCom's and EntCom's services were pretty similar; both IncCom and Ent-Com had a solid market reputation; and even though EntCom operated in a different geographic market, it had plenty of credible reference customers. As a consequence, one might expect that customers would switch easily. At least, that is what most salespeople thought when they were interviewed in Step 1 of the project. From the interviews held with customers in Step 2, however, it turned out that most customers would churn to the new entrant only at a price difference between 10% and 25%; while some customers were ready to switch at a 0% price difference, it was surely not the case that a 1% or 2% price difference would induce many current customers to switch (see Figure 5.3). These values were obtained using the trade-off method that we explained in detail in Chapters 3 and 4.

Segmentation

IncCom had segmented the market based upon company size (small, medium, large and corporate customers). While size matters from a sales segmentation perspective (there is just no point in allocating plenty of resources to very small customers), it is less appropriate a dimension from a marketing segmentation perspective. In this very case, customers within any given segment did not reveal anything close to similarity of preferences,

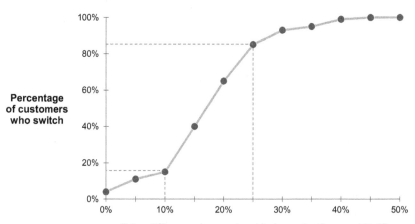

FIGURE 5.3 Switching behavior as a function of price difference

for instance when it came to the value that they attached to the service features or changes in the service levels.

For instance, a large bank and a large library really have very little in common, and therefore should not be considered to belong to the same segment. When the private network is not functioning at a bank, whether large or small, it is a total disaster, meaning that all banks put a high value on mean-time-to-repair. But libraries, whether large or small, value mean-time-to-repair much less: to be a little facetious, when the network is temporarily down, patrons may just want to read a book.

As the same observation applied to other features, it was blatantly clear that large libraries had a lot less in common with large banks than they had in common with small libraries. Similarly, large banks had a lot more in common with small banks than they had in common with large libraries. Based upon that information, the segmentation of customers into groups with similar preferences was redefined, leading to three segments: Quality Buyers, Price Buyers and Value-for-Money Buyers. While the sample size was admittedly small, it turned out that these patterns were quite closely linked to the customer's industry and some other objective factors such as the number of locations to be connected.

While we have the information on the willingness-to-pay of any customer in the sample, it is instructive to see a summary thereof for two of the three segments (see Table 5.8 for the Quality Buyers segment, and Table 5.9 for the Price Buyers segment; for confidentiality reasons, the definition of the services has been edited and the actual figures have been modified). The tables show a list of differentiating features, along with the proposed improvements in service level. When a service level improvement is marked by an X, it means that at least 30% of customers were willing to pay more than $30 (fourth column) or more than $50 (fifth column) for that improvement. Again, the values were obtained not through direct questions about willingness-to-pay but through trade-off questions, as explained in Chapter 3.

While the content of the table does not have to be taken at face value (as the definitions and figures have been disguised), and while we are not showing the unit variable costs, the pattern is close to what we observed in reality. First, for a given segment, some features are valued significantly more than they cost, while others are not. Thus, some are value creating differentiators, while others are value destroying differentiators. Second, customers differ

TABLE 5.8 Willingness-to-pay of "Quality Buyers" segment for feature improvements

Feature	Service level improvement		Feature price	
	From	*To*	*$30*	*$50*
Mean-time-to-repair	4 hours	2 hours	X	
	8 hours	4 hours	X	X
	Best effort	8 hours	X	
Service window	Store hours	24 × 7		
	Office hours	Store hours		
Overbooking	1:4	1:1	X	X
	1:10	1:4		
	1:20	1:10		
	Best effort	1:20	X	X
Security level	Level 1	Level 2	X	
Bandwidth	Current	Double		
Router management	Reactive	Proactive	X	X
	None	Reactive		
Feature 7	99.95%	99.98%	X	X
	99.90%	99.95%	X	
	< 99.90%	99.90%	X	
Feature 8	No	Yes	X	X
Feature 9	No	Yes		

Note: X = At least 30% of customers is prepared to pay more than the indicated price for the service level improvement

significantly in their valuation of the features. In particular, price buyers have a high willingness-to-pay for only a very few features. Knowing these exceptions is key to developing a defense strategy. In fact, it is the information itself as to what these few value creating differentiators are that is the source of competitive advantage, not the mere fact of being able to offer them.

These findings in general confirm the logic that we explained before: differentiation per se is not the answer to low-priced entrants, and may even make things worse when the differentiation is value destroying.

Bundles of optional features

A common question is whether a feature should be added to the base package or whether it should be offered as an option, possibly in a bundle with

TABLE 5.9 Willingness-to-pay of "Price Buyers" segment for feature improvements

Feature	Service level improvement		Feature price	
	From	To	$30	$50
Mean-time-to-repair	4 hours	2 hours		
	8 hours	4 hours		
	Best effort	8 hours		
Service window	Store hours	24 × 7		
	Office hours	Store hours		
Overbooking	1:4	1:1		
	1:10	1:4		
	1:20	1:10		
	Best effort	1:20		
Security level	Level 1	Level 2	X	
Bandwidth	Current	Double		
Router management	Reactive	Proactive		
	None	Reactive		
Feature 7	99.95%	99.98%	X	
	99.90%	99.95%	X	
	< 99.90%	99.90%	X	
Feature 8	No	Yes	X	
Feature 9	No	Yes		

Note: X = At least 30% of customers is prepared to pay more than the indicated price for the service level improvement

other features. When a differentiating feature costs more than it is valued by some customers, it is important not to add it to the base package, that is, not to create a new augmented base package. For instance, moving from best effort to 8 hours for mean-time-to-repair is apparently not valued much by most price buyers, and less so than its marginal cost. Hence, it is better to offer that feature separately (at a charge, in line with the logic explained in the two-customers case example earlier in this chapter) than to include it in the base package with an accordingly adjusted price.

Given the overall diversity in the willingness-to-pay for the differentiating and not so differentiating features, only some features would have to be added to the base package. These are the features that most customers value more than they cost. Others should be offered as options, and prices will be set based upon the method explained in Chapters 3 and 4.

If it turns out that pretty much all customers of a segment (i.e., many more than the "at least 30%" shown in Tables 5.8 and 5.9) value a combination of features (say, proactive router management, availability of a utilization report, and 1:1 overbooking) by more than its marginal cost, it makes sense to create a bundle to simplify the life of the customers in that segment. This practice is similar to the practice of automakers who offer optional business packages to the business customer segment, so that these customers do not have to select option by option; the automakers assume that most business customers value all the features in that business package.

Price levels that maximize margin

In the industrial pump case that we used in Chapter 4 to discuss new market entry, we did not program an optimization model to determine the offering and price to be used at launch. We could have done so but chose not to, as the programming effort was quite severe for what was ultimately a one-time decision: one enters a specific market only once, and optimizes the choices at that time, given the preferences of customers, competitors' likely reactions and unit costs. Rather than making a program, we actually looked at six distinct possible pumps (with different combinations of features and price levels) and selected the one that generated the highest margins for the entrant. We did so simply by forecasting how many customers would buy each of the pumps at what price, and by computing the ensuing revenues and margins. We then adjusted the preferred offering (the "best pump so far") and simulated whether margins could be increased by making small changes to this pump.

In the private networks case in this chapter, however, we actually did optimize the new offering, using an optimization program, thereby also assuming that the sample of interviewed customers was representative. Table 5.10 gives a sense of what this looked like. It shows a snapshot of the distribution of willingness-to-pay (WTP) for a number of customers from the sample and for just one feature (we only show 17 out of 50 customers and have fiddled around with the actual figures for confidentiality reasons, but the pattern is about the same as that of the true raw data).

The chosen feature is "service window," which refers to the time slots during which repair to private networks can be performed. This feature has three possible service levels: office hours, store hours (which are longer

TABLE 5.10 Calculation of margins for a given combination of price levels

Cus-tomer	Willingness-to-pay			Customer deal value				Customer choice (Y = Yes)			Contribution margin			
	Office	Store	24/7	Office	Store	24/7	Max	Office	Store	24/7	Office	Store	24/7	Max
1	0	33	37	0	-3	-35	0	Y			0	0	0	0
2	0	16	32	0	-20	-40	0	Y			0	0	0	0
3	0	54	56	0	18	-16	18		Y		0	17	0	17
4	0	30	40	0	-6	-32	0	Y			0	0	0	0
5	0	5	5	0	-31	-67	0	Y			0	0	0	0
6	0	18	44	0	-18	-28	0	Y			0	0	0	0
7	0	17	17	0	-19	-55	0	Y			0	0	0	0
8	0	12	12	0	-24	-60	0	Y			0	0	0	0
9	0	36	37	0	0	-35	0	Y	Y		0	17	0	17
10	0	56	75	0	20	3	20		Y		0	17	0	17
11	0	18	73	0	-18	1	1			Y	0	0	50	50
12	0	10	20	0	-26	-52	0	Y			0	0	0	0
13	0	35	36	0	-1	-36	0	Y			0	0	0	0
14	0	47	50	0	11	-22	11		Y		0	17	0	17
15	0	12	15	0	-24	-57	0	Y			0	0	0	0
16	0	34	40	0	-2	-32	0	Y			0	0	0	0
17	0	25	37	0	-11	-35	0	Y			0	0	0	0

than office hours) and 24-hours-7-days-a-week (24/7). Using the trade-off method of Chapter 3, we have an estimate of each customer's WTP for increasing the service window from office hours to store hours and from store hours to 24/7.

Since office hours is in the base package, we set its WTP value equal to zero. What we did measure, then, was customers' increase in WTP for store hours relative to office hours, and their increase in WTP for 24/7 relative to store hours (and hence, as a result, relative to office hours). Taking, for example, customer #3, it turns out that he is willing to pay $54 more per month for increasing the service window from office hours to store hours. He also has a WTP of $56 for 24/7 service over service during office hours only, and, as a result, his WTP for 24/7 is just $2 more than that for store hours. That is so because this specific customer is closed outside of store hours, and thus puts little value on the opportunity to have maintenance work done on his premises when the office is closed. Again, other customers have *different* preferences, and we argued from the very beginning that these differences, pardon the pun, make all the difference.

Table 5.10 shows the results of the contribution margin calculation if the price for the service window feature is set at $0 when "office hours," $36 when "store hours" and $72 when "24/7," assuming a unit variable cost of $0, $19 and $22, respectively.

Let us see how we can optimize margins, first in the simple case without a real entry threat, and then in the complex case with a real entry threat.

Simple case: no real entry threat

In the simple case, there is no real entry threat, that is, we assume that at current prices all customers stay with the incumbent and buy the base package. In this no-churn case, optimizing prices for the store hours and 24/7 service levels boils down to maximizing profits. This is easier said than done. We first define the range within which the price can be optimized. For a given feature, that range goes from its unit variable cost (minimum level) to the maximum WTP across customers (maximum level). The reason is that it does not make sense to price either below the unit variable cost or above the amount that any customer would want to pay. That range is from $19 to $56 for store hours, and from $22 to $75 for 24/7. We then simulate, for every combination of prices within the range, which of the three feature levels each customer would select to maximize his deal value. For instance, if the price of store hours is $36 and the price of 24/7 is $72, customer #3 would select store hours, as his deal value is $54 – $36 = $18, which is larger than the deal value of staying with the office hours of the base package (zero), and surely more than the deal value of selecting 24/7 (–$16).

How much contribution margin does the company make from customer #3's selection? The price of the selected feature ($36) minus its unit variable cost ($19) equals $17, which can be seen in the last column. The total contribution margin made at this combination of prices ($36 for office hours, $72 for 24/7) is the sum of the margins made across all 17 customers, given that they are all maximizing their deal value. At these prices, total contribution margin is (4 × $17) + (1 × $50) = $118.

The program then tests all possible combinations of prices (that is, (56 – 19) × (75 – 22) = 1961 combinations, assuming that price increments are equal to $1), and returns the combination that gives the company the highest total contribution margin.

Whether store hours and 24/7 are offered would depend of course not only on the contribution margin from these services, but also on other factors such as their development costs. If development costs for these services exceed the present value of the extra contribution margin generated from having extended service windows, this extended service should not be offered.

Complex case: real entry threat

The preceding exercise is insufficient when we move from the simple to the more complex case, that is, when the entry threat in fact is real. In that case, a customer's deal value (net of switching costs) of buying the base package from the new entrant could be larger than his deal value of buying it from the incumbent. And some customers would still switch at the optimal price that we derived in the simple case. Hence, the margin from the service windows that these customers would have selected without competitive alternatives will in fact not materialize for the incumbent if the customers do have competitive alternatives. That being said, optimizing prices taking competitive alternatives and switching values into consideration is not much more difficult than in the simple case. The principle remains basically the same. The same applies to the more complex case when we have to optimize many potentially differentiating features, as opposed to just one.

The net outcome of this exercise is a new optimized base package and a set of options and prices that allows some customers to get more deal value from staying with the incumbent than from moving to the entrant. In this very project, the base package itself was actually not augmented, that is, no extra features or service levels were included in the base package (see Table 5.11). As the distribution of preferences across customers was rather wide (as in the good old demand curve), it did not make sense to include things in the base offering that some customers did not want to pay for.

In fact, some features were removed from the base offering, in the same way that airlines take away from coach class passengers pretty much everything except the one thing that everyone needs: a seat. For example, the bandwidth feature was double in the original base package, in the belief that it would super-please the customer. As in reality few people valued this double bandwidth, it was removed from the base package. To put it in airline terms: we took away the extra legroom from those customers who did not

TABLE 5.11 Changes in base package, options and prices

Feature	Current offering		Optimized offering	
	Level	Price	Level	Price
Mean time to repair	Best effort	Base	Best effort	Base
	8 hours	10	8 hours	5
	4 hours	N.A.	4 hours	15
	2 hours	N.A.	2 hours	30
Service window	Office hours	Base	Office hours	Base
	Store hours	N.A.	Store hours	35
	24 × 7	N.A.	24 × 7	40
Overbooking	Best effort	Base	Best effort	Base
	1:20	20	1:20	30
	1:10	40	1:10	60
	1:4	60	1:4	70
	1:1	80	1:1	150
Security level	Level 1	Base	Level 1	Base
	Level 2	N.A.	Level 2	30
Bandwidth	Single	N.A.	Single	Base
	Double	Base	Double	N.A.
...	...	...	...	...

Note: "Base" = Feature level is included in the base package need it and did not value it; in return, we reduced the base price somewhat and made the extra legroom optional at a charge.

Customer communications

The original segmentation by customer size was replaced by a segmentation by industry. For instance, banks were allocated to the Quality Buyers segment, while libraries were allocated to the Price Buyers segment.

The purpose of the segmentation was not to create specific bundles for specific segments (e.g., a low-price bundle for the Price Buyers and a high-price bundle for the Quality Buyers), since the offering was transparent and the Quality Buyers could then buy the low-price bundle.[16] Instead we unbundled and charged for the different feature levels, based upon the distribution of willingness-to-pay (the demand curve) of all customers in the sample and upon our estimates of their switching values to their best alternatives.

We used the segmentation to assist in targeting and communicating to customers. As Price Buyers are by and large only interested in a low price, why should the salespeople visit these customers? To them, there is really nothing other than price to talk about, which is anyhow non-negotiable. It is different, however, with the Quality Buyers. From the information on their needs and, most importantly, willingness-to-pay, we know which features they value the most (see Table 5.8 again). For instance, more than 30% of customers in the Quality Buyers segment were willing to pay more than $50 to upgrade from reactive to proactive router management. Obviously, if they do not understand or are not aware of the existence of this improvement or upgrade, they will not buy it. Hence, it is a feature that the salespeople may want to explain during a call at Quality Buyers. Conversely, feature 9 may not be the first thing the salespeople want to talk about, since less than 30% of the customers in the Quality Buyers segment were willing to pay more than $30 for it.

We would like to remind you, though, that a segment is not as homogeneous as is often portrayed in marketing textbooks. After all, Table 5.8 only shows that 30% or more of customers in the sample are willing to pay $30 (or $50) for a particular upgrade in service. That means that it is quite possible that some Quality Buyers do not value the improvement from reactive to proactive router management, whereas some are not willing to pay for the protection against overbooking. The information summarized in Table 5.8 is useful in deciding which customers to target and visit, and to give an indication about what to talk about (i.e., the options that are likely to create most value for the customer). It does no more than that, given the unavoidable sub-segment heterogeneity. The only totally homogeneous segments we know of are those consisting of just one customer.

▶ THE CEMENT CASE AS AN EXAMPLE OF A "FIGHTING BRAND" DEFENSE STRATEGY

In the preceding telecommunications case, we showed how to respond to a low-priced entrant by optimizing the definition and the prices of the base package and the possibly differentiating features that are added as options. One other much-heralded defense strategy is the development of a fighting brand, sometimes also called a fighter brand or flanking brand.

All respectable marketing textbooks have some chapter on fighting brands. They cover plenty of examples, primarily in B2C industries, such as Eurowings, the low-price carrier of Lufthansa; Celeron, the fighting brand of Intel in microprocessors; Renault's Romanian-built Dacia, which launched the Sandero hatchback at £6000 in the UK in 2015, at that time the UK's cheapest new car;[17] or P&G's Cheer brand in laundry detergents. These same textbooks naturally highlight the benefits of launching a fighting brand, which usually includes some form of regaining sales from the low-priced entrants; dutifully, the textbooks also point to various drawbacks, of which cannibalization of the flagship brand is said to be the most important one.[18]

When we got our first fighting brand project, and our client asked us to develop a concept for the fighting brand along the four-Ps-of-Marketing lines, we were fortunate enough to be relatively senior so that we could ask a newly hired consultant to tell us what she learned in business school about fighting brands. We needed to know how to decide whether the fighting brand should have the same product or service features as the low-priced entrant's brand; or whether it should be slightly better in order to attract more customers or worse, to reduce cannibalization? And what about the price: as low as the entrant's, or lower, or a tad higher? And what about the critical issue of branding: should the association with the umbrella brand be clear, as is the case with Eurowings, the low-cost airline of the Lufthansa Group; or should it not, as with P&G's Cheer (which could as well have been labeled Budget Tide, or something along those lines, to make the link with the flagship brand) or 3M's Highland self-stick notes. Still other questions include: should we use a different salesforce from the one that sells the flagship brand? Should we use a salesforce at all? And what about the channel: do we sell the product through the same channel or through a different one?

Our young and eager consultant came back, you guessed it, with examples and anecdotal evidence about successes and failures. But nowhere could she find an operational framework for decision-making. As a consequence, we developed one ourselves for our first of several fighting brand cases.

The case took place at a large stock-listed cement company that we call Cemco. It had autonomous divisions in Landia and Neighbonia, one of Landia's neighboring countries. We were asked by Cemco Neighbonia to help the company regain some of its lost margins as the company was bleeding. The focus was on bags of cement (typically between 25 kg and 50 kg) that are sold to wholesalers, who in turn sell those bags to small construction companies and sometimes to DIY enthusiasts, if they are handy enough. Large construction companies or companies that manufacture ready-mix concrete typically buy cement directly from the cement company, and do so in bulk, not in bags. Bulk cement is obviously less expensive than bag cement.

From a history of stability to the eruption of a price war

One would expect the market structure in Landia and Neighbonia to lead to stable and high cement prices due to a combination of three factors.

First, the product is a commodity: cement is cement, with different grades (CEM I, II and III and the like; we spare you the details). In the absence of switching costs, this means that a small price difference would make buyers of branded cement switch quickly from one supplier to another. That switching value depends on the segment of buyers, with wholesalers having roughly a 1% switching value, and, for instance, ready-mix concrete companies having on average a switching value of about 3%. Second, the market is concentrated, definitely at the local level, as it is uneconomical to transport cement for more than 200 miles. Third, market demand is not driven by market price but by non-price factors such as construction activity. That is, if for a given level of construction activity, the average price of cement were to drop, total market demand would not increase significantly. Just imagine: would you buy or offer anyone a bag of cement, should bagged cement prices drop by 50%?

In view of these three factors, lowering prices by a few percentage points will surely lead to a significant gain in market share. Due to the low switching values, customers who operate in the same region as the company lowering prices will switch in droves, at the expense of their current supplier. The supplier that loses customers can of course try to differentiate, but there are very few service dimensions in this industry that will allow anyone to raise the switching values by more than they cost. The best response is thus to match the price cut immediately and minimize the churn of customers to the aggressive competitor.

This is obviously not a win-win, since the size of the market does not grow with the price cut, given the third market characteristic mentioned previously. Both players lose. One would expect all players to understand this, and hence not to initiate price cuts. That had been the case for a very long time. In fact, prices were high at about €80/ton at the time of the case, as companies were smart enough not to cut prices, understanding the disastrous implication for all. Price-fixing agreements that have been wielded for a long time in the cement industry and for which companies have been fined heavily, are not even necessary to keep prices high.[19] It simply requires to think through one's competitors' minds, and keeping their incentives and likely behavior or responses in mind.

Often companies even consciously decided not to enter particular territories, though not through explicit market sharing agreements as in the past, as these are totally illegal.[20,21] It happened by communicating to customers close to the competitor's plant that the company would not serve them, which is in no way illegal.[22] That the competitor as a result decides not to serve customers around the plant of the other company is just intelligent behavior. Intelligent behavior requires not to attack competitors' customers, hoping (but not communicating in one way or another) that competitors will not attack your customers either. Intelligent behavior is as yet not illegal, but for all you know, there comes a time. What is illegal is to engage in market splitting (territory A is mine, territory B is yours) through explicit or tacit communication (press announcements and the like) with the aim of splitting the market. But being intelligent does not fall under tacit communication.

Apparently, cement companies had been intelligent for a long time: markets and market shares were stable, and prices were high, both in Landia and in Neighbonia. But then, something went wrong, so to speak, when one player in Landia's capital region, MegaMix (disguised name), lowered prices, initially by €3. The move was initially not even taken seriously, as it had never been experienced before. The ball really started rolling when competitors reacted and lowered prices by €5, in an attempt to regain lost customers. In response, MegaMix kept on decreasing prices in steps of €5. Twelve months later, prices in some regions were 50% below what they had been a year earlier. Meanwhile, the downturn spiral continued, down to the level where no company made any money. The price war had spread from the capital region to the whole of Landia. Market shares were roughly unchanged, while sales value had dropped by over one-third in a year's time.[23] Notice that MegaMix only intended to increase its market share in the capital region, but that prices dropped throughout Landia. This is because of the domino effect, with waves of price cuts stretching outwards.

We can only speculate why that price war happened. In any case, the net effect was that prices for bulk cement in Landia were rock-bottom (around €25–€30/ton), whereas prices for cement in Neighbonia stayed high (around €70–€80/ton for bulk, and €85–€95/ton for bag cement). Despite the vastly different price levels between Landia and Neighbonia, MegaMix's nearest and most important competitor in Landia, which we call Landia Cement (LC), did not attack Cemco's customers in Neighbonia. While LC's prices had equally plummeted, and LC was sufficiently close to the border with Neighbonia, it effectively understood that attacking Cemco's wholesalers in Neighbonia might make matters even worse. Both LC and Cemco were intelligent players and did not enter into each other's territory, however tempting it may have been for LC at that time.

However, some of LC's customers in Landia, namely the traders, were not as nicely behaved as LC. They sent faxes and emails to Cemco Neighbonia's customers, asking if they wanted cement (actually Portland cement 42.5) at a significantly lower price than Cemco Neighbonia's. When the Cemco Neighbonia customers agreed to buy, traders simply bought that cement in bulk, packaged it in unappealing low-quality bags, and ordered a transportation company to deliver the cement to the Cemco Neighbonia customer "whenever the truck got there." They offered no services at all: cement could only be ordered via fax or email, and there were no specific delivery dates, no supply reliability, no weekend deliveries, no rush orders, and no special logistical services. Bag quality was equally low: there was only one bag size, namely 25 kg, and when the bags, which were put on disposable pallets, tore apart at delivery, it was the customer's problem – the Landian traders would not replace them. This was in sharp contrast with Cemco, which pampered its customers: it accepted orders not only by fax or email but also over the phone or directly through the sales representative; it offered weekend deliveries and rush orders; and, of course, it replaced torn bags, even though this did not happen so frequently, given their higher quality.

The traders' customers who got the faxes played this off against the Cemco Neighbonia sales representatives, mentioning the traders' offer and asking for a price concession to stay with Cemco. If Cemco did not cut (not necessarily match) prices, they threatened to switch part or all of their bag volume from Cemco to the traders. Cemco's policy so far had been to keep prices pretty much unchanged (to be precise, it dropped its average price after rebates by only 1.1%). Unsurprisingly, the net effect was disastrous: in just one year, Cemco Neighbonia had lost 24.7% (!) of its volume. In such a stressful and emotional environment, the position of Cemco Neighbonia's general manager was at stake.

Cemco Neighbonia did not quite know how to deal with this new type of competitor, which is quite different from retaliating against an established player like LC. Regarding the latter, we had in fact set up a pricing model for Cemco that allowed, with one click of a button appropriately labeled "retaliation," to search a database of LC customers. As soon as LC attacked one of Cemco Neighbonia's customers, the model revealed LC's customers that were of approximately equal size to the Cemco Neighbonia customer being attacked. Thus, if needed, Cemco Neighbonia could retaliate immediately and proportionally. Cemco Neighbonia of course never initiated an attack on LC's customers in Landia, whether Landia's cement market was at war or at peace.

Things were totally different with traders. Traders are like guerilla fighters who come down from the mountain to attack the regular troops, and then hide back into the mountains where they cannot be found and hence retaliated against. So, when the traders attacked Cemco's wholesalers in Neighbonia, Cemco had no way to retaliate, as these traders in fact had no single customer in Landia: buyers in Landia obviously preferred to buy directly from a cement company such as MegaMix or LC.

So, if retaliation is not possible, what should Cemco Neighbonia do? Interviews with Cemco Neighbonia managers revealed that the proposed responses could be clustered into four categories, which can be simplified as follows: (1) do nothing, (2) respond with price cuts, (3) launch a fighting brand under the Cemco umbrella brand name, such as Cemco Budget, and (4) launch a fighting brand without reference to the Cemco umbrella brand name, such as Budget Cement. We will not elaborate on the first two options. While they are quite interesting in their own right, they would lead us too much astray from the analytical issues involved in launching a fighting brand in a B2B setting. In what follows, we will solely focus on the question of launching a fighting brand and omit any details that are not necessary to follow the analytical arguments.

The objectives and risks of launching a fighting brand

To understand what was needed to launch a fighting brand in this peculiar B2B setting, we first had to agree on Cemco Neighbonia's objective with the fighting brand. That objective was neither to regain market share nor to eliminate the Landian traders, for instance.

Regaining market share is simply an unreasonable objective, at least for a stock-listed company, as it may well mean sacrificing profits. For sure, dropping the price to Cemco's unit cost level would do the market share job, as the Landian traders, at the end of the day, are low priced but high cost, despite their lower bagging and service costs. That is because the traders buy bulk cement at LC's price, which is above LC's unit variable cost, and because Cemco's unit variable cost is similar to LC's unit variable cost in this mature industry. Furthermore, the traders have higher transportation costs than Cemco, as Cemco is in closer proximity of the targeted customers.

Likewise, eliminating competitors cannot be an objective in its own right, as that may well be at the expense of profits and, at times, even illegal. Management eventually agreed with these arguments. A consensus was reached that the objective of launching the fighting brand was to regain share *profitably* from the traders, while minimally affecting profits from selling the flagship brand. This, one can say, is a reasonable, well-defined objective.

Launching a fighting brand also carries some risks. Many would mention the cannibalization of the flagship brand's sales (while meaning profits, really). At the end of the day, however, cannibalization in the absolute sense might be less pronounced than one would think: at the time of the launch, Cemco had suffered a lot of damage, in that many price-sensitive customers had left Cemco Neighbonia already. Thus, it would be better to think about the incremental cannibalization beyond the damage done by the low-priced entrants.

There were some other threats to be aware of, such as the possible responses by other established players, the deterioration of Cemco's company image, or the risk that the demand for the fighting brand emerged in areas not affected by the Landian traders. As incremental cannibalization turned out to be the main threat, we will focus on that issue in the remainder of this section.

The defense options

In order to simplify the discussion about the defense options, we assume that there are two types of customers buying the bags of cement: price-sensitive and price-insensitive customers. In the past, without the Landian traders, the wholesalers had no choice, and bought all their needed volume from Cemco. But as soon as the Landian traders appeared, some of the price-sensitive wholesalers left Cemco for one of these traders, or at least got one of them as a second supplier. This is shown as the today situation in Figure 5.4. That figure also compares the first two options (i.e., do nothing; respond with price cuts) with the option of launching a fighting brand (with or without reference to the Cemco umbrella brand name).

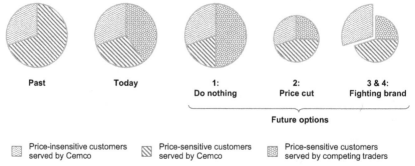

Price-insensitive customers served by Cemco

Price-sensitive customers served by Cemco

Price-sensitive customers served by competing traders

FIGURE 5.4 Comparison of revenues in various defense options

Option 1 (do nothing) is likely to induce even more price-sensitive customers to switch from Cemco to the Landian traders, as Cemco is not offering them an incentive to stay. The advantage is, of course, that the value
extracted from the customers that stay, and in particular the price-insensitive customers, is unaffected.

The advantage of option 2 (price cut) is that some of the customers are
likely to return to Cemco, as it was precisely the low price that made the
Landian traders attractive to them. The disadvantage is that the revenues
and margins extracted from the price-insensitive customers will shrink, as
illustrated by the smaller size of the total pie.

With the launch of the fighting brand (options 3 and 4), it is hoped that the
best of both worlds is achieved. It has the benefits of the "price cut" option,
in that a fighting brand by Cemco will make the alternative offered by the
competing traders less attractive, inducing a larger number of price-sensitive
customers to stay or to return to Cemco. It also has the benefits of the "do
nothing" option: if price-sensitive customers switch to Cemco's fighting
brand, and price-insensitive customers do not switch, total revenues from
the flagship brand are not affected. This is illustrated by the last pie where,
ideally, the size of the slice of the price-insensitive customers is the same as
in the "do nothing" option and the two slices of the price-sensitive customers
have the same (smaller) size and split as in the "price cut" option.

In conclusion, launching a fighting brand appears to be a sensible option.
But we still need to answer various questions about the differentiation and
price of the fighting brand, the salesforce to deploy, the geographical area to
serve, and the specific brand to use.

Differentiating the fighting brand

The most difficult question is about the differentiation of the fighting brand
from the Landian traders' product on the one hand, and from Cemco's flagship brand on the other hand. In this case, there are two dimensions to differentiation that cater to the needs of the end customer (i.e., the wholesaler's
customer) and/or the direct customer (i.e., the wholesaler).

The first dimension relates to the product itself. Product differentiators are
primarily the features that influence the end customers who buy the bag of

cement. There are very few product differentiators, though, as the cement inside the bag is the same: remember that the Landian traders bought Portland Cement from LC, which is exactly the same as Cemco's Portland Cement. One possible differentiator could be the type of quality label used (in addition to the required CE mark). Another possible differentiator could be bag quality, because it affects the extent to which cement absorbs moisture when stored. In addition, it is also possible to influence the perceived quality of the cement through branding. More specifically, Cemco could use an umbrella Cemco brand name such as Cemco Budget. To the suspicious end customer this would increase the perceived quality compared to a neutral brand name (Budget Cement, for instance, which would have no quality connotation).

The second differentiation dimension relates to the service associated to the product. Service differentiators primarily play to the needs of the wholesalers. Significant differentiation from the Landian traders was possible on a range of services related to logistics and ordering, as mentioned before. For example, just allowing the wholesaler to order over the phone was already a differentiator.

But what is the actual real goal of differentiation here? The goal of differentiation is not to have zero or minimal cannibalization of the flagship brand. In the ideal world, one should differentiate the Cemco fighting brand from the Landian traders' brand as long as the incremental margin gain from the differentiation (as a result of stealing share back from the Landian traders) exceeds the incremental margin loss from the cannibalization (as a result of suspicious, price-insensitive Cemco customers switching from the Cemco flagship brand to the Cemco fighting brand).

This information is, however, very difficult to figure out empirically, especially when the company is bleeding and has to act quickly, as in the decision to launch a fighting brand. The answer to the differentiation question does not only depend on the marginal impact on price-sensitive and price-insensitive customers but also on the number of customers in those two categories. We did not have those figures, nor the money and time to gather the information in detail. In addition, we were supposed to think about both product differentiation and branding (affecting the end customer and, indirectly, the wholesaler), service differentiation (affecting primarily and often uniquely the wholesaler) and pricing.

Given those circumstances, we adopted the following reasoning. Both price-sensitive and price-insensitive customers have a number of *minimum require-ments*, as already defined in Chapter 3, about the product (or service), and value a number of improvements beyond the minimum requirements. How-ever, the minimum requirements for the price-insensitive customers are higher than those of the price-sensitive customers. Understanding these differences is totally critical because it is very difficult to figure out how to differentiate the fighting brand product from the Landian traders' product in the ideal way, that is, to identify features that differentiate the fighting brand and hence make it more attractive to the current price-sensitive buyers of the Landian traders' cement, yet that do not make the fighting brand more attractive to the price-insensitive customers (who currently tend to buy the Cemco cement). In fact, any differentiation tends to be valued more by the price-insensitive customer than by the price-sensitive customer, who knows that "cement is cement" and goes for the lowest price. The few differentiators of the fighting brand that exist will make that brand marginally more attractive than the Landian traders' cement to the price-sensitive customer, but unfortunately not by much, pre-cisely because she is price-sensitive and does not value differentiation much, if at all. That is why the marginal effect of differentiation on the price-sensitive customer is likely to be smaller than its effect on the price-insensitive customer.

Taking the preceding into account, and considering that margins on Cemco's flagship brand were much higher than they could be on its fighting brand, Cemco decided not to differentiate its fighting brand from the Landian trad-ers' product at all. Thus, the exercise is one of resisting the temptation to differentiate, as differentiation triggers incremental cannibalization. What-ever worked toward the price-sensitive customers who had defected to the Landian traders would work even more forcefully toward the price-insensi-tive customers who had stayed with Cemco's flagship brand.

The takeaway from this reasoning is important. To launch a fighting brand that differentiates relative to the low-priced competitor, one should be look-ing for product features and services that are valued by the price-sensitive customers but that are not valued by the customers of the flagship brand, that is, the more price-insensitive customers. For simple products like cement, one is unlikely to find many such differentiators, if any at all.

For more complicated products, this is not necessarily the case, as there are more dimensions to play with. Admittedly, identifying these differentiators requires an in-depth understanding of differences in customer preferences. For instance, many price-sensitive leisure travelers may value nightly entertainment in their budget hotel, whereas it may not create any value, and possibly even negative value, for the business traveler who prefers a quiet place. If this hypothesis is validated through customer interviews, established branded chains could add this type of entertainment to their fighting brands. By doing so, they would attract customers from low-priced entrants that target the leisure traveler, yet without inducing their business travelers to switch.

Funeral services are another business where one can play with several dimensions. Price-insensitive customers (that is, the deceased person and/ or his family) tend to value the memorialization and prestige that come from a personalized white-glove service. Conversely, price-sensitive customers are looking for a no-frills solution (e.g., a less expensive cremation) away from a funeral home. But they also may value the possibility of buying, evidently when they are still in this world, a so-called preneed contract, that is, an insurance policy that guarantees the availability of sufficient funds for covering the cost of their funeral. Such a preneed contract may be a differentiating feature that price-insensitive customers look down on ("Rest assured, by the time I pass away, there will still be enough money left in my bank account"), but that an established funeral service provider may use with its fighting brand to keep price-sensitive customers away from no-frills entrants.

Removing a minimum requirement from the flagship brand

As we explained earlier, the differentiation route has serious limitations when applied to a fighting brand, especially when the product or service is rather simple. In our experience, a more fruitful and prevalent route is to look into the minimum requirements of both price-insensitive and price-sensitive customers.

Remember from Chapter 3 that a customer will not buy a product if it does not satisfy a minimum requirement, whatever differentiating bells and whistles the product may otherwise have. Hence, if one can identify minimum requirements that most price-insensitive customers have but that are not minimum requirements for price-sensitive customers, one has a solid basis for positioning the fighting brand. It then suffices to remove that minimum requirement from the fighting brand, as those customers buying the flagship brand will then certainly not switch to the fighting brand. At the same time, one can then also differentiate the fighting brand without triggering the dreaded cannibalization, as explained in the previous section. Whether it is worth it depends of course on the cost of such differentiation relative to its benefits. But at least, in this case, it won't trigger switching by the price-insensitive customers.

The only remaining issue, then, is to find out what those minimum requirements are and what, if anything, differentiates the fighting brand most from the entrant's brand. Ideally, this is done by means of trade-off interviews with a representative sample of customers, as explained in Chapter 3. In practice, it could be that the decision has to be made quickly and that it is just not feasible to do such trade-off interviews. In that case, it is necessary to gather the estimates indirectly, for instance from lead customers, salespeople, technical sales staff or marketing.

As its sales were down by nearly 25%, Cemco indeed did not want to spend more time and resources on extensive customer interviews. Cemco decided to take the shortcut and dig into the minimum requirements of end customers first. The starting point was a simple observation: while the volume of Cemco's flagship brand had dwindled significantly, 75% of the flagship brand volume was still sold at high prices. Why did so many end customers not switch to the Landian traders' product? In all (internal) likelihood, it was because of the absence of any known brand on the Landian traders' bag. *Some* end customers are suspicious of using an unknown brand of cement, whereas a known brand is likely to give them the assurance that they can use the product safely for their construction projects and that their walls won't fall apart, so to speak. In other words, the minimum requirement for the price-insensitive end customers was the presence of Cemco's brand on the bags.

The agreement on this issue was invaluable information for the launch of the fighting brand. Cemco had to remove its umbrella brand from its fighting brand, that is, the fighting brand would not be called Cemco Budget but Budget Cement (a disguised name, obviously). Once this was done, it was in fact no longer necessary to differentiate the Cemco fighting brand, provided direct customers (that is, the wholesalers) preferred the Cemco product over that of the Landian traders' cement for other reasons that proved to be of a differentiating nature. In this case, it was the better reputation of Cemco over the Landian traders (more on this in the following service discussion). With this strategy, it was pretty much guaranteed that the original objective would be achieved: take market share back from the Landian traders profitably (as long as the differentiator does not cost too much, which was the case, as the reputation came from Cemco's actual standard operating practices), while minimizing the effect on the flagship brand (as long as the minimum requirement of the buyers of the flagship brand is removed from the fighting brand).[24]

The identification of the minimum requirements for the buyers of the flagship brand is easier when the products are more complicated. For instance, in a case related to pacemakers, the buyers of the flagship product wanted the best possible product, that is, a product with all the gauges required to give the physician and hence the patient the right information about the patient's heart condition; for them, a pacemaker is not just an electromechanical device that boosts the heart to beating at the right rate. So, the fighting brand product was made by removing some of the more sophisticated functions from the high-end pacemaker, which minimized the risk of cannibalization. Again, this was quite counterintuitive, as removing these functions was costlier than leaving them in. But it guaranteed that the more worried and more price-insensitive buyers would not switch to the fighting brand. Obviously, the decision to remove important gauges raised some ethical issues.

Still another case related to the launch of a fighting brand in speed camera alert systems. Such a system allows drivers to signal the existence of fixed and, much more importantly, mobile police radars. The minimum requirement of the high-end segment (i.e., users who drive more than 30,000 miles a year) was that all traffic information was available on their device: not only the radar warning signal, but also traffic hazards, speed limits on the roads, and the optimized journey as a function of all conditions that can affect it.[25] Entry-level users did not have all of this as a minimum requirement. As a consequence, it was decided to remove the minimum requirement of the high-end users from the new fighting brand device, and to differentiate it from the new entrant's device so as to make users switch back (or stay, whatever the case may be) without cannibalizing profitable sales to the high-end segment.

The preceding examples clearly demonstrate the value of an analytical approach when launching a fighting brand. It is much more effective than having endless discussions about hollow statements such as "creating a superior solution while minimizing the impact on the flagship product" or the even more frequently heard "capitalizing on the value of the brand." The analytical approach focuses on what is critical to make the right decision:

▶ Identify the minimum requirements of the customers of the flagship product that are not minimum requirements of the price-sensitive customers.

▶ Define the fighting brand product by removing at least one of these minimum requirements, and identify differentiating elements over the new entrant's offerings that are valued by the customers at risk, i.e. by the price-sensitive customers.

▶ Should the minimum requirements of the customers of the flagship product coincide with or be a subset of those of the price-sensitive customers, then launching a fighting brand may be damaging in terms of cannibalization, unless differentiating features can be found that are valued by the price-sensitive customers but are not or negatively valued by the buyers of the flagship product.

That is the core of the analysis. Ideally, it is done by using customer data; and if that is not possible, by using a priori guesstimates thereof. But again, and this is the guideline and common theme in this book: in Operational Strategy, it is critical to know what to look for, based upon a sensible model of customer behavior. In such a model, customers have minimum requirements as well as features that they value above those minimum requirements; and they look for the best deal relative to their best alternative. Once we agree on this model, we know what to look for to decide whether or not to launch a fighting brand, and if so, how. The data to look for can be gathered in a quick-and-dirty way, or in a more elaborate manner, depending on the time and resources available, and, we are sure you guessed it, on the marginal value of investing this time and resources compared to the marginal cost.

We just want to conclude by telling what eventually happened with Cemco's launch of its fighting brand. As mentioned, Cemco did not use an umbrella brand. That was easier said than done, though, because Cemco needed to create a separate legal entity, so as to avoid that the Cemco name appeared in fine print on the bag. In addition, in this very case it was not entirely necessary to differentiate the Cemco fighting brand. Cemco only needed to minimize cannibalization through the absence of the Cemco name on the bag of the fighting brand. Compared to the Landian traders' product, Cemco's fighting brand product turned out to be nothing much different: the same cement in the same dirty bag.

Other than that, Cemco had to resist the temptation to grow this low-end market: they only launched one type of bag (the same as the Landian traders), they did not have a range (they only had Portland Cement, just like the Landian traders), they made sure that the CE mark was the only quality label (just like the Landian traders), again, because doing better might give the price-insensitive customers the idea to switch from the flagship brand to the fighting brand despite the absence of a Cemco brand, and so on.

Pricing the fighting brand

The more difficult decision was actually the price Cemco should charge for its fighting brand to the wholesalers, knowing that the latter typically charge a particular margin on top. Cemco could have chosen to add differentiating features and charge a higher price. They decided against it, as the wholesalers knew that price-sensitive customers buy only based upon the very lowest price, not the second lowest price. Hence, a higher price would have led the wholesalers to switch from Cemco's product to the Landian traders'.

How about lowering the price to attract customers? Here again, remember what we said at an earlier stage in this chapter: only in exceptional circumstances does it make sense to cut prices to gain share, but surely not in this case, given Cemco's size. In addition, the lower the price of Cemco's fighting brand, the more attractive this product would be relative to Cemco's flagship brand, which was to be avoided. Obviously, if all buyers of the flagship product required a Cemco brand as minimum requirement, it would not have mattered. But if that is not the case, then, obviously, the marginal customers (that is, those that waffle between Cemco's flagship brand and its fighting brand) would switch to the fighting brand. And that risk was real, for two reasons. First, segments of customers are rarely as homogeneous as we had assumed in order to simplify the core ideas of the analysis. Second, the conclusion that the Cemco brand was a minimum requirement of price-insensitive customers was in fact a mere hypothesis based on a limited number of mostly internal interviews.

So, instead of lowering the price of its fighting brand, Cemco chose to match the price offered by the Landian traders. Nothing prevented the Landian traders from undercutting Cemco, but that risk was low, given the traders' high costs. Actually, to minimize the risk of undercutting by the Landian traders, Cemco could have given up some market share, so that the traders' incentive to cut prices would be eliminated too, but that turned out not to be necessary.

The end-result was that Cemco's fighting brand product was almost the same as that of the Landian traders, both in terms of content, bag, brand and price. They just made sure that their product was preferred by the direct customers (that is, the wholesalers) just enough for these to prefer Cemco's fighting brand over the cheap Landian traders' cement. That was actually relatively easy because the wholesalers of course knew that Budget Cement was a Cemco product, even if the Cemco name did not appear on the bag. It is the end customer who did not know, and that was the way to keep it. After all, the wholesalers had been dealing with Cemco for years, and Cemco could proactively inform them that they had a product that was the same as the one offered by the Landian traders.

Other fighting brand decisions: services, scope, salesforce and advertising

A similar conclusion was reached regarding Cemco's services toward the wholesalers. Here again, the very clear message was to resist the temptation to differentiate from the Landian traders. Anything that Cemco did to increase the attractiveness of buying its fighting brand would be at the expense of its flagship brand, as the total volume purchased by the market was stable. Cemco therefore opted for a no-service policy (just like the Landian traders), no weekend deliveries (just like the Landian traders), no sale on premise (Cemco copied the Landian traders here too, and told the wholesalers that the sale of the fighting brand was solely done by fax), and a longer delivery time than for the flagship product (3 to 4 days, just like the Landian traders). That no-service commitment was quite difficult, because Cemco was used to pampering its customers.

Cemco also used disposable pallets (you guessed it, just like the Landian traders). The pattern should be clear by now: Cemco's fighting brand should be attractive enough to the wholesalers to make them select Cemco rather than the Landian traders, but nothing beyond that. Cemco's goal was not to grow the low-end market but to take share away profitably from the Landian traders.

At the end of the day, the reason why wholesalers preferred Cemco's fighting brand was the intangible value of Cemco being Cemco, which at least meant supply reliability, a reputation that Cemco had established over the years. With such a supply reliability, why would a wholesaler buy from unknown traders that have been around for just a year, and may not deliver on time or, at some point, not deliver at all, or even go out of business? So, all that Cemco needed was to make the wholesalers flip. With Cemco being preferred, given its historical relationship with the wholesalers, and everything else being equal (the product and the price in this very case), it was not needed to differentiate further on services. That could only lead to damage, as it could incentivize some wholesalers to buy more of the fighting brand at the expense of the flagship brand. As a result, Cemco had to resist the temptation to add services. That mantra had to be rubbed in over and over again, by revisiting the objectives and the risks of launching the fighting brand.

Since the goal was not to grow the market for low-priced cement, Cemco should only offer its fighting brand to wholesalers that were attacked by the Landian traders. However, Cemco did inform its loyal wholesalers of its fighting brand approach, so that they did not feel abused because of their loyalty. And if they so desired, they could of course also buy the fighting brand, but Cemco definitely did not promote that option. Likewise, Cemco should not and did not launch its fighting brand in areas unaffected by the Landian traders.

Another difficult choice related to Cemco's salesforce. Usually, it is recommended to use different salesforces for the flagship brand and the fighting brand, because it is very difficult for salespeople to put on two different hats: the service commitment hat when selling the flagship brand, and the no-service hat when selling the fighting brand. Eventually Cemco chose to have just one salesforce, whose primary objective was to sell the flagship brand. Given that choice, it was of paramount importance to train this same salesforce in sequential selling. This basically means that the salesperson tries to sell the flagship brand first. At the same time, he should know to pull the Cemco fighting brand option from his other pocket should the wholesaler boast with a better offer from the Landian traders and consequently refuse to buy the flagship brand (for all or part of its needs).

Finally, do you think that Cemco spent anything on advertising the fighting brand? You guessed it: not a dime, as Cemco obviously did not want to grow the low-end market. In fact, Cemco invested more extensively in advertising the flagship brand when it launched the fighting brand: they wanted to pull customers toward buying the flagship brand as opposed to the fighting brand that they were going to launch. This was totally counterintuitive but sensible given the objective.

▶ CONCLUSIONS

Developing a defense strategy against an aggressive new entrant is Operational Strategy at its best. We have shown that seemingly convenient managerial beliefs, such as "always match prices," or generic if-then decision rules are to be avoided. Quite to the contrary, such beliefs and rules may lead to decisions that are no better than those based on flipping a coin. Think, for example, of the decision to differentiate, when doing so destroys margin; or the decision to cut price, when in fact raising the price, or not doing anything, would generate a higher margin despite the volume loss.

The only defense logic that makes sense is one that is based upon a sensible model of customer behavior and reflects the particular conditions of the situation at hand: as an incumbent, what objectives do we want to achieve, and what risks are we willing to take; how do customers prefer the new entrant's offerings over ours; what are the differences in preferences between customers; what choices and alternatives do customers have to maximize their deal value; what are customers' switching costs; and what are the entrant's incentives and likely responses to our defense actions?

The answers to those questions should be based – inasmuch as possible, both time-wise and resource-wise – on information derived from customers, either by talking to them directly, or indirectly by leaning on other sources such as the salesforce. In any case, it is better to do the right thing with imperfect information, than take a shortcut that is easy to work with but has no behavioral foundation and turns out to be dead wrong.

▶ NOTES

1 Adrian Ryans, "When Companies Underestimate Low-Cost Rivals," *McKinsey Quarterly* (June 2010).

2 See 18th Annual Global CEO Survey: A Marketplace Without Boundaries? Responding to Disruption (PWC, 2015). See https://www.pwc.com/gx/en/ceo-agenda/ceosurvey.html

3 For a product to be part of their core business, it had to meet four mandatory conditions: a well-known therapy that has been on the market for several years; with full clinical acceptance and clear indications established; a significant portion of the population has access to it through reimbursement; and competitive products are seen as good substitutes.

4 The price trend was in fact downward not only in the stents market but in pretty much all of the company's mature product markets.

5 Michael E. Porter, *Competitive Strategy* (New York: Free Press, 1980). For a more general discussion about the lack of generalizability of the effectiveness of such high-level generic strategies, see Garth Saloner, Andrea Shepard and Joel Podolny, *Strategic Management* (Hoboken, NJ: Wiley, 2001): 59–63. In this textbook, Professor Saloner, Professor at Stanford University's Graduate School of Business, and his coauthors forcefully argue that taking on an extreme position such as "differentiate" or "cost leadership" is no more a guarantee for business success than the "stuck-in-the-middle" position that for decades has been dreadfully abhorred in those same textbooks. Just think about it. What have been the most successful vehicles in, for instance, the US or Canada? The low-cost no-frills ones? The very differentiated ones? Nope, the very much stuck-in-the-middle vehicles such as the Honda Accord, Ford Taurus, Ford Explorer, Toyota Corolla and Toyota Camry, to name a few. These are not the lowest-cost vehicles and not particularly differentiating either but are appealing to a large audience.

6 Michael Treacy and Fred Wiersema, *The Discipline of Market Leaders: Choose Your Customers, Narrow Your Focus, Dominate Your Market* (Boston: Addison-Wesley, 1995).

7 Nirmalya Kumar, "Strategies to Fight Low-Cost Rivals," *Harvard Business Review* (December 2006): 104–112. We build on this example solely for illustrative purposes, not because we find this particular article more or less interesting than others.

8 Tit-for-tat is not about starting a price war. A price war is about unilaterally lowering prices in an attempt to gain share.

9 Irrationality is not that exceptional, as at some point emotion may take over or because people just think very short-term. We do recall a case in the cement industry where the general manager of a particular country wanted to respond to a new entrant that was undercutting. He said, literally: "We go below them by 20%, just to give it to them." In this very case, the best response by the general manager of the incumbent should have been to match the entrant's price cut.

10 Some people may be in favor of a "do nothing" scenario, with the argument to "preserve the value of the market." The fact is: the value of the market may be preserved, but it flows entirely to the new entrant.

11 To avoid unnecessary complexity, we assume that there are no development costs for feature A. But even if there were development costs, the argumentation would not change.

12 We assume that no competitor responds with a price cut.

13 Differences in switching costs are, incidentally, quite standard, just like it is quite standard that some people would switch to a new hitherto unknown dishwashing liquid brand for a price difference of just 10%, whereas others would need perhaps a 40% price difference, and yet others would never switch.

14 The fact that customer 2 values both features more than customer 1 is not relevant to understand the logic of the analysis and, in particular, the best response for the incumbent in this case.

15 Timothy D. Wilson, Christopher E. Houston, Kathryn M. Etling and Nancy Brekke, "A New Look at Anchoring Effects: Basic Anchoring and Its Antecedents," *Journal of Experimental Psychology: General* 125 (1996): 387–402.

16 This topic could elicit plenty of discussions that are a bit beyond the scope of this book.

17 Andy Sharman, "European Carmakers Fight Back Against Premium and Low-Cost Rivals," *Financial Times* (March 15, 2015).

18 See, for instance, Mark Ritson, "Should You Launch a Fighter Brand," *Harvard Business Review* (October 2009): 86–94.

19 See for instance the rulings in Brazil where six companies have been fined heftily for two decades of price fixing (see "UPDATE 2-Brazil Fines Cement Firms $1.4 bln for Price Rigging, Orders Asset Sales," *Reuters* [May 29, 2014]). The situation in Europe is not any better. Historically, according to the European Commission's press release IP/10/1696 of December 10, 2010,

> [t]he markets for cement and other building materials have been scrutinized both by the Commission and national competition authorities in the past. The Commission has fined a European-wide cartel in the cement sector in 1994 (see IP/94/1108). The German and Polish competition Authorities have also fined cartel agreements in the cement market in 2003 and 2009 respectively. Furthermore, in 2007 the French competition Authority fined anti-competitive practices in this market.

In that same press release the Commission announced that

> The European Commission has opened an anti-trust investigation into suspected anti-competitive practices by several manufacturers of cement and related products in Austria, Belgium, the Czech Republic, France,

Germany, Italy, Luxembourg, The Netherlands, Spain, and the UK. . . .
The Commission will investigate indications that the companies acted
to restrict trade flows in the European Economic Area (EEA), including
restrictions of imports into the EEA from countries outside the EEA, market sharing, price coordination and connected anti-competitive practices
in the markets for cement and related products.

20 See for instance http://ec.europa.eu/competition/cartels/cases/cases.html

21 Besides, the antitrust authorities in Europe are waiting in the wings to carry out
    unannounced inspections at the premises of companies that are suspected of
    market sharing, price fixing or other anti-competitive practices. See for instance
    European Commission Memo/09/409, "Antitrust: Commission Carries Out
    Unannounced Inspections in the Cement and Related Products Sector" (Sep-
    tember 23, 2009) or Memo/08/676 "Antitrust: Commission confirms unan-
    nounced inspections in the cement sector" (November 5, 2008).

22 If it were illegal, then one of the authors could sue his favorite pizza parlor in
    Cambridge, MA for refusing to deliver "across the bridge" to customers, includ-
    ing himself, in Charleston. What the pizza or cement company does is simply to
    communicate to customers that their delivery is limited to particular areas. For
    the cement company, it was indeed consciously excluding for instance customers
    close to the competitor's plant.

23 See Daniel Deneffe and Ferdinand Hoyos, "Pricing in Downturn Economies,"
    Prism (first semester 2003): 40–55.

24 There is an interesting analogy with Bayer's trademarked pain reliever Aspirin™.
    If Bayer were to launch a fighting brand called "Bayer Budget Aspirin," it is highly
    likely that they would lose pretty much all sales on their flagship product: peo-
    ple who are worried about buying the real stuff would feel comfortable buying
    "Bayer Budget Aspirin" because of its association with the trusted Bayer brand.

25 We disguise the figures and the information for confidentiality reasons.

6

Operationalizing a strategy when having zero competitive advantage

"Sustainable competitive advantage" is the core concept of traditional strategy textbooks. But the last time that we used that very expression in this book was back in Chapter 2. One of the reasons why we have not used it more frequently is that achieving sustainable competitive advantage in the real world is more the exception than the rule, as discussed in this chapter.

All along this book, our thesis (well, common sense it is) has been that a company will be successful if (1) it uses its capabilities to offer unique deal value, and if (2) that value exceeds the switching costs of a sufficiently large number of customers, and if (3) the company can realize such an offering at a reasonably low cost. If all three conditions are fulfilled, the undertaking should be profitable for the company concerned. Furthermore, if competitors cannot or do not want to emulate the deal value created by the company, nor offer a different value to reduce customers' incentives to switch, then one can say that the company has some sort of advantage. That advantage will persist as long as other companies do not annihilate the value created.

We called that an as-long-as-possible competitive advantage, but what is in a name? We are talking here about the process of identifying what customers value, based on predictions of customer choices, and of putting cost and profit figures on the efforts to bring that offering to market. If you like to call that ability competitive advantage, be our guest. But at the end of the day, what counts is whether these profit figures are acceptable to the company, given its alternatives of spending its cash.[1]

The notion of an as-long-as-possible competitive advantage makes sense if the company, through a Grand Strategy exercise (as explained in Chapter 2), has first discovered a promising strategic option, and subsequently has identified some form of customer value, by using the Operational Strategy trade-off method (as explained in Chapter 3). But what if the company cannot even identify any promising strategic options? Think, for instance, of companies making metal rods, or gelatin, or chlorine, or any other base chemical. These companies are really not excelling at anything relative to their competitors: all they know is to produce products that are no different from competitors.

And yet, these companies also feel the constant pressure to increase profits. Unfortunately, traditional strategy books rarely talk about developing a strategy to improve profits in (near) commodity markets. That is probably because such markets just do not fit the mold of sustainable competitive advantage. Because of its importance to many companies, we do not shirk that challenge. In this chapter, we will explain how to improve margins despite the absence of competitive advantage. We will first go into the notions of cost cutting and value pricing, solutions that are often put forward for commoditizing markets. We will point to some of the shortcomings of the value pricing solution (often described as the price waterfall), and then offer a more comprehensive framework for margin improvement. We will do so first for B2B markets and then for B2C markets.

▶ COST CUTTING AND VALUE PRICING

For a long time, managers of companies in commoditizing markets thought that the only way to increase margins was to cut costs to the bone. Hence, they also sought to minimize marketing expenses and, with it, the number or often the fraction of staff employed in marketing. We won't focus on cost cutting here, simply because we have little to add: it is a no-brainer that for a commodity product that is close to or exactly the same as competitors' products, and where one has no or little influence on the price of the product, production should be maximally efficient. But in fact, this statement applies to any product, even a high-end differentiated product. Doing so is just more critical if differentiation of the base product is impossible and prices are driven by supply/demand conditions.

While the need for cost efficiency has been well understood for a long time, in the first decade of the millennium managers' attention shifted to value pricing as an additional source of margin improvement. The idea of value pricing is that one should price a given component of an offering to a customer according to the value of that component to that customer. Such value pricing can apply to improvements in the performance of the product (e.g., a specific chemical grade that for instance dries faster) but that is not always feasible in view of the commoditization of the product (e.g., chlorine is chlorine is chlorine). However, even if the base product itself is a commodity and its price determined by supply/demand conditions, value can still be created and extracted through value pricing of all kinds of services on top of the base product.

The idea of value pricing is that services that have value to the customer should be priced accordingly, instead of giving these away for free, as often happens. The objective is to create a fair balance in the value that the customer receives and the value that accrues to the company as a compensation for helping out its customer (see Figure 6.1). In B2B markets, such services primarily are logistical services such as rush ordering, vendor-managed inventories, special logistics, and even things like order cancellations.

The value pricing concept applies also to many B2C industries that sell commodity products or services. Think of the airline industry, where a particular type of seat (say, a middle seat in coach class) on one particular airline

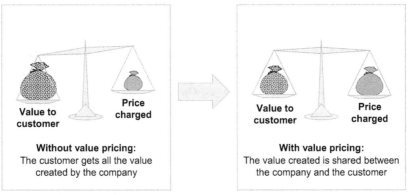

FIGURE 6.1 The notion of value pricing

is pretty much the same as the same seat on another airline. It may even be exactly the same, which obviously limits an airline's ability to price it differently from a competing airline on a competing route. However, many services or product improvements that the airlines used to give away for free can be charged for, as these have value to customers (e.g., extra legroom, baggage, earphones, and the like). Airlines initially included all these elements in the booking class (i.e., first, business, coach and many subclasses, such as Y, B, H, M, K, L, W, S, N, Q or O). Over the last two decades in particular, they have been unbundling their offering, thereby value pricing all of those ancillary services separately. The fees for these benefits appear as surcharges on top of the price for the base package.

More generally, value pricing starts by defining and pricing a standard offering (often also called the base package), which includes some quantity of the base product (e.g., a full truck of fertilizer) plus some minimum service levels (e.g., standard delivery within three business days). Everything on top of the standard offering (e.g., a request for a shorter delivery time or a rush order) is charged on top. A simplified version of a pricing structure for a company selling commodity products in B2B markets is illustrated in Figure 6.2.

In the airline industry, one can envision the base package as that infamous middle seat in coach class, plus whatever is included in it. And as we all know, that is not very much: a minimum amount of legroom, no food (barring the occasional microscopic bag of pretzels), and, in a fair number of airlines, no drinks. All the extra benefits, including priority boarding, get a charge. The value of priority boarding is not the reassurance it gives to

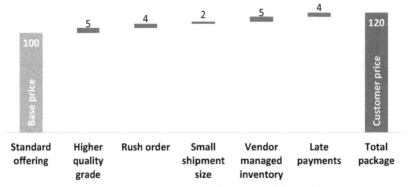

FIGURE 6.2 Typical pricing structure for a specific package

customers who apparently fear that the airline would take off without them; the value is that it allows those customers to pre-empt others for the overhead bins, stuff it up with their oversized bags, and have plenty of legroom during the flight.

The price waterfall way of explaining value pricing

When Figure 6.2 is made in reverse format, the pricing structure is called the price waterfall. A price waterfall starts with the price for the order when all extra services are included, and then rewards the customer for not making use of some of these services. In our original figure, by contrast, the structure starts with a price for the order when only the base services are included, and then adds on surcharges to customers who request extra services.

From a behavioral economics perspective, the price waterfall is the better way to communicate the idea of value pricing to customers. First of all, behavioral economics tells us that people typically exhibit loss aversion: they prefer avoiding losses to making equivalent gains. The dissatisfaction of losing $1 is larger than the satisfaction of making $1.[2] Coupled with another behavioral economics phenomenon called framing, the phenomenon of loss aversion implies that a transaction should be formulated as a gain (in this case: a discount) rather than as a loss (in this case: a surcharge), even if the final price is exactly the same. For example, the actual price of a hotel room is always much lower than its list price (check the price on the back of your room door, and you will feel good) because people prefer to get a discount over the worst possible day for booking a room (say, a weekday when both the president is in town and it is marathon day) rather than a surcharge over the best possible day for booking that same room.

Let us go back to the example shown in Figure 6.2. Suppose a customer makes a rush order (at a price of $4 per order) for a higher-quality grade (at a price of $5 per order). In that case, the preceding pricing structure suggests that the customer pays a base price of $100 plus a surcharge of $9 for making use of these services. In price waterfall terms, by contrast, the customer obtains the order at a base price of $120, with a discount of $11 for being well behaved, which here means paying on time, managing his own inventories, and having large order sizes; in the communication to the customer, the penalization for rush ordering and a higher-quality grade is not mentioned. While the outcome is exactly the same, customers are more likely to buy the package when the offering is formulated in price waterfall terms, that is, as a gain.[3]

The risks of value pricing

Looking at value pricing in addition to cost cutting in these types of markets is certainly a good step forward. But value pricing (whether communicated through the price waterfall format or otherwise) can also be very risky. That is the case when market conditions do not allow the service to be value priced. In that case, competitors can mess it all up.   .

Let us assume, for a moment, that the company has a standard offering (i.e., the commodity product plus a number of base service levels) that is identical to that of its competitors. If, in addition, the company offers some optional product feature or service level that is unique and has value to the customer, then it does make sense for the company to charge a premium for this benefit.[4] However, as soon as the company value prices a product or service feature that is not unique, and if competitors decide not to value price it (for whatever reason, for example because they simply are late to see the value pricing potential, or because they see the initiator's value pricing initiative as an opportunity for them to gain share), then such value pricing may lead to bigger margin losses than just doing nothing.

This situation is illustrated in Figure 6.3. The company charges the customer properly for the option of getting superior quality relative to the best alternative product. However, it errs in charging for the extended payment terms above and beyond what is included in its standard offering (say, 30 days end of month). When competitors do not charge for such extended payment terms (or charge less), then the total price of the company's package will be higher than the price of the competitor's equivalent offering. In a commodity or commoditizing market, where customers do not see many, if any, differences between products of alternative suppliers, such value pricing is thus no longer appropriate. The company that charges a premium for the (absolute) value of the extended payment terms to the customer is in fact not in a position to do so, since it adds no value relative to its competitors that do not charge. And since customers are looking for the best deal (the difference between their willingness-to-pay and the price), the company will end up losing plenty of customers. Theoretically, it will lose all customers

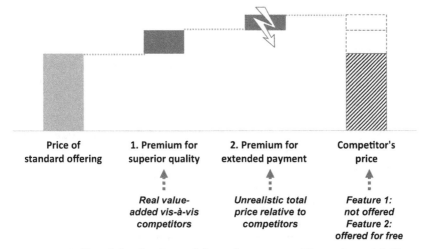

Price of standard offering	1. Premium for superior quality	2. Premium for extended payment	Competitor's price
	▲	▲	▲
	Real value-added vis-à-vis competitors	*Unrealistic total price relative to competitors*	*Feature 1: not offered Feature 2: offered for free*

FIGURE 6.3 The risk of value pricing when competitors do not follow

who make use of the extended payment terms, including those who value the superior quality option. As a consequence, it does not make any margin from the latter customers, and its total margins must go down.

A totally different risk of value pricing relates, strangely enough, to competition law. It is no surprise that companies that start value pricing services that used to be free are quite vocal about it, as they hope that other players in the industry will do the same. For example, American Airlines was the first traditional carrier to introduce a value price of $15 for the first checked bag.[5] It announced its baggage fee policy weeks before it became effective, seemingly in the hope that other major players would follow. It turned out that others did, to begin with United, who effectively introduced the $15 fee two days before American Airlines. US Airways followed a bit later.

But sometimes companies are too vocal about their initiatives, thereby running the risk of infringing competition laws. To mitigate that risk, a careful approach within the strictest limitations of applicable competition laws is required. Attempts at "price signaling" may well be scrutinized by antitrust authorities, as there is a fine line between transparent price announcements and anti-competitive information exchange.[6] Law firm Baker McKenzie puts it mildly as saying that "there is significant interest in price signaling from competition authorities around the world," and concludes with a set of dos and don'ts from a review of numerous legal cases of price signaling worldwide.[7]

The shortcomings of value pricing

In commodity or commoditizing markets, value pricing (whether communicated through the price waterfall format or otherwise) is not the magic formula for margin improvement. To the contrary, value pricing of services or features has three major shortcomings. First, as explained earlier, value pricing is too simplistic. It does not take into consideration competitor behavior and can do a lot more harm than good. Second, value pricing focuses primarily on services or features that we offer to our customers. But margins can be improved also by considering services or features that our customers could offer to us, if properly incentivized. We will come back to that alternative in detail later in this chapter. Third, by definition, the focus of value pricing is on charging more, which is simply not the correct objective: the objective is to increase margins, not price per se.

The latter sounds like a platitude. But from experience we know that many managers still assume that margins increase when prices increase. They probably forgot what they learned in college or grad school about price elasticities. Maybe they forgot because they got bored to tears when the microeconomics professor explained a simple phenomenon: when you raise prices, you tend to sell less volume, and thus earn less in total if the gain in unit margin is undone by the volume loss. In any case, the bottom line is that increasing prices is a bit too simplistic a mechanism for margin improvement. Beware of consulting companies that show that the effect of a 1% price increase is much larger than the effect of a 1% decrease in fixed or variable costs or a 1% increase in volume, "everything else constant." Yeah right, everything else constant. . .

We hope that the preceding is sufficiently convincing to move from a value pricing solution to a more sophisticated approach, which we will illustrate in the following pages. We will work first with a concrete example in B2B markets. At the end of the chapter, we will consider the implications for B2C situations in general, and will use the airline industry as an example.

Let us be clear: our approach does not brush off value pricing, or disregard it altogether. To the contrary, value pricing is retained as one vehicle for margin improvement. However, it is only effective when specific conditions hold. We will clarify when we can go ahead with value pricing, and also recommend sound actions for margin improvement under conditions where value pricing is risky.

As the proof of the pudding tends to be in the eating, we just add two quotes from the Chief Marketing Officer of a global chemicals company who had gone through a value pricing project: "The price waterfall does not work" and "What you are saying is at the heart of the issues in the chemical industry." We heard similar stories at other companies in other industries. Based upon such customer feedback, we have fine-tuned our approach to margin improvement over the years, as explained next.

▶ A FRAMEWORK FOR MARGIN IMPROVEMENT IN B2B MARKETS

Let us go back to the worst of all possible worlds that a company can face: selling a commodity product whose price is driven by supply/demand conditions. This is the case for products such as polypropylene, ethanol or phosphate, for which prices are recorded on a weekly basis by market information providers such as ICIS.[8] They base their information upon interviews of buyers and sellers of said commodities. These prices are often used as benchmarks in contracts, as no buyer wants to pay more than the market price for the commodity, and sellers do know that they cannot charge more than this market price. Marketing managers are thus lucky if market prices are high, and unlucky if they are low (see Box 6.1).

BOX 6.1 LUCK VERSUS MANAGERIAL ACUMEN IN COMMODITY MARKETS

In commodity or commoditizing businesses, luck is a bigger contributor to success than managerial decision-making. Solid windfall gains can materialize when markets happen to be short (i.e., there is a shortage of supply relative to demand) and market prices consequently soar to equalize supply and demand. Conversely, companies can suffer severe losses when markets are long and prices plummet due to the oversupply. What is common in both scenarios is that the business unit manager primarily rides the market, with little influence on the financial performance of the company.

Admittedly, we simplify a bit, as the business unit manager still has a critical task, that is, to forecast next year's market equilibrium prices (you can call them future prices, if you like). Using current market (ICIS) prices in a one-year contract covering next year will lead to lots of regret, at the side of the business unit manager, if supply/demand conditions change favorably for the seller during the contractual period. We remember the case of a major producer of diols (an intermediate chemical) that had picked up the rumor that a Taiwanese player was going to leave the geographic markets into which the producer was sell-ing. That reduction in supply was anticipated to raise next year's equilibrium price by about 30%, from $1.00 to $1.30/kg. We recommended to propose a contract to the producer's major customer at a price of $1.30/kg, much to the dismay of some salespeople, who flattered us with reactions such as "you guys don't understand commodity markets," or "this is crazy," or "believe me, we will lose the customer." In their mind, it was not possible to increase prices for these commodities by more than 2% or 3%, while we went for a 30% increase.

Was it the right recommendation? Absolutely! And was it possible that the pro-ducer would lose its major customer? Absolutely too! Let us assume that a com-petitor indeed decided to take that customer away at, say, the current market price. In that case, one or more of the competitor's own current customers would become available for the producer to serve, because at the equilibrium price quan-tity demanded must be equal to quantity supplied. The beautiful thing is that the producer could now sell the quantity at the true future market equilibrium price of $1.30. This is surely a lot better than selling at a price that is only 2% higher, and experiencing ex post regret next year for having sold at too low a price. In a business with revenues of about $1 billion, the revenue increase from anticipat-ing higher future market prices and refusing to sell at today's market price was $81 million. Not bad for a commodity business, even though the situation was a little bit more complicated than how we described it here (for instance, there was uncertainty about the likelihood that the Taiwanese player was going to leave the market, and about the actual capacity and cost levels of the competitors).

Many companies in these types of businesses have been operating in this way for decades. They have gathered a base of repeat customers that one could label loyal. That term is really a misnomer, though, as customers in these businesses are really only loyal to the extent that there are no price differences with competing suppliers. These so-called loyal customers are ready to switch as soon as price differences reach values as low as 0.5%, since the products are the same and there are no or few switching costs. The same applies to the company itself: it is loyal to a customer as long as the latter pays the market price. The preceding means that neither buyer nor seller is truly loyal. In commodity or commoditizing markets, buyers and sellers are just loyal by convenience, so to speak.

Next we explain the four steps required to optimize margins in commod-ity or commoditizing markets. In that margin management framework, we assume that the standard offering, which consists of a certain quantity of the base product (e.g., a full truck of fertilizer) plus some minimum service levels (e.g., standard delivery within two days), is priced at the competitive equilibrium market price. Margin management, then, is about improving margins from additional services or other features to and from the customer.

Step 1. Recognize services from company to customer and from customer to company

Our clients often tell us that there are no services in their commodity businesses, as everything is about price. When digging into the issue a bit further, it turns out that they often do offer services to their customers, but neither our clients nor their customers recognize these services as such. For instance, the possibility for a customer to cancel orders is often not recognized as a service because everybody in the industry offers it free of charge. As a result, order cancelling is not perceived as a customer benefit that is suitable for margin improvement.

We do not quite concur with this. The possibility to cancel orders is a service offered by the seller to the buyer. And even if no one charges for this service, it does not mean that margin improvement from this service is impossible, as we will explain. That is why it is important to first recognize the existing or potential services that are offered in the business. Box 6.2 shows an illustrative list of groups of services that we often encounter.

BOX 6.2 EXAMPLES OF SERVICES TO AND FROM THE CUSTOMER

▶ Technical service: providing detailed production-related assistance to the customer for the start-up or improvement of production.

▶ Supply and purchase guarantee: establishing a gentlemen's agreement between supplier and customer on targeted volumes.

▶ Supply and purchase obligation: making a contractual commitment between supplier and customer to supply and demand certain volumes.

▶ Supply reliability: making a commitment, as a supplier, to deliver individual shipments in time and at the right place.

▶ Rush ordering and order cancellations or changes: handling customer requests for rush orders, order changes, order delays and order cancellations.

▶ Forecast accuracy and order regularity: taking actions, as a customer, to forecast properly and to exhibit or stick to a regular order pattern.

> ▶ Customer-specific logistics: making investments, as a supplier, in optimizing delivery mode, quantities, packaging (e.g., (big) bags), pallets, concentration, etc.
>
> ▶ Safety stock, vendor-managed inventory and consignment stock: keeping and owning, as a supplier, customer-specific stock levels at various places in the chain.
>
> ▶ Payment terms and bad debtor insurance: agreeing on invoicing schemes, payment terms, related credit lines and insurance requirements to be respected by the supplier.
>
> ▶ Early ordering: placing customer orders much earlier than implied by the standard lead-time between order and delivery.
>
> ▶ Electronic purchasing and download of certificates: establishing e-commerce and web-based interactions between customer and supplier.
>
> ▶ Limited size of order: requesting the supplier to deliver, for instance, half-trucks due to limitations in the customer's own storage capacity.
>
> ▶ Analysis certificates: requesting the supplier to provide specific analysis certificates to the customer.
>
> ▶ Weekend shipment: requesting the supplier to deliver its product to the customer during the weekend.
>
> ▶ Promotion of brands: requesting the customer to promote the supplier's brand to the customer's customer (e.g., having a promotional video of the supplier's product at its customer's (retail) store).

Some of the listed services are from the company to its customers, such as the provision of a supply guarantee, rush ordering, order cancellations and other pretty straightforward things. Less straightforward are the services in the opposite direction, that is, services that a customer could offer to the company, if properly incentivized. Forecast accuracy is one of these services: the better the forecast by the customer, the lower the company's production planning costs, variable storage costs and working capital costs, to name a few.

Early ordering is another example of a service that a customer could offer and that provides tangible benefits to the company. If a customer orders much earlier than the standard order lead-time (say, a week instead of three days before the expected delivery time), the company can benefit from optimized routing and using slower yet cheaper means of transporting the products to its destination (multimodal transportation as it is called, consisting, for instance, of a combination of cargo ship plus truck as opposed to just using a truck or truck-and-train). Customers rarely offer these services, primarily due to the lack of incentives: why would a customer, for instance, order early if there is no gain and a potential loss from doing so? And early ordering can obviously not be included in the standard offering, as it is more of an exception than the rule.

Step 2. Define the standard offering

Once the company has defined all existing or potential services to and from the customer, it can define its standard offering, which covers the product plus the base service levels. Table 6.1 shows a simplified example of the standard offering at a small polypropylene producer.

Unless the company defines what service levels are included in its standard offering (or, worse, if it leaves that decision in the hands of its salespeople), it cannot define the extra service levels that are excluded from the standard offering. As an example, if the meaning of the service level "regular order" is not clear, the meaning of the service level "rush order" cannot be clear either.

That sounds like a platitude, but we have seen many companies that have not defined their standard offering. In such cases, salespeople naturally consider that everything is included in the price of the standard offering. They never even wonder whether they could value price service levels on top of

TABLE 6.1 Simplified example of standard offering

Dimension	Standard offering	
Product	Polypropylene	
Shipping conditions: packaging; destinations	Bulk; to countries X, Y and Z	
Payment terms	60 days net	
Purchase guarantee	None	
Order size	Full truck	
Order lead-times (days)	West South-Central states	≥ 2
	South Atlantic States, East South-Central States	≥ 3
	Midwestern States, Mountain States	≥ 4
	Pacific States, Mexico	≥ 5
	Central America	≥ 14

the standard offering, as the latter is undefined. Seemingly in an effort not to have to bring up the issue with their customers, in their mind everything is included in the price, just like everything is included in a first-class airline seat, with the notable difference that a first-class seat is much more expensive than our dreadful middle seat in coach class.

Step 3. Set up a margin management structure for services from the company to the customer

The question now is how to improve margins from the services that the company offers to the customer, knowing that its standard offering is competitively priced, and that value pricing is not the unique solution or not a solution at all actually. In Step 4, we will address the same question for services that flow in the opposite direction, that is, services offered by the customer to the company. Figure 6.4 shows examples of both types of services.

Let us consider one of these services, and see how we should price that service, if at all, to customers as a function of the offerings of the company's competitors.

Case 1: the service is only offered by the company

Assume that we are the only company to offer the service, say weekend deliveries, and that these weekend deliveries have a particular value to a

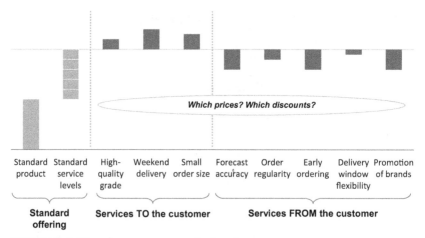

FIGURE 6.4 Margin management structure

customer. If that value exceeds our cost of weekend delivery, we should simply value price the service. The level of the value price should be somewhere between the cost of the service and the value to the customer (see Figure 6.5). In other words, we do not make the customer pay for all the value delivered. Theoretically we could extract all value minus 1%, but in our experience this is not always a good practice, as the customer feels doublecrossed. This is likely to backfire whenever the balance of power shifts from the company toward the customer. After all, value pricing is about sharing value between the company and its customer, not about accruing all that value to the company.

Note that the company's costs of delivering the service determine only its walk-away price, and not the actual price it charges. This implies that value pricing is sensible even if costs are zero. That would be the case, for instance, if the company were the only one to offer the order cancellation service and if the goods have not yet left the plant. Even in that case, the company should charge the value price as a reward for offering a service that is of value to the customer.[9]

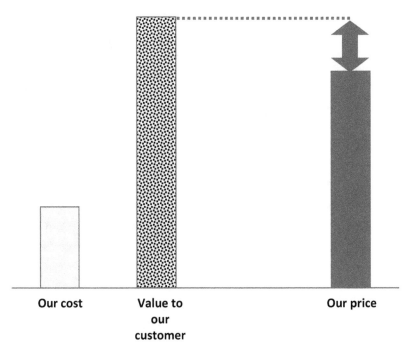

FIGURE 6.5 Price in case 1

Case 2: the service is offered by both the company and its competitor, who charges a particular price (that is less than the company's value price)

Imagine that our value price for weekend deliveries is $100 per order, while a competitor does cost-plus pricing and charges only $60. In that case, we should simply charge the competitor price (see Figure 6.6). Our price cannot be higher because we have no added value over the competitor. And it should not be lower because price cuts can be matched easily, and we do not want to set a price war in motion.

That argument also applies whenever, for some base service, our price, whichever way calculated, is higher than that of our competitors. In all such situations, we should match the competitor's price. To illustrate the point, let us consider the specific case of a base chemicals company that we call company X. It produced granules in a plant located in a particular town A. From there, it normally transported its granules to its customers in bulk (the base offering). For customers who wanted the granules in bags, it charged on a cost-plus basis. The bagging facility was in a different town, town B.

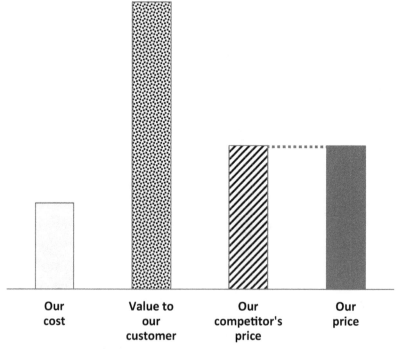

| Our
cost | Value to
our
customer | Our
competitor's
price | Our
price |

FIGURE 6.6 Price in case 2

The cost of bagging thus had three components: (1) the cost of transporting the required volume of granules from A to B, (2) the bagging costs, and (3) the transportation costs from B to the customer. As the competitor, company Y, had its production plant and bagging facility located on a single site, its transportation costs were significantly lower (see Figure 6.7).

Let us put some simple numbers on this. Imagine that company Y's total costs were $600 for a full truck of bagged granules. It set its prices on a cost-plus basis, ending up with a price of $800. The amount of $800 barely covered the sum of all the components of company X's total costs, which were $750. As company X was not yet familiar with the value pricing concept and its drawbacks, it wanted to at least charge $900, that is, 20% above its costs. While doing so, it was hoping that the explanation of its extra transportation costs to and from the bagging facility in town B would be sufficiently convincing for the customer to buy. Unfortunately, the customer did not care a bit, as company X's cost components were totally irrelevant to him. If the price of the granules of company X is the same as that of company Y (which should be the case, given the commodity nature of the product), then the only price that the customer is willing to accept is that of his best alternative, namely $800. Anything else is irrelevant, as it is the total price of the package (product plus service) that will be compared, whatever so-called loyalty may exist.[10]

Some readers may wonder what happens if company X's total costs are actually above company Y's price. For example, imagine that company X's total costs are no longer $750 but $850, while company Y still charges $800. Also

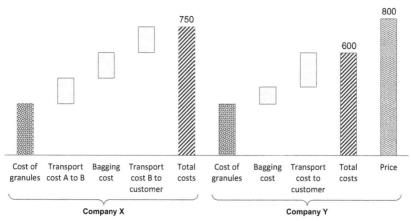

FIGURE 6.7 Price ceiling set by competitors

in this situation, company X should charge the competitor's price, provided that its total contribution margin (that is, the margin from both the base product plus bagging) is positive. If it is not, it should just not offer bagging to that customer. If that means letting go of the customer, be it that way, as zero contribution margin is still higher than a negative one.

Case 3: the service is offered by both the company and its competitor, who offers the service for free

Imagine that our competitor offers weekend deliveries for free, in an effort to super-please his customers with the generously sounding statement "we don't charge extra for weekend deliveries to important customers like you." This behavior in fact is just a dangerous short-term share-stealing tactic that can and will be copied. Do the initiators of such tactics really think that their competitors will just stay put and accept losing their profitable customers? Most competitors do not, and the tactic will result in lower profits for all.[11] Even though that behavior is risky, it still does happen in the real world. The question is what to do in that case (see Figure 6.8).

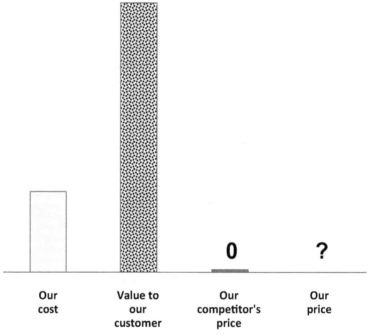

FIGURE 6.8 Price in case 3

Each time we ask that very question in a workshop or a lecture, the participants come up with all kinds of solutions. One of these is to offer an alternative service that (1) only we can provide, (2) has the same or higher value to the customer than the service that competitors offer for free, and (3) has a lower cost than the original service. Our answer to that suggestion is: should such alternative service exist, then it should be optimized in its own right, which means that it should be value priced, as we are back in case 1.

So, our initial question still remains: what do we do with the price of our service if competitors give it away for free? When really forced to focus on that question, the participants eventually give up and say that one cannot do anything, apart from offering the service for free too. And it stops right there.

We differ, in that it just does not stop right there. There are solutions that are better than just giving the service away for free. But the solutions are not simple and depend on numerous factors, for example whether we are the market leader. Next, we walk you through the logic to follow.

Subcase 3.1: we are the market leader

Imagine that the following two conditions are met: (1) we are the market leader, and (2) our competitor, while customarily giving the service away for free, can be anticipated to follow our price leadership for the particular service. These conditions were met in the case of American Airlines (with its clear announcement about charging a baggage fee). In such case, we should definitely try to exercise our market leadership and value price the service, in the expectation that our competitor understands the logic of the approach and the futility of undercutting the value for all, and hence decides to follow the price leadership. This is the best of all possible worlds.

Unfortunately, the real world is rarely the best of all possible worlds. The fact of the matter is that market leaders are few and far between. Being the largest player does not suffice. And if there is one thing that we have learned in this context, it is this: if you are not the market leader, do not act like a price leader. We remember a medium-sized player in the PVC industry who tried to set and announce prices, in the hope that others would follow. As nobody did, the company quickly changed its strategy from price leadership to good followership, which turned out to be a great move.[12]

Subcase 3.2: we are not the market leader

If we are not the market leader and we unilaterally charge for the service, then we will lose at least all customers who value that service. We then fall in the value pricing trap that we explained up front in this chapter. So, in reality, we have no choice but to offer the service for free as well.

But what happens when things are free? Let us just give an analogy that is well understood by any student who rents a furnished apartment around campus for the length of a course or program. If one of the appliances (say, the refrigerator) does not function properly, the student does not want to mess with it, and calls maintenance. It usually takes the technician little time to diagnose the problem and explain the solution to the student. It often boils down to things like "To get the fridge cooler, you just need turn the temperature control dial clockwise and check the temperature gauge five hours later." Or even worse: "The power button is right here. Just press it and the fridge will turn on." What happened? The student did not bother to check the basics, because there is only an incremental cost in doing so and no benefit when maintenance is free. If the student had had some sort of incentive to check first, the technician's wasteful driving back and forth would not have taken place.

The same thing happens in B2B settings: when things are free, people abuse. Take the example of rush order service. Imagine that with regular ordering a customer gets the goods 3 days after the order has been received; with a rush order, the customer gets the goods a day later. If rush orders are free, then why would a customer place regular orders? There is no gain in doing so, and only a possible loss due to new information that may trickle in during the course of the 2 extra days and that may obviate the need for these orders. That is, the customer no longer makes a difference between situations in which he really does need the goods quickly and situations in which he does not. Even if the customer is really sure about the orders he needs, and even if he has a well-established relationship with the supplier, there will be rush orders as long as rush orders are free. The problem is that placing rush orders that are not really needed constitutes a waste.

Fortunately, there are ways to eliminate this waste, to the benefit of both the company and its customer. The first thing to do is to offer the rush order service for free, for the reasons that we explained. The second thing to do is to assess the frequency of use of rush orders by the customer, as well as your cost of handling rush orders.

If the frequency and cost are insignificant, your best stance is to do nothing. The simple reason is that you do not want to upset customer relations for something that is immaterial. That is the same stance that credit card companies take when they waive the interest charges to a customer who exceptionally happens to pay a few days late but otherwise always pays on time.

If the frequency and cost are significant, you should still offer the rush order service for free. But you should also sit down with your customer and propose an additional option. That option consists of an end-of-year discount for the proportional reduction in the number of rush orders relative to the number of rush orders last year, whereby that discount is less than your marginal cost of the rush order. The idea is to give the customer an incentive to think twice about using rush orders going forward: as the rush orders are free, she is not penalized for using them; but she gets a money-back reward for reducing the number of rush orders. As a consequence, she will have a tendency to order regularly when she can and will only place a rush order when she really needs it.

You may wonder why we do not just give the same discount each time she places a regular order instead of a rush order. Why do we instead recommend to give a discount for *reducing* the number of rush orders relative to last year? Giving a discount for a regular order is indeed an option, but it has an important drawback: one actually rewards the customer for placing regular orders; if the customer already places a fair amount of regular orders (even when rush orders are free), you are in fact giving money back to the customer for doing things that she is already doing. In that case, the cost savings from changing the customer's behavior toward more regular orders may be smaller than the financial losses from rewarding the customer for placing regular orders. This does not happen in the scheme that we recommend: the customer only gets rewarded for improvements, not for behaving well to begin with.

This incentive scheme only works if a number of conditions are satisfied, which we will explain in a minute. That being said, if these conditions hold, the scheme always leads to better results. Let us walk you through an example to illustrate the point (see Table 6.2). To keep things simple, yet without any loss of generality, we assume that there is just one competitor. In the starting year (2016), the price per order (based on the ICIS market price) is $40, and markets are so aggressive that everyone gives rush orders away for free. Our marginal cost of a regular order is $20, and turning a regular order into a rush order costs us an extra $10. As a result, we make a contribution margin

TABLE 6.2 Original situation

Year	Competitor X		Our company					Our customer orders	
	Price per order ($)	Extra charge for rush order	Price per order ($)	Marginal cost per regular order ($)	Extra charge for rush order	Marginal cost per rush order ($)		Regular	Rush
2016	40	Free!	40	20	Free!	10		100	20

TABLE 6.3 Situation one year later

Year	Competitor X		Our company					Our customer orders	
	Price per order ($)	Extra charge for rush order	Price per order ($)	Marginal cost per regular order ($)	Extra charge for rush order	Marginal cost per rush order ($)	Discount for reduction in # rush orders ($)	Regular	Rush
2016	40	Free!	40	20	Free!	10	N.A.	100	20
2017	40	Free!	40	20	Free!	10	4	115	5

of $20 (40 − 20) on a regular order, and of $10 (40 − 20 − 10) on a rush order. Under these circumstances, a customer places 100 regular orders and 20 rush orders per year. In other words, 1 order out of 6 is now a rush order, which can be assumed to be an abuse over what that figure would have been, should the company and its competitors have charged for the rush orders.

Let us now work through the proposed scheme for 2017. Our account manager suggests to the customer that rush orders will still be free in 2017, but that she would get a discount of $4 per proportional reduction in the number of rush orders (see Table 6.3). We can expect two things to happen. First of all, and most importantly, the customer will stay with us, since she has no reason to switch. Second, she will reduce the number of rush orders in 2017: she will tend to reduce the number of needless rush orders, while continuing to place rush orders when she really needs them. That is, as a result of this incentive, rush orders could decrease from twenty in 2016 to, say, five in 2017. These five are the real rush orders. The gain to the company in 2017, compared to 2016, is thus equal to $90, that is, the reduction in the number of rush orders ($20 - 5 = 15$) times the net savings per averted rush order ($\$10 - \$4 = \$6$).

We can now compare the gains from the four possible schemes (see Table 6.4). The four schemes are: (1) give a discount of \$4 for reducing the number of rush orders, as previously explained; (2) do nothing; (3) charge just the marginal cost of \$10 for the rush order so as to (seemingly) recover that cost; and (4) give a discount of \$4 for placing a regular order.

The marginal gain from the second scheme (do nothing) is obviously zero: the customer will behave the same way in 2017 as she did in 2016. The third scheme (charge \$10 for a rush order) will typically induce the customer to place her rush orders with the competitor, as he does not charge for rush orders. As a result, the company loses the margins it would have made on the 20 rush orders ($20 \times \$10 = \$200$).[13] But it could also be that the customer, to keep things simple, places all her orders with the competitor. If that happens, the company loses much more ($100 \times \$20 + 20 \times \$10 = \$2200$).

The fourth scheme (give a discount of \$4 per regular order) will induce the customer, as in the recommended first scheme, to reduce the number of rush orders (from 20 to 5). Hence, the company first gains \$90. However, the company is also giving \$4 away for each of the 100 regular orders that the customer would have placed as a regular order even without the discount. In other words, the company rewards the customer for being well-behaved by her own initiative. The margin losses thereof ($100 \times \$4 = \$400$) are larger than the total margin gain from changing the customer's behavior toward regular orders (\$90).

From the preceding comparison, it turns out that our margin gain is largest when we give the customer an incentive for improving her performance. It should be noted, however, that such a scheme is only feasible and effective

TABLE 6.4 Comparison of the benefits of the four schemes

Scheme	Margin gain
1. Discount for reduction in number of rush orders	$(20-5) \times \$6 = \$90$
2. Do nothing	0
3. Charge \$10 for a rush order	At least: $-20 \times \$10 = -\$200$
4. Discount \$4 if not a rush order	$(20 - 5) \times \$6 - (100 \times \$4) = -\$310$

under four conditions. The preceding conditions are, in our view, not too stringent and can fairly be assumed to apply in many B2B markets.[14]

Condition 1: the proposed incentive is not set as a general policy but is negotiated with each specific customer

The improvement incentive is part of the end-of-year negotiation between the company and a specific customer. It cannot be a general public policy because, at the end of the day, we do not reward the well-behaved customer; we only reward the poorly behaved customer for improving her behavior. The scheme is fair in that the same options are proposed to every customer; it is unfair in that the poorly behaved customer will exercise the option more frequently, and benefit more from the incentive. Hence, this scheme can only work in markets where the service negotiations are relatively non-transparent between customers. Consequently, the proposed option does not work in B2C markets where price policies are public.

Condition 2: the customer sustains her good behavior over the years

The customer will benefit from the incentive scheme in the subsequent year (2018) only if she keeps on being well-behaved. For example, if the customer increases the number of rush orders from 5 in 2017 to 10 in 2018, her reward for good behavior will decrease. She will only get the $4 discount on the improvement relative to the initial year (2016), that is, her total reward in 2018 will be $40 (($20 - 10) \times 4$) compared to $60 in 2017. The customer needs to keep on performing.

Condition 3: gaming can reasonably be assumed not to happen

One could argue that a customer would have an incentive to place very few regular orders in the initial year, so as to gain a lot in the subsequent years. Such gaming is unlikely to happen in the real world, though, if the preceding condition 1 is met: the scheme is not announced as a policy but only brought up to poorly behaved customers during the end-of-year negotiations. There is in fact no base year that the customer can anticipate. Besides, most buyers do not think two years ahead anyhow.

Condition 4: costs must truly be marginal, not fixed

If the costs of the service are fixed (that is, our costs do not go down when the customer converts a rush order into a regular order), it is best to do nothing.

When explaining the incentive scheme and conditions here, we have used rush ordering as an example, because it is a situation where value pricing is often difficult. And it applies to all kinds of industries, not just commodity chemicals. For example, a distributor of professional barber supplies to wholesalers had a policy of shipping everything via courier. The outcome was that the wholesalers kept a minimum of stock, and ordered all supplies just-in-time, even supplies that they could have ordered much earlier.

Another example of how giving things away for free leads to significant abuse occurred at a company in the medical devices industry that produced and sold a specific type of life-saving device. The industry standard is to deliver these devices either at 8 am (rush order) or after 3 pm (regular order). One could argue that rush orders are very important because it is critical to have a life-saving device on time at the hospital. Upon reflection, though, the device is *too* important to be rush-ordered: when a patient suddenly gets in a critical condition at 7:55 am, then 8:00 am is just like 3 pm, that is, too late. Hospitals obviously know that. Hence, they have the devices, owned by their supplier, in consignment stock at the hospital. Under these conditions, rush orders are no longer required, and the value of rush orders to the hospital is minimal. Nevertheless, in this case, hospitals continued to place rush orders to replenish the consignment stock, as rush orders at 8 am did not cost anything more than regular delivery at 3 pm. Seeing this, the medical device company sat down with the hospitals, proposing to give them a discount at the end of the coming year for the reduction in the number of rush orders. And indeed, almost all rush orders were eliminated after one year.

Let us conclude the discussion of the proposed incentive scheme by summarizing its benefits, keeping in mind that the alternative is to do nothing.

> *Benefit 1: you do not upset customer relations.* This benefit flows from the fact that you do not penalize the customer for being poorly behaved. To the contrary, you reward the customer for being well-behaved.

> *Benefit 2: no one ever loses.* The incentive scheme includes an option that the customer can exercise. If the customer does exercise the option, both the customer and the company will be better off. If the customer does not exercise the option, no one will be worse off.

> *Benefit 3: you will never lose the customer or the volume.* That is so because the customer has the option to buy the same package of product and services under exactly the same conditions as before and, hence, at no extra charge.

Benefit 4: you do not unnecessarily give money back to customers who do not use the extra service much in the first place. This benefit is the outcome of rewarding the customer based on her improvement in performance, as opposed to rewarding her for being well-behaved.

Benefit 5: waste between the company and its customer is eliminated, thus strengthening the relation between the two. The scheme is designed to eliminate waste that makes no one really better off but still occurs by lack of incentives to eliminate it.

Benefit 6: the benefits of the scheme hold even if competitors imitate it. This is probably the most important benefit, as any form of price discount is typically ineffective due to it being easily imitable by others. When such imitation of price discounts takes place, it leads to lose-lose situations where no one gains volume while everyone loses margin. It is exactly the opposite, though, in the scheme that we have proposed here. Should competitors introduce the same incentive, each company's customer becomes more loyal (well, the loyal-by-convenience sort that we discussed before), since the benefit of improving behavior is dependent on staying with one's current supplier. And each company improves its margins, since the discount is less than the marginal cost of the service.

The key takeaway from this section is that value pricing the company's services is not necessarily the best option for improving margins. Other margin improvements options are: match the competitor's price, do nothing, or include an option to reduce the usage of the service. The best margin improvement option for any specific service can only be determined after answering a number of questions: Is the company recognized as a market leader? Do customers use the service frequently? Does the service have a sizeable variable cost component? Do competitors offer the service too? And do competitors charge for the service? As a function of the answers to these questions, some services to customers will get a surcharge, while others will be offered for free together with an option to improve.

Step 4. Set up a margin management structure for services from the customer to the company

In the previous section, we looked at margin improvement options for services that the company offers to its customers. But margins can also be improved by optimizing the services from the customers to the company.

Such opportunities are often overlooked, probably because of a chicken-and-the-egg situation: no incentives are offered for the services; hence, the customer does not offer the services; hence, they are not observed; hence, the opportunities are overlooked.

The logic for setting up a margin management structure for services from our customers to the company is exactly the same as the logic explained in the previous section: if we are not the market leader, we will not penalize the customer for not providing services to us. The reason is also the same: if we are the only one to do so, and competitors do not follow, our customer will simply switch, since our total offering becomes too expensive.

As before, the first practical step is to think out of the box, and consider all the services that our customers could offer to us, as well as the benefits that would flow to us. Some of these benefits can relate to lower costs, for example through services such as ordering early, ordering regularly, fore-casting accurately, and the like. Other benefits relate to increased revenues, for example as a result of your customer placing your point-of-sales market-ing material at his premises. For instance, a security solutions company had produced videos that highlighted the benefits of its products. Some of the company's wholesale customers were incentivized to play the videos in their showrooms. The incentive was needed because the benefits to a wholesaler of playing the videos are relatively limited, whereas most, if not all, benefits accrue to the security solutions company: any extra security product that the wholesaler sells as a result of the video would most likely cannibalize the sale of a similar product of a competitor of the security solutions company, whereas for the security solutions company the benefits are the margins generated from this extra sale.

To explain the approach in some more detail, let us take the service "fore-cast accuracy." Customers typically do not forecast their supply needs well, simply because they have no incentive to do so. Even worse, some customers not only forecast inaccurately, but often forecast more than necessary, with the argument "to be sure to get the materials." For them, this makes sense, since there is no penalty for forecasting too much. The seller, to the con-trary, would benefit from better customer forecasts, since these would lead to lower costs (e.g., production planning time, variable storage costs and working capital charges). Even if all these costs cannot be calculated accu-rately, it is possible to estimate the minimal cost reduction that an increase in forecast accuracy would bring about.

TABLE 6.5 Estimate of cost savings from higher forecast accuracy

Cost item	Input data	Savings per extra ton accurately forecasted
Working capital	Working capital costs for keeping extra inventory are estimated at 3.5%. Company could reduce inventories by 10,000 ton through better forecasting.	10,000 ton times $750/ton times 3.5% divided by 440,000 ton = $0.60/ton
Physical storage	Storage costs for external capacity amounted to $750k in 2017 (5,000 ton). Annual production volume in 2017 was 440,000 ton. Costs savings are only realized over the first 5,000 ton.	$750k divided by 440,000 ton = $1.70/ton
Production planning	Improved forecast accuracy allows for more efficient production planning, but this is hard to calculate.	Not included
Total		**$2.30/ton**

Table 6.5 shows the cost savings estimate of a chemical company that was looking into a scheme to incentivize its customers to forecast more accurately. Even though it could not calculate the effect of higher forecast accuracy on its production planning costs, it could calculate some other effects, leading to a total savings estimate of $2.30/ton. This seems like a small amount, but in a low-margin business where one has very little to play with to improve margins, this is sizeable and more than welcome.

In order to explain how to define the optimal margin management structure for this chemical company, assume that the company is not a market leader. In that case, we will not initiate a penalty for poor forecasting, as no one else is applying penalties. would be the only company to do so, and no one would be likely to follow our lead. Neither will we reward the customer for good forecasting, as our goal is margin improvement. Instead, in the end-of-year negotiations with the customer, we will propose an incentive scheme. We will formulate our discussion along the following lines:

> It would be great if you could improve the accuracy of your forecasts
> somewhat, as that allows us to eliminate some avoidable costs. We
> are happy to share the benefits thereof with you. So here is the deal:
> if your forecast accuracy does not improve, nothing will happen. But if
> your forecasts do improve at the end of next year, we will be happy to

give you a discount of $1 per extra ton of materials that is forecasted better than last year (assuming total volumes are the same).

Through this proposal, the company shares the value of the improved forecasting ($2.30) with the customer ($1.00). As a result, the customer has an incentive to improve the forecasts of the purchases for which he can make a better forecast with minimal effort (when there was no incentive, even a minimal effort was not worth it). The customer will still not improve the forecasts that are difficult to make accurately. The net effect hereof is that the waste between the company and its customer is minimized or eliminated: the forecasts that can be improved at low cost are improved, while the more-challenging-to-forecast or impossible-to-forecast purchases are not, as there is no win-win incentive to do so.[15]

To conclude this section, we give an example from a playing card company that manufactures all types of cards: regular playing cards, baseball and soccer trading cards, and more recent gaming cards such as Pokémon and Yu-Gi-Oh (we are sure there are even more recent ones, but neither of the authors is up to date). Here again, the company's customers (retailers, etc.) do not forecast well, whichever game they purchase. There are two types of reasons for this: (1) laziness and/or the absence of an incentive to forecast accurately, and (2) the difficulty of forecasting well.

The first reason applies to regular playing cards and sports trading cards. It really is not that difficult for companies that sell these cards to forecast demand for these cards, particularly since there is a wealth of historic data to work with, and history is a good predictor of the future for these types of cards. But why would companies do so if poor or overly optimistic forecasts can be made without any single negative consequence? After all, they apply simple microeconomic thinking: the slightest positive marginal cost incurred for better forecasting should not be incurred, since the marginal benefit is zero.

Things are different when it comes to the new gaming cards. For these games, forecasts are difficult to make, as any useful historic data are missing. In addition, a new game can either take off spectacularly or never get off the ground. Even after the first year of the launch of a new game, forecasts tend to be at best unreliable. The implication is that the proposed scheme to incentivize the customer to improve forecast accuracy will help improve the forecast accuracy of the first type of cards but not of the second type.

Wasteful inaccurate forecasts will be eliminated, whereas some inaccurate forecasts will remain because it is too difficult or costly to improve them.

And again, the idea is to reward for improved forecasting, not to reward for good forecasts. If the customer forecasts 70% right to begin with, and we reward him for that, then the gains from the expected forecast improvement (from, say, 70% to 85%) may very well be smaller than the losses incurred from rewarding him for the 70% good forecasts.

▶ A FRAMEWORK FOR MARGIN IMPROVEMENT IN B2C MARKETS

By and large, the logic for margin improvement in B2B markets that we explained in detail in the previous section applies also to B2C markets. Some adaptations are needed to take into consideration that B2C markets in general are more transparent than B2B markets. In transparent markets, it is no longer possible to reward customers for improvements in behavior. This is not only so in B2C markets, but in any market where the pricing of services is transparent, including in some B2B markets.

Let us pick up the airline example to see how we adapt the way of thinking. As discussed earlier in this chapter, there are plenty of services that an airline can offer to its customers. And airlines have been trying to value price these services through à la carte pricing, for example by charging baggage fees and the like. There are, however, a number of risks associated with being the first airline to introduce such fees (see Table 6.6).[16,17]

The first risk of à la carte value pricing is generic, and was already mentioned for B2B markets. If we are not the market leader and others do not follow, then we may well become too expensive for a large number of customers. Many customers are likely to switch to competitors who do not charge for the service.

The other risks of à la carte pricing are specific to the airline industry. Nevertheless, they are noteworthy, and in various degrees applicable to other industries as well. For instance, airlines too frequently engage in so-called value pricing when competitive conditions do not allow. Witness indeed US Airways, which at some point did charge for soft drinks, but was the only airline to do so. When no one was following, they dropped the new beverage pricing policy.

TABLE 6.6 Examples of risks associated with introducing fees

Area of risk	Impact on customer behavior	Example
Competitor response	Customers switch to competitors that do not charge for the service	In 2010, Southwest Airlines credits its domestic market share gains partially to its "Bags Fly Free" campaign, as other carriers increasingly charged for checked baggage
Customer response	Customers seek escape from the fee, so that the expected revenues do not materialize while costs increase	When American Airlines started to charge extra for checked-in baggage, significant departure delays occurred as passengers carried more luggage on board
Brand image and positioning	Customers are less loyal	In 2009, US Airways reversed its decision to charge passengers for non-alcoholic beverages because of negative passenger reactions and the impact on brand perception
Operations	Customers attempt to take a free ride, leading to unexpected costs that outweigh the revenue gains	When JetBlue introduced differentiated prices for preferred seats, its cabin crew at one point had to police passengers moving to empty seats, causing high dissatisfaction amongst passengers and extra work for the cabin crew

Source: Southwest Airlines, US Airways, authors' research

Airlines also tend to overlook one major opportunity for margin improvement that is similar to what we discussed before. Instead of value pricing or charging for a service, airlines should incentivize customers to change their behavior in ways in which the airlines benefit. Let us take an example that we discussed with the CFO of a major Star Alliance member. When we started talking about business class services, the CFO was in fact afraid that we would propose to charge for all kinds of services that are included in the business class offering. In other words, he was afraid that we would subject business class passengers to the same regime as coach class passengers. We reassured him that this was not our goal, for we did understand that business class passengers value the convenience of being able to use all kinds of services that are otherwise charged to coach class passengers (lounge access, priority boarding, food, alcoholic beverages, blankets, headphones, and the like). We told him it was about something totally different, that is, not à la carte pricing but à la carte *options*.

Consider lounge access, for example. This service is free for business class passengers, and we are not recommending to start charging them for this service. Still, margin improvement is possible. Here is how. Many lounges of the Star Alliance members are owned by the Star Alliance member airlines, but others, particularly in smaller airports (say, Bucharest in Romania) or in smaller African countries (say, Banjul in Gambia), are owned by the airports. When a business class passenger of a Star Alliance member then makes use of that lounge, the airport charges the airline a fee of about $20.

We doubt that most business class passengers value this service by more than a few dollars. Most of these lounges are usually crowded. Yes, there is the free drink and a few chips, but that is about it. Possibly the biggest benefit for some may be the feeling of exclusivity of walking in the lounge with a sense of disdain for those who are supposed to wait outside.

But when things are free, the same pattern emerges as mentioned before: passengers use and abuse the lounge more than they would if they had some incentive not to. That is exactly why we proposed the following scheme: when telling the business class passenger at the check-in counter that the lounge is between gates 23 and 24, the agent should also mention the option: "But if you choose not to use the lounge, we will give you 200 points in frequent flier miles."

Chances are that a big chunk of the business class passengers will avoid going to the lounge altogether. We have no idea about the "mileage-elasticity" of lounge visits, but we can imagine that the number of visits may well drop by an easy 50% to 80%. Why is that? The first reason is linked to the preceding abuse argument: people visit the unpleasant lounge simply because it is free, without really enjoying being there. The second reason is that many people just love miles, and sometimes are even obsessed by them.[18] Some irrational fixation seems to have gotten a hold on many of us, because the reality is that the value of airline miles is low, somewhere between 1 and 2 cents, depending on the carrier.

By contrast, the benefit to the airline of people not using the lounge is huge. Per passenger who decides to exercise the option of not using the lounge, the airline makes $20, minus some very small amount for the cost of the 200 frequent flier miles, surely less than $1.[19,20] Some back-of-the-envelope calculation shows that this scheme could translate to tens of millions of extra pre-tax profits.[21]

One can think of many other areas where the absence of incentives not to use free services leads to waste. For example, for international flights to popular destinations (say, Boston–Frankfurt), six check-in counters are often open, just to ensure that there are sufficient agents for the check-in of passengers at peak time, which is usually between 1 and 2 hours prior to departure. But the counters open already 3 hours prior to departure. During that off-peak period, the agents are busy talking to other agents, but it is more likely to be about their home improvement or weekend plans than about serving passengers. This wasteful situation thus points to an opportunity for mile-sensitive airline customers in economy class to provide a service to the airlines, that is, to check in between 3 and 2 hours prior to departure. Of course, they will not do so unless the airline offers them an incentive, for instance in the form of extra frequent flier miles.

This scheme is a little trickier than that in the previous examples, because the airline does not want all passengers to accept the offer. Hence, it is important to experiment with a small number of incentive miles first (perhaps 100 per passenger) and increase them gradually should the bulk of check-ins still take place close to departure. In any case, as with the business lounge service, the gains of this scheme for the airline can run into the millions.[22] And by now, you have also understood that penalizing passengers for checking in closer to departure time definitely is not a margin improvement solution.

Most airlines are hesitant to offer à la carte options such as the ones described previously.[23] They are hesitant despite the no-risk nature of à la carte options. The options increase the satisfaction and loyalty of passengers who exercise the option, while not making the other passengers worse off. At the same time, they increase airline revenues (more loyal passengers mean more revenues in the long run) and definitely decrease airline costs. When incentivizing customers in the airline industry, various questions need to be looked into, such as: how do the variable costs of the services offered vary across flights, airports or regions? What is the current usage of a given service? How sensitive is passenger behavior to changes in incentives? What would be the complexity and costs of implementing a win-win option?

Working with options is very sensible and underutilized also in many other B2C industries than airlines. Think, for example, of telephone operators who offer a new smartphone when a customer purchases a particular plan. Again, offering a phone for free is not the smartest move: it could very well be that many people do not value the phone as much as it costs to the operator, because they do not like the brand or model, or because they just bought a new phone themselves. So, rather than offering the phone for free, it may be wiser to offer the customer the option of either taking the phone or having, say, some free minutes should they decide not to take the phone.[24] Again, waste is eliminated because for all one knows some people may buy the plan (and get the phone for free) and toss out the new phone when coming home.

The same applies to the beverage industry. Often an alcoholic beverage company offers a free glass with the purchase of a bottle. Some customers value this, and decide to buy the bottle as a result, which is the actual intent of the company's promotion campaign. But other customers may start getting second thoughts about buying the bottle, because they do not value the free glass, or because they have their own high-end glasses at home and believe that the cost of the so-called free glass is somehow included in the price of the bottle. Still other customers may buy the bottle with the glass, only to toss it out back home.

To get rid of this abuse and waste, the beverage company can follow two approaches. Approach 1 is to offer customers the option not to take the glass and get a $0.20 discount. With this approach, customers who do not value the glass will exercise the option. Approach 2, which is a slight variation on approach 1, is to offer customers who buy the bottle the option to buy the glass at a price of $0.20. With this approach, only customers who value the glass will exercise the option. Both approaches make sure that "free" disappears, that waste is eliminated, and that margins improve.

The bottom line of the discussion on margin improvement in B2C markets is that the logic explained for margin improvement in B2B markets still holds. This includes the conclusion that value pricing is often not the solution. The big difference between B2C and B2B markets is that it is difficult, if not impossible, to offer B2C customers the option to *reduce* the (ab)use of a costly service that is offered by the company and/or the option to *increase* the service offered to the company. Incentives in B2C markets should typically be based on absolute levels only, not on improvements.

▶ CONCLUSIONS

Margin improvement is the ultimate goal of a company's business strategy. Contrary to what many traditional strategy textbooks seem to imply, the ability to improve margins is not contingent on the company having superior resources or capabilities, and obtaining sustainable competitive advantage. If it were, most companies that are just middle-of-the-road or that operate in commodity or commoditizing businesses would be eliminated.

In this chapter, we took the worst-of-all-worlds case, that is, companies that own nothing special. They just own planes that are the same as their competitors', or chemicals that are the same as their competitors', or anything else that is just the same. We have shown that in these markets the concept of sustainable competitive advantage is unrealistic for most, if not all, participants, but that margin improvement is still possible.

Beyond cost cutting, value pricing is one of the approaches to improve margins, but it is rarely effective when competition is fierce. In that case, other more complex margin improvement approaches should be applied. These approaches are based on eliminating waste that emanates from the free availability of things. Such waste can be eliminated by providing incentives to customers to (1) reduce their use of features of the company's offering that cost more to the company than they are valued by them, or (2) improve the services they offer to the company so that it can generate cost reductions or realize revenue gains.

▶ NOTES

1 In principle, it boils down to looking at the Net Present Value (NPV) of future cash flows, using the appropriate weighted average cost of capital (WACC). But keep in mind that the longer-term future, at least beyond five years, is very difficult to forecast.

2 According to Kahneman and Tversky, most studies suggest that a given loss is perceived twice as negative as the same gain is perceived positively. See Daniel Kahneman and Amos Tversky, "Advances in Prospect Theory: Cumulative Representation of Uncertainty," *Journal of Risk and Uncertainty* 5 (1992): 297–323.

3 In some instances, such a communication is not feasible (e.g., in airlines) and, hence, the surcharge communication may still occur.

4 Obviously, if the standard offering of the company is different from that of its competitors, the assumption of commoditization of the offering no longer holds, and price differences will emerge between the standard offerings of different companies. This could be due to either truly different products (e.g., a chemical that dries faster) or due to different service levels included in the standard offering.

5 Low-fare and regional Spirit Airlines had already introduced baggage fees at an earlier stage.

6 Law firms are aware hereof, witness for instance the recommendation of Slaughter and May to "not make public announcements which refer to other competitors or which are contingent on how they (or the industry more broadly) will react." See Anna Lyle-Smythe and Poppy Smith, "When Is a Price Announcement Not a Public Announcement?" *Slaughter and May Newsletter* (July 2016).

7 See Kurt Haegeman and Grant Murray, "Price Signaling and Global Antitrust Enforcement: Practical Counselling Tips," *Baker McKenzie Publication* (January 1, 2017).

8 See www.icis.com

9 Whether the price charged to the customer should be the same across all customers is a long discussion that should be covered by books on pricing. Overall, though, it is most sensible to have structured and non-negotiable prices (i.e., one price for all customers) for products and services that are simple and repetitive.

10 By the way, if you hear this argument, do use it gently against the customer when he asks to break down your costs when prices are too high.

11 A second, less aggressive reason for competitors not charging for services is simply that no one is doing it yet.

12 Besides, the PVC industry is actually too fragmented to identify a clear market leader.

13 One could argue that the customer would reduce her rush orders to about five as well, and place these at the competitor. This is unlikely, since the 15 rush orders that are not truly rush orders have some value to the customer. Hence, there is no point for the customer to rationalize her rush orders if the competitor offers them for free while our company does not.

14 If the conditions do not apply, one has to adapt the solutions accordingly. It is beyond the scope of this book to go through all possible exceptions.

15 Whether the waste is minimized or eliminated depends on whether the incentive offered is larger than the incremental cost of improving the forecast.

16 Dennis Schaal, "Southwest Airline's Kelly Calls on Competitors to Increase Bag Fees," *Tnooz* (January 21, 2010).

17 See "US Airways to End Fees for Non-alcoholic Drinks," *USA Today* (February 23, 2009).

18 Just watch the movie *Up in the Air* to see the obsessed George Clooney doing everything possible to accumulate miles.

19 According to some accounts, airline companies value points in their financial statements at less than one one-thousandth of a cent per point, but, in any event, it is a fraction of a cent. See https://en.wikipedia.org/wiki/Frequent-flyer_program

20 In addition, given the low cost of the miles to the airline, should 200 miles not do the job, raise it to 500 miles, and if that is still not enough, raise that figure again.

21 The calculation is based on some reasonable figures for elasticities and on publicly available information for an airliner whose profits turned slightly positive in 2016 after six years in the red. The ballpark figure points to an increase in pre-tax profits of about $28 million, which is sizeable given the low profitability of such airlines. From this figure, we would need to subtract the administrative and set-up costs of this scheme, but it surely appears worth investigating.

22 If a sufficient number of passengers take up on the offer, and the check-in agents are busy all the time, the airline could probably do with four instead of six agents for this international flight. If we consider the costs of two agents, the number of similar popular international destinations, and the number of take-offs each year, a back-of-the-envelope calculation based on publicly available data points to gains for the airline that run in the millions of dollars. And any million counts in an industry where there is so little to play with.

23 Airlines rather seem to expect passengers to offer services to the airlines (like obtaining the boarding pass at home) without incentivizing them. Sometimes, airlines even penalize passengers for not offering a service. Ryanair, for example, charges a hefty fee to passengers who want to get their boarding pass at the airport.

24 Alternatively, the operator could offer the phone at a price of $5 to customers who decide to buy the plan. As a result, only customers who value the phone will exercise this option, and hence no phones are needlessly given away.

7

The real-world way forward

With this book, we have attempted to bring business strategy back to its very essence: it is about a company making decisions that, first, are likely to influence customers to prefer its offering over competitive alternatives; and second, that will allow the company, if a sufficient number of customers do have such preference, to cover its costs well enough to deliver the return that its stakeholders expect.

We hope that we delivered on the promises that we had put forward in Chapter 1. If after reading this book you are indeed convinced of the merits of the principles and methods that we have explained, we hope that as a manager you will apply these with gusto in your daily business life.

By the same token, we hope that you will also want to share those principles and methods with your colleagues and business partners – because life is so much more efficient and fun for all when mental models and vocabularies are aligned. To that effect, we have summarized the seven key takeaways of this book here.

▶ NO WALK IN THE PARK

We can assure you that it was laborious for us, authors, to write this book. And we reckon that it was also demanding for you, reader, to absorb this material. So, we congratulate you for your perseverance to make it to this very end. At times, it must have been rather brain-taxing to master the various conceptual principles explained in this book, and to work your way through its many numerical examples.

If that is the case, it is not because we take pleasure in complexities per se. It is simply because business strategy in the real world does require hard thinking and rigorous analysis. There is no escape. Easy slogans ("annihilate competitors!," to take one) and fast talk ("the secret is to super-please customers," to take another) at a business conference or a visioning off-site may give a pleasurable shot of dopamine, but they do not provide any reassurance of a reasonable chance of success back home.

As is clear from this book, doing business strategy is more of a tough mountaineering expedition than a refreshing walk in the park. We advocate the abandonment of catchy yet simplistic recommendations. We favor a more complex yet behaviorally founded way of thinking, because the reality is that the world is complex and that customers do make choices. Therefore, we need to try to capture the essence of this complexity and of the factors that influence customers' choices.

▶ IDEOLOGY IS OF LITTLE PRACTICAL USE

There is a great parallel between lifestyle magazines and (many) business strategy books. Both appeal to people's yearning for simple solutions to timeless desires, such as "how to have a genuinely fulfilling love life" or, more prosaically, "how to be a truly strategic business leader." We all admit that these desires are elusive, and that the solutions are futile – yet we keep clicking on titles like these, vaguely hoping that, this time, we will find a kernel of wisdom that will propel us toward a genuinely fulfilling love life or truly accomplished strategic leadership.

The problem, at least for business strategy books, is that the foundations for the solutions brought forward by their authors in many cases are rather fragile. Their almost ideological claims-to-truth are often founded on mere anecdotal examples of exceptional situations, which are then generalized into widely applicable recipes. With hindsight, every business manager of course wishes she had the foresight that, say, Amazon appears to have had in the mid-1990s. We are immensely respectful of Amazon's achievements, but theirs are so specific and exceptional that we are highly skeptical of any management theory that uses – or better, abuses – Amazon as "evidence." And it does not help that author X, today, may use the Amazon example to prove management theory A, while author Y, tomorrow, may use the Amazon example to prove exactly the opposite management theory B.

Management theories tend to degrade into ideological debates captured by soundbites such as "constraint-based" versus "ambition-driven," "inside-out" versus "outside-in," "technology-push" versus "market-pull," "fast-follower" versus "early-adopter," and many other hyphenated strategies. We realize that behind these soundbites often stands a consumer marketing machinery that thrives on simplification and provocation, given the need to have a voice that carries above the brouhaha of the entertainment and opinion industry. But these simplified, if not simplistic, approaches rarely lead to effective business strategies.

An effective business strategy ultimately cannot be based but on one observable fact about homo sapiens: when he is offered two alternatives that could help him meet a need, he will choose the one that he thinks will give him the higher value. In other words, if a company considers, for example, to enter a new market, it "only" needs to validate that a sufficient number of potential customers will want to choose the company's product given their best alternative, and at a price at which the company will make money. As we have shown in this book, this company does not need any ideology to arrive at a proper strategic entry decision.

▶ RETHINK MARKET SEGMENTS

No two potential customers can be claimed to be identical, at least not up front. Two different customers a priori have different preferences. Even if they have a number of common characteristics (in terms of age, gender, income, hometown, professional occupation, or any other parameter that is used to categorize people or companies in homogenous groups) and if they thus are often lumped together in so-called "segments," they may choose totally different offerings. Belonging to a commonly defined segment is not a good predictor of the trade-offs, preferences and choices that a given customer will actually make. That is an observable fact.

As a consequence, it makes little sense, when starting to define an Operational Strategy, to reason at the level of segments. It is the individual customer level that counts. Ex post, once we have identified the preferences of all individual customers in our chosen sample, and once we then have aggregated and extrapolated these preferences to the entire market, then it may be possible to define groups of customers with relatively common needs (yes, "segments"), for example to be able to organize our salesforce activities and our tailored marketing pitch at the segment level. But such segmentation is not needed to define a meaningful strategy to begin with.

In other words, Operational Strategy reasoning should essentially follow a one-to-many-to-all process: start with the individual customer, aggregate at sample level, and extrapolate to the entire market. Most business strategy books reason exactly the other way around, i.e., all-to-many-to-one: segment the market, define an offering for each segment, and possibly tailor the offering to individual customers. As we have explained in this book, making an accurate assessment of how customers will really behave when confronted with a company's offering is crucial to forecast future volumes, revenues and profits reliably. Such accurate assessment can be made only through what we have called a totally customerS-centric approach.

▶ THE END OF THE AVERAGE

Many strategy books point to the creation of customer value as the key to business success. As you must have gathered by now, we will be the last ones to minimize the importance of thinking about customers' needs. But beneath the notion of "customer value" lies one precarious idea: that there is something like average customer value. There is not. What counts are customer values, that is, differences in customer value.

Recognizing this distinction, when doing Operational Strategy, fundamentally affects (1) the kind of market information we need to gather, (2) the strategic choices and decisions we make, and (3) the bottom line results we eventually achieve. We are not talking small potatoes here. We have shared quite a few real-world examples thereof, including one that shows that setting a product's price on the basis of average customer value may well cut profits by a factor of two to three.

The fallacy of the average applies also to strategy formulation more broadly. Many strategy books are centered on general rules, which in turn are based upon "on average" results from the research done by their authors. Think, for example, about the rule "if a competitor cuts prices, then respond by tit-for-tat." We find such general rules utterly risky. In strategy, averages never matter. Strategy is about recognizing the specific circumstances and conditions of the particular situation at hand, and about identifying profitable ways to offer customers a deal that they find more attractive than any other alternative.

Managers are misled when they apply rules that are positioned as unconditionally applicable but are in fact non-generalizable. In that case, they may make decisions that lead to outcomes that are not any more desirable than those that would follow from flipping a coin.

▶ IT'S ALL IN THE PRODUCT

Potential customers have needs, and we aim to meet these needs through our product (here we use the term "product" in the broad sense of "offering," that is, it includes services and intangibles such as the brand). The product is the means by which we create value, and by which we can possibly capture a significant part of the value created. It is through our products that we enter new markets, or that we defend our current market position against new entrants, or that we maintain our customers' loyalty even when they care about price only.

In other words, business strategy, at least in the sense of Operational Strategy, essentially is product strategy. Product strategy is not a subset of business strategy, let alone an afterthought consigned to the guys in product planning or marketing, once the big shots in the C-suite have concocted the company strategy. When discussing our take on business strategy and talking about this book in particular, some people try to pigeonhole us into the "so, you guys are marketing specialists" hole. When this happens (and assuming we are having a good day, which is usually the case), we patiently explain and re-explain our strategists' view, starting with the seven takeaways summarized in this chapter.

It also means that the other topics that are customarily addressed when operationalizing a business strategy should logically come second place: the investments to make, the organization to design, the partnerships to establish, the acquisitions to make, the financing to arrange, the values to spread, the stakeholders to involve, the communications to manage, etc. It does not mean that in the greater scheme of things these topics are less important, but in terms of strategic reasoning they are subordinated to "the products to meet customers' needs."

▶ DEAL VALUE IS THE SINGLE MOST IMPORTANT NOTION

As we have said earlier, let us forget about segments, and rather think about an individual customer and the choices he makes. In particular, we want to know whether he will prefer our product over his best alternative, which may be the product he currently uses. The answer depends on what we have called the "deal value" of his alternatives. If the deal value of our product is higher than any of the alternatives, we've got, well, the deal. Deal value is defined as the difference between the customer's willingness-to-pay (alternatively called "customer value") and the price he has to pay.

There is one crucial refinement to the preceding. It is called switching costs. When confronted with a new product, the customer will not only consider the deal values of the new product (including all of its components, such as brand value) and the product he currently uses (if any is at all a "substitute") but also the monetary and non-monetary costs he has to incur when switching from his current product or from "nothing" to the new product. If that switching cost exceeds the difference in deal values, he will stick to what he currently has or does not have.

The notion of deal value is so important that we have summarized it again in an example (see Figure 7.1). It compares the deal value of the customer's

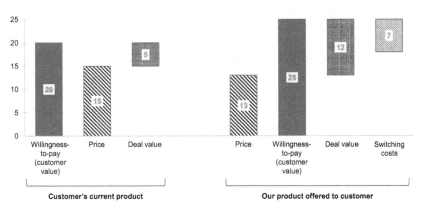

FIGURE 7.1 Summary of the notion of deal value

current product ($5) with the deal value of the new product we are offering ($12). Based on that information, the customer would prefer our product, not so much because it has a lower price ($13 versus $15), but because his willingness-to-pay for our product is so much higher ($25 versus $20). Our product apparently has a combination of tangible and less tangible features (including its look-and-feel, brand, perception of hassle-free dealing, etc.) that provides a higher utility than his current product.

Unfortunately, the customer would also incur high switching costs ($7), leading to a situation where he is indifferent between the two alternatives: the deal value of his current product ($5) is the same as the deal value of our product minus the switching costs ($12 − $7 = $5). If we want to make a deal with this customer, we will have to improve the utility of our product to the customer, help him lower his switching costs, and/or lower our price. Or we can also work with a combination thereof; for example, we can provide more utility and at the same time raise our price, as long as the monetary value of this increased utility is higher than the price hike.

The preceding example relates to the situation where the customer currently uses already a product that is a substitute of ours. But the logic of deal value applies also to the situation where the customer is offered a novel product that no supplier has ever offered before (as an example, take the GPS location device when it was first launched on the market). In those cases, the customer will compare the deal value of the new product with his "nothing" alternative.

▶ OPERATIONAL STRATEGY AND GRAND STRATEGY GO HAND IN HAND

After hearing all of the preceding, you may argue that it is all logical and sensible, but just unworkable in practice. There is, you may argue, no way in the world that your company could take the time and go through the pain of trade-off interviews with customers and the subsequent analyses each time a strategic opportunity pops up.

You are right about that, and that is why we propose an end-to-end process in which Operational Strategy, that is the method explained herein, is preceded by Grand Strategy. The purpose of Grand Strategy is to use the traditional strategy toolbox (that is, the notions of industry attractiveness, competitive advantage, and the like), in combination with minimal market and competitor evidence, to assess the merits of strategic opportunities in a quick-and-dirty way. As a result of that assessment, some opportunities will easily be discarded as non-attractive and/or non-feasible. Others may appear to be both attractive and feasible, at least at first sight. Those selected possibilities, and only those, are then taken as hypotheses to be tested in depth in the subsequent Operational Strategy process. The Operational Strategy either confirms, adapts or rejects the Grand Strategy hypothesis and then details the implications thereof. The benefit of this approach is that Operational Strategy protects managers from implementing high-level strategic decisions that turn out to be wide off the mark afterwards, that is, costly to their company and detrimental to their career.

As we have argued in this book, Grand Strategy and Operational Strategy are not opposites. They go hand in hand, and are part of an end-to-end strategy formulation process. Even better: the principles and concepts of both Grand Strategy and Operational Strategy should guide the strategic judgments and decisions that managers must make on a continuous basis as they go about their company's daily business. And we do hope that, with this book, we have contributed to providing more solid foundations for making strategic decisions in the real world.

Index

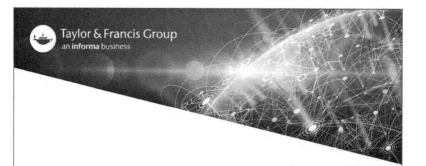

CPSIA information can be obtained
at www.ICGtesting.com
Printed in the USA
LVHW050738150120
643428LV00009B/122